PROSPER

Major Francis Alfred Suttill, DSO. Photo taken when a Lieutenant in 1941/42. (Author's collection)

PROSPER

MAJOR SUTTILL'S FRENCH RESISTANCE NETWORK

FRANCIS J. SUTTILL

*For his grandchildren Emma and Sami and the families of
all of those who fought with him for the freedom of France.*

'Truth does not do as much good in the world as the
semblance of truth does evil.'
François VI, Duc de La Rochefoucauld

First published as *Shadows in the Fog* in 2014
This revised and updated edition published in 2018

The History Press
The Mill, Brimscombe Port
Stroud, Gloucestershire, GL5 2QG
www.thehistorypress.co.uk

British Library Cataloguing in Publication Data.
A catalogue record for this book is available from the British
Library.

ISBN 978 0 7509 8937 4

Typesetting and origination by The History Press
Printed and bound in India by Thomson Press India Ltd

CONTENTS

FOREWORD

The Special Operations Executive (SOE), one of a handful of wartime British secret services, was only in existence for less than five years, but its activities and personnel have attracted undiminished scrutiny and controversy ever since it came into the public gaze at the end of the Second World War. Discernibly less secret than its wartime colleagues (and sometime rivals) MI6 and MI5, its activities started to become public knowledge scarcely before hostilities had ended. The SOE's work in France drew particular attention as a result of the country's strategic importance and the special resonance drawn from the fact that many, if not most, of the agents of its F Section were British citizens. Publishers soon grasped that there was a ready market for tales of British secret agents engaged on clandestine operations in Occupied France and, as early as 1945, George Millar became the first member of F Section to write his memoirs. Interest was further increased with the highly publicised gallantry awards made to SOE heroes and heroines such as 'Tommy' Yeo-Thomas, Odette Sansom and Violette Szabó. Subsequent biographies of these agents became best-sellers. But soon, darker tales began to circulate. While ghostwritten autobiographies of the agents and hagiographic biographies described sometimes real, sometimes exaggerated and sometimes even fictional feats of derring-do, other writers started to make more critical assessments of SOE's achievements in France.

Perhaps the most controversial debate in Britain and France concerned the rise and fall of SOE's largest circuit (or network), PROSPER. It was created and led by Francis Suttill who had been brought up in France and England, and in peacetime had practised as a barrister. He was married with two young sons. While serving in the British Army, his language skills marked him out as a potential recruit for SOE and, after specialist training, he was parachuted into enemy territory in October 1942. Thereafter he developed a very substantial circuit that eventually spread throughout much of the old occupied zone of France. As speculation grew on both sides of the Channel that an Allied invasion was imminent, the increased recruitment of local personnel and the delivery of stores by the RAF's supply drops began to turn PROSPER into a veritable army. Perhaps the circuit grew too large too soon; the bigger it got, the more vulnerable it became to the implacable and relentless German security forces. Through a variety of circumstances, a wave of arrests took place amongst Suttill's followers and then in the ensuing weeks the Germans exploited the leads with ruthless efficiency. Ultimately the network was completely dismantled with more than 150 members of PROSPER falling into German hands.

The destruction of this pivotal feature of F Section's plans for fomenting resistance in Occupied France attracted post-war controversy and the circumstances behind PROSPER's collapse inspired a profusion of official and personal enquiries. Formal post-war French investigations failed to identify any single cause or culprit while a variety of British authors offered sundry theories and speculations. A major limitation of these analyses of the 1950s and 1960s was that they were conducted without the benefit of access to SOE's official archives. These remained classified and therefore closed to private researchers. An 'SOE Advisor' was appointed in 1959 by the Foreign Office to answer questions from the closed archive but he applied his brief largely to inhibit the increased probing of SOE's secrets (although, thankfully, his successors proved much more forthcoming). Finally, in 1966, an official history, *SOE in France* by M.R.D. Foot, was published. Drawing upon the closed SOE archive and a range of published secondary sources and interviews with a selection of veterans, the book provided an unprecedented and radically clear view of SOE's structure and activities. But this 'definitive' version of events failed to still the debate over the PROSPER controversy and writers continued to dissect the story with their further, 'unofficial' examinations of the affair.

In the 1970s a series of revelations began to emerge about intelligence in the Second World War and, in particular, the British exploitation of deception stratagems. Speculation began to be voiced that PROSPER had been sacrificed on the altar of Operations BODYGUARD and FORTITUDE, the schemes devised to mislead the Germans of the time and location of the Allied invasion of the Continent. Amongst the more fanciful conspiracy theories to emerge were allegations that MI6, the British Secret Intelligence Service, had conspired to betray the work of its SOE 'rival' to the enemy in order to achieve the success of its D-Day deception plans and maintain its primacy in Whitehall.

In 2002 the last of the formerly secret SOE files were released to The National Archives and whatever official evidence about PROSPER that had survived the years was finally available to researchers. Although the number of veterans had sadly diminished and opportunities to garner their oral testimonies has all but ended, the amount of data on the PROSPER tragedy is now substantial and perhaps complete. Seventy years after the events, we stand the best possible chance of learning what really happened.

Francis J. Suttill has written a remarkable book about his namesake father. It is a memorable achievement on many fronts, not least that while it constitutes the story of a son's journey to discover the truth about a father he never knew, it avoids any drift into self-indulgence. His personal drive to find the real facts is evident on every page but the investigation is handled in a clear-headed, forensic manner. The author is not looking for someone to blame nor is he seeking simply to whitewash any criticisms of his father's decisions and actions. As a result of this rigorously analytical perspective, the book is a far from conventional account of an SOE agent's life. Unlike the sometimes fanciful and novelistic approaches of other authors, Francis J. Suttill's text is replete with facts and detail ranging from the timing and location of RAF supply drops to an in-depth analysis of the German security offensive launched against PROSPER. While others might have drifted into speculation about what personalities might have thought or said, the story has an exemplary grounding in fact derived from a mass of documentary evidence and the oral testimonies of survivors. The book is a genuine voyage of discovery rather than a validation of preconceptions.

This book will surely be the definitive account of Francis Suttill and the tragic story of his PROSPER circuit. The focus upon blame and guilt that dominated previous studies has been replaced by recognition that there are few 'blacks' and 'whites' but largely a variety of 'greys'. The SOE agents were volunteers and, although they were given the best available training to meet the tasks ahead of them, they were only human. Some of the characters proved stronger than might have been expected in meeting the ghastly challenges confronting them, while others, sadly, did not. The mistakes and failings of the British agents and their French colleagues are generally characterised as human weaknesses not treachery, although such a word still seems applicable to the double agent Henri Déricourt. The book sensibly represents the view that it is not surprising that scared, brutalised and skilfully manipulated agents should have succumbed to the menacing, persuasive powers of their captors. Most accounts of the PROSPER story have focused upon the fallibilities of these agents and made scant recognition of the efficient practices (all too often achieved through brutal coercion) of the German security forces. While British historians have celebrated the successes of MI5's handling of their 'Double Cross' operations and the 'turning' of German agents sent to find the United Kingdom's secrets, it is rarely conceded that their Nazi opposite numbers were sometimes achieving similar results against SOE networks in France.

In conclusion, this work serves two main purposes. Perhaps the most important is that it might have laid to rest the ghosts that attended a family tragedy. Secondly, it finally puts to rest a 70-year-old debate and, one hopes, will stifle the persistent, indiscriminate conspiracy theories that have continued to besmirch the memories of a group of brave, volunteer secret agents who risked their lives for the liberation of France from Nazi tyranny.

Mark Seaman, SOE Historian
2014

From my time as the last SOE Advisor to the Foreign and Commonwealth Office, I know for how long and hard Francis J. Suttill has worked to bring this book to completion. I also know that the late Professor M.R.D. Foot, the doyen of historians of SOE's operations in France, supported his conclusions and strongly encouraged their publication. I am sure that Mark Seaman is right to describe this as the 'definitive account' of the tragic story of the PROSPER circuit and that it will be accepted as such. The book is, moreover, excellently presented, with a liberal and original use of illustrations, which add vividly to the picture of the circuit and its personalities and geographical spread. Above all, the reader is able to understand with unusual intimacy the humanity of the French resistants: the dedication and heroism of ordinary people who were willing to risk their all for liberty. I am delighted that this book has finally been published and I am confident that it will find the success its author deserves.

Duncan Stuart
2014

INTRODUCTION

One night in November 2000 I happened to catch part of a television programme about prisoners-of-war whom the Germans thought might be used as hostages in peace negotiations towards the end of the Second World War.[1] One of them was 'Jimmy' James who had taken part in the famous 'Great Escape' from Stalag Luft III in 1944. Fifty of the seventy-six escapees had been shot by the Germans and four of the survivors were sent to a special camp just outside the concentration camp of Sachsenhausen, some 35 kilometres north of Berlin, where other potential hostages were held. They of course tunnelled out again but were all recaptured and this time they were thrown into the prison block inside the camp – the Zellenbau.

I did not know a great deal about my father's wartime activities at this time, except that he had been part of something called the Special Operations Executive (SOE). He had been parachuted into Occupied France towards the end of 1942 to organise resistance groups and supply them with arms and sabotage material. He had been caught by the Gestapo in mid-1943 and nothing more was known except that he was last seen in the Zellenbau at Sachsenhausen in March 1945, where he was officially assumed to have been killed together with a fellow SOE agent known as Charles Grover-Williams.

I had always thought that the Zellenbau was where prisoners were held prior to their execution, so I was surprised to hear that someone had survived. More in hope than in expectation, I asked the makers of the programme to pass on a letter to Jimmy James. Within a week, I had a telephone call from Jimmy saying that he lived not far from me at Ludlow. He was delighted to receive my letter but somewhat surprised as he had been trying to trace any relatives of the British and Commonwealth personnel killed at Sachsenhausen for the erection of a plaque there in their memory to be unveiled in a few months' time. He had contacted the Foreign and Commonwealth Office and had been told that there was no record in the files of my father having any children.

Although Jimmy's time in the Zellenbau had coincided with part of the time my father was there, he had not met him as the prisoners were all in solitary confinement and kept strictly separate, but he suggested we meet so that he could tell me about the conditions in which prisoners were held. He told me his amazing story, which I later discovered more about in his book.[2] He confirmed that the Zellenbau was a place where you did not know from one day to the next whether you were to live or die.

I wrote to Duncan Stuart, his contact in the Foreign and Commonwealth Office, who worked in the Records and Historical Department with the title of SOE Advisor. I discovered that although some SOE files had been released to the Public Record Office at Kew (now The National Archives), these did not include the files of individual agents. He was, however, able to let me have a copy of most of the documents that remained in my father's file. These related mainly to the post-war search for my father, which was complicated because Sachsenhausen was in the Russian Sector and the arrival of the Iron Curtain meant that information about former prisoners of the camp was extremely difficult to find.

The situation became somewhat confusing when Duncan Stuart told me there was a story circulating that Grover-Williams, my father's fellow SOE prisoner, had somehow survived and returned to France under a pseudonym, only to die when he was run over and killed by German tourists in the 1980s! If Grover-Williams had survived, perhaps my father had as well?

The only evidence for the death of my father and Grover-Williams was in two documents that I found in War Office files relating to the 'killing and ill-treatment of allied nationals' in Sachsenhausen concentration camp.[3] Paul Schroeter was a fundamental Christian who had been a prisoner in Sachsenhausen since early in the war and was one of those who were trusted to work in the prison block, bringing round food. In an interview on 5 July 1946 he stated, 'I saw Suttill and Williams for the last time round about the 15th to the 18th of March 1945. At approx the end of March they were transported by ambulance car to the Industriehof where they were most certainly executed.' He added, 'As a further proof of the death of the prisoners, their prison garb was handed back to us by mistake. We then sent it to the Q.M. stores where it ought to have gone in the first place.' In a second interview on 21 August 1946, he adds that, 'as such prison garb was unimpaired, the victims must have been hanged or gassed, since shooting would have left its mark on the clothing'. (The Industriehof, also known as Station Z, was a small group of buildings outside the main camp walls where prisoners were killed by shooting, hanging or gassing and then the bodies burnt.)

On the basis of this document, the British issued a Death Certificate that my father was 'Presumed Killed in Action' in 'Western Europe on or shortly after 18 March 1945'.

By this time, I felt the need to visit Sachsenhausen. I had contacted one of the researchers who worked at what is now a Place of Remembrance (Gedenkstsatte) and Museum. Dr Winfried Meyer was unfortunately not going to be there on the day I visited, but he left two documents for me to collect when I arrived. These were interrogations by the British of Kurt Eccarius who had been Chief Warder of the Zellenbau.[4] I read these before going any further and found that Eccarius told a completely different story from Schroeter. He stated he believed that Suttill and Grover-Williams had been sent, with all their kit, to the Gestapo HQ in Berlin sometime early in 1945.

Somewhat bewildered by this contradiction, I went into the camp and found the remains of the Zellenbau. Some parts had been rebuilt but Eccarius had said that my father was in Cell 10 and this was only marked by an outline of the foundations. I stood in what remained of that cell and found it difficult to believe that he had lived in this small space for well over a year. I was very glad that my wife was with me as the emotion of the moment was overwhelming. I later found the Industriehof, where all that remained were again the foundations and two small incinerators.

I was given a leaflet about the trial for War Crimes of Anton Kaindl, the Camp Commandant, and many others.[5] After they liberated the camp on 22 April 1945, the Russians started to assemble evidence for a trial. They were particularly keen to investigate Sachsenhausen because some 10,000 Russian prisoners-of-war had been shot there in late 1941. However, most of those they wished to prosecute had ended up in the hands of the British, who also had a particular interest as two of their Commando units had been killed there. They set up a Special Investigation Team, which had found sufficient evidence by early 1946 to indict twenty-three of the main

SS leaders from Sachsenhausen. It was then decided to hand over all the evidence and the prisoners to the Russians and, after months of further interrogation, including 'psychological and physical pressure', all of the defendants gave general confessions. A War Crimes Trial finally started in Berlin in October 1947 and after only eight days, thirteen of the most important criminals were sentenced to life imprisonment. If they had been found guilty in one of the Allied War Crimes Trials, they could have been sentenced to death, but this penalty was not available in a Russian court under their penal laws applicable at the time. Those convicted were sent to work in the northern coalmines and six of them died in the first winter, including Kaindl. Eccarius and other survivors were released back to Germany in 1956, where they were tried again and heavy sentences imposed.

I returned home confused. The experience had been cathartic in some respects, but the unanswered questions as to my father's fate were disturbing. I spent a couple of days at the Public Record Office looking through the files about Sachsenhausen. A really frustrating discovery was the file that had contained all the evidence gathered by the British team; it was now empty, as all of the documents had been sent to the Russians and no copies kept. The only interesting document I found was a statement dated 15 May 1946 by one of the Zellenbau guards, Heinrich Meyer, which corroborated and expanded Eccarius' story. I noted that the British had held Meyer in the same camp as Eccarius, which would have given them the opportunity to ensure that their stories were consistent.

This uncertainty also caused a problem for the wording of the memorial plaque proposed by Jimmy James. The relevant German authorities would not accept wording that stated that the people to be commemorated had necessarily been killed at

Memorial at Sachsenhausen. (Author's collection)

Sachsenhausen. A compromise was agreed so the inscription read: '*In Erinnerung an die tapferen Mitglieder der britischen und Commonwealth Streitkrafte, viele noch heute unbekannt, die im KZ Sachsenhausen gefangen gehalten und hier oder an anderen Orten getotet wurden.*' (In memory of those brave members of the British and Commonwealth forces, many still unknown, who were interned in Sachsenhausen and perished here or elsewhere at the hands of their captors.)

A date was finally fixed for the unveiling of the memorial – 6 July 2001 – and I returned to Sachsenhausen with my younger daughter, Sami, then aged twelve. Her older sister, Emma, could not come as she was sitting her GCSEs. It was all very moving and we both cried. When she returned to school that autumn, her teacher asked the class to write about a day that had changed their lives, thinking that they would all write about the destruction of the twin towers in New York, but Sami considered that what she had been through on her trip to Sachsenhausen where her grandfather had been killed was more important to her. She said that she was determined to go back to Sachsenhausen in 2045 to make sure that the memory was kept alive.

At the end of that year, an article appeared in *The Sunday Times Magazine* for 16 December in which the arguments for Grover-Williams' survival were expanded. It had a suitably dramatic title – 'The Spy who came back from the Dead'. A one-time filmmaker called Jack Bond had somehow come across the story and thought he might be able to make a film about it to restore his reputation. The first hint that he found to support the story was that, unlike the widows of other agents who had been killed, the widow of Grover-Williams was not receiving a war pension.[6] Then he found in Grover-Williams' SOE file some rather curious correspondence from 1947. This started with a request from an Intelligence Officer in Germany to the then SOE Advisor, Major Norman Mott, asking for information as to the fate of an SOE agent called Williams. It appeared that a letter from a W. Williams had been intercepted by the Censors in which he expressed his fear of returning to France as he would be liable to arrest. This seemed to be related to an earlier memo on the file, dated 10 February 1945, from the Security Services in London to the head of the French Section of SOE, Colonel Maurice Buckmaster. It said that an enemy source now in this country, whose information was considered to be reliable, had made the following statement: 'A certain Benoit formerly of 47 Avenue Brocard, Paris, worked for the Germans and denounced to them the well-known racing driver Grover-Williams who was parachuted into France in 1942 and was working under Gestapo control in May 1943.' The source had also stated that Grover-Williams was now in Germany.[7]

With my father before he joined SOE – 1941.

Encouraged by these leads, Bond decided to employ researchers to look more closely at the archives in the Public Records Office and in France and he claimed to have found evidence (although this has never been presented) that Grover-Williams had been transferred to another camp in Poland from where he was able to walk free when the German guards abandoned it as the Russians approached. He surmised that Grover-Williams had worked in some capacity for MI6 after the war. It was then discovered that a man called Georges Tambal had moved into the house of Grover-Williams' widow in 1948. The article claimed some very tenuous likenesses between photographs of Grover-Williams and Tambal and between some writing found on a post-war document and documents he was known to have written before the war.

It seemed to me that Bond and his team were trying to make something out of nothing in an attempt to persuade investors that there was an exciting story to tell. Looking back at the conflicting statements of Schroeter and Eccarius, I felt that Schroeter was more likely to be telling the truth as he had no reason to lie. Eccarius, on the other hand, was still in British hands when he made his statements and would have been aware that if the British had tried him, he would have faced the death penalty: a good reason not to admit killing people.

It was clear to me at this stage that it was time to start trying to find out more about my father and his extraordinary role in the war. Little did I know that I was embarking on an incredible journey that continues to this day as, although I have now found most of the outline and some of the details, many of the details are still missing or sketchy and I hope that others will now help me to fill in the gaps.

Notes

1. *The War behind the Wire*, Hartswood Films for BBC2, 17 November 2000.
2. B.A. James, *Moonless Night*, William Kimber, 1983.
3. WO 309/439, TNA.
4. Interrogations 21 and 27.02.1946, WO 309/853, TNA.
5. Information Leaflet 24, Gedenkstatte und Museum Sachsenhausen, 1999.
6. I discovered later that his widow did, however, claim compensation for his death under an agreement with the German government in 1965.
7. HS 9/1596/8, TNA.

THE CALL OF FRANCE

The Suttill name is an old one originating in Yorkshire. My father had carried out some research and the oldest record he found dated from 1207 when a Michael de Suthill appears in the Pipe Rolls. Standardised spelling of names is relatively modern and the first official recording of the Suttill spelling was a reference to John Suttill who was Sheriff of York around 1730. Before that there was an enormous range of spellings: Sootell, Sotell, Soothill, Sothell, Sothile, Sothill, Sothille, Sothulle, Sottell, Sotthill, Southehill, Southill, Sowtell, Sowthyl, Sutel, Suttle and probably others.

There are two ideas for the origin of the name. It could have come from the ancient French '*sotil*' meaning clever and cunning, still occurring as 'subtle' in English. This might suggest a Norman origin. The alternative is that it comes from 'south of the hill', which might suggest an English origin for the name. There is still an area of Dewsbury in Yorkshire that is called Soothill.

In the parish church of Dewsbury or The Minster Church of All Saints there used to be fourteenth-century stained-glass windows showing the arms of Sothill, but the Reformation and time have taken their toll. There is still a late twelfth-century de Soothill grave in the church and the great bell is said to have been given by Sir Thomas de Soothill, in penance for the murder of a servant boy whom he threw into the forge dam in a fit of rage. The bell is known as Black Tom and is rung each Christmas Eve, one toll for each year since Christ's birth, a tradition dating back to the fifteenth century and known as The Devil's Knell.

My father had found some intriguing records from the thirteenth and fourteenth centuries. Sir John de Suthill is recorded as owning land in York in 1266 and is accused of homicide in 1282. The next year he is recorded as a knight fighting for the Bishop of Durham and in 1298 he goes with King Edward I to Scotland. He is pardoned as an adherent of Thomas, Earl of Lancaster, in 1318 and as a rebel in 1326. At the same time, Sir Henry de Suthill, a Lord of Laxton, is also pardoned but then imprisoned at Nottingham on a charge of rebellion, being released on bail and having his lands and goods in Yorkshire and Nottinghamshire restored to him in 1322. Another record shows that he fought at the Battle of Bannockburn in 1322 with Edward II against Robert Bruce, where his arms were 'gules un aigle argent', which translates as a silver eagle on a red background. Then in 1324, as a non-resident knight of Lindsey in Lincolnshire, he was summoned to the Great Council at Westminster.

In 1520, when Henry VIII of England met Francis I of France on The Field of the Cloth of Gold (Le Camp du Champ d'Or) near Calais, his queen, Catherine of Aragon, went with him. She had her own separate retinue and among the 'Gentilmen' appointed to her train was a Gerves Suttel.

The fortunes of the family declined during the Reformation as they refused to leave the Roman Church and in Camden's *Brittania* in 1607 it states, 'Not far from Dewsbury is Suttill Hall, an ancient seat of the family of Suttill. It is now greatly ruined and the estate belongs to the Duke of Montague.'

The family Bible contains a record of births and deaths, which overlaps with, but does not include, the John Suttill who was Sheriff of York around 1730. The earliest date in the Bible is 1761 when William Suttill was born at Masham in Yorkshire, but his father is named as Francis and his grandfather as William and the latter must have been a contemporary of John. On an internet site, I was able to trace this line back to a David Suttill born in Yorkshire in 1580.

There seems to have been a tradition in our branch of the family of naming the first son William and the second Francis, although the situation is confused by the fact that some of them are called William Francis. The William born in 1761 was a flax spinner who worked with his second son, John, in Pateley Bridge in Yorkshire, but they moved first to Plymouth and then to Dorset where they eventually set up their own business. William's first son, William, born in Pateley Bridge in 1789, was also a flax spinner. He went to Plymouth with his father and brother, but he then parted company with them and is next heard of living in Moscow, but he appears to be the start of the family connection with France as he died in Lille in 1854. However, in 1830 he must have been in Yorkshire, as this is where his son, another William, was born and he in turn had a son in 1858 called William Francis, my grandfather.

The area between Lille and Belgium is renowned for its textile industries and so would have been an area of opportunity for my great-great-grandfather and the family seem to have prospered there. My grandfather, although born in Manchester, lived in Lille and managed a textile business there. It was here that he married a near-neighbour, Blanche Marie Louise Degrave; he lived at No 13, she at No 28 rue de Roubaix, Mons-en-Baroeul, which is just to the north of the Lille Eurostar Terminal.

They had four children, the youngest being my father, Francis Alfred, born on 17 March 1910. My father was sent to England to be educated by the Jesuits at Stonyhurst College in Lancashire. Initially he appears to have done

My grandfather and grandmother. (Author's collection)

My father and mother. (Author's collection)

well; I still have two of the books that he won as prizes. Then tragedy struck when he was 16. He was found to have poliomyelitis and told that he would probably never walk again. His mother did not accept this possibility and for a year she devoted herself to getting him to walk, including making him take up golf. The results were remarkable as, despite ending up with one leg 18mm shorter than the other, he could walk without a perceptible limp. At the end of the year it was time to go back to school, but this time locally so that his rehabilitation could be continued, and he gained his Baccalauréat at the College de Marcq, a Catholic school nearby, where he was described as a brilliant laureate, winning five prizes. He then read law at the Université de Lille and at University College London and was called to the Bar at Lincoln's Inn in 1935. Ironically, as it turned out, he claimed British nationality in 1931 to obtain exemption from military service in France.

Also in 1935, he married a fellow student who had read medicine, Margaret Montrose, and they had two children. I was born in 1940, three years after my brother. By this time they had bought land in the village of Newdigate near Redhill in Surrey and had a house built. This outlay proved to be excessive in the pre-war years when the legal profession, like so many others, was in decline and this probably contributed to him volunteering in September 1939, some time before he would otherwise have been called up. He started in the ranks of the East Surrey Regiment but was soon selected for Officer Training in Colchester, resulting in his appointment as a second lieutenant in May 1940. He was not very impressed by this training, writing home on 2 May:

We have had an awful day. Out this morning and this evening an exam. I did quite well in the exam, in fact, the best yet but the whole thing leaves one most frightfully tired and exhausted so this letter will probably be a short one. I shall try and get out for a stroll while the light is still good. It might do me good. I don't think I like this Company much. One feels they don't give a damn for you. The young officer we had at first is in hospital with a poisoned leg and we keep getting different officers.

A year later he attended an Intelligence Course in April/May 1941, was promoted to Acting Lieutenant and posted as Intelligence Officer to 211 Brigade based near Plymouth. The rest of the family also moved to Devon, first staying in Tiverton, where my mother worked as matron in Blundell's School, and then to a farm outside Plymouth.

His next posting was to SOE, but how did he get there? There was no fixed selection process and it was not possible to apply as no one knew that such jobs existed. In my father's case, the only clue that I could find was a letter that I found on his file. His Service Record shows that he was medically assessed in Chesterfield in November 1941 as a potential paratrooper. In January 1942 he was approached by a Colonel Hope Thompson. In his reply to the colonel on 24 January 1942, my father wrote:

I have received your letter and am very grateful to you for having remembered me. I was interviewed by the CO of the 1st Battalion at Chesterfield a fortnight ago. He put me on his A1 plus list. I also passed my medical. I am still very much a volunteer for paratroops and hope that you will remember me if a vacancy occurs in your battalion. Please recommend me for special duties if you can. My one wish is to be used in France. [He then repeats his military history to date and ends by saying] I lived near Lille for 9 years and speak native French. I am not concerned about rank except, being a family man, from the financial point of view.[1]

I assume that Colonel Hope Thompson was in the 1st or another Parachute Battalion, as on 9 March my father was promoted to Temporary Captain and posted to the 1st Battalion, The Parachute Regiment. But Hope Thompson must have known about SOE and passed on my father's letter as on 16 March this order was cancelled and he was ordered to report to Room 055A at the War Office; he had been selected for interview by SOE.

There was competition for French-speaking officers at this time as they were also needed as translators and Intelligence Officers for the invasion of Madagascar, which started on 5 May. The Allies were concerned that, if the Japanese were to take over the island, supply lines to the Far East would be seriously threatened. A mention in a letter to my mother that month records that he had been considered for Madagascar but not selected.

Many agents' files contain detailed reports on their training and these are often so revealing that it is surprising that some agents ended up in France. My father's training records are no longer on his file and so I have had to try and recreate his training programme by discovering who trained with him and then seeing what their files revealed.

Training was by language group, which posed the risk that agents meeting again unexpectedly in the field might know each

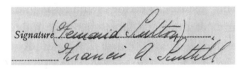

My father's signature on the Official Secrets Act.

other's real names. They were therefore given code names for training, although these often used the same initials as their real names. Thus my father became 'Fernand Sutton' and I noticed that when he signed the Official Secrets Act on 19 May, he used this name rather than his real one, which surprised me.

Each training group had a Conducting Officer who escorted them on, and took part in, their courses so that they often ended up becoming agents themselves. This is what happened to Lieutenant André Simon who accompanied them on their first course but left for France on a mission soon afterwards. His replacement was Lieutenant Robert Searle who did not go to France. A note on his file suggests that my father worked as a Conducting Officer initially, but this seems unlikely as the previous training group had started in mid-February, which is before he joined SOE, and two days after joining, he started his own training.

My father's training group was labelled 27N and started out with eleven recruits. They were sent to Wanborough Manor near Guildford in Surrey, known as Special Training School 5, or STS 5, for a hard training course of military and physical training. This course finished on 15 April and two of the group were failed, leaving nine. Eight of this group then went to Scotland using as cover membership of the Inter Services Research Bureau for even more intensive training. STS 23 was based in Meoble Lodge near Arisaig and this course ended on 17 May to be followed by a short parachute course at STS 51, Ringway airfield near Manchester.

My father's companions were now: 'Clement Bastable' – Claude de Baissac who would organise the Scientist circuit around Bordeaux; 'Hilaire' – Harry Peuleve who was to be de Baissac's first radio operator; 'Robert Lang' – Roger Landes who initially took over as de Baissac's radio operator when Peuleve was injured and later became the circuit's organiser; 'Louis

Legranges' – Louis Lee-Graham, a radio operator captured following a crash-landing; 'Michel' – Marcus Bloom who joined the Prunus circuit as a radio operator; 'Frederick Chalk' – Fergus Chalmers-Wright who initially worked with the Political Warfare Executive; and 'Noel Hines' – Norman Hinton who was sent on a solo mission the purpose of which remains unknown.

At this point, the trainees were finally told that they were not being trained as Commandos but as potential agents to be sent into France to organise sabotage and resistance networks and this was when they were asked to sign the Official Secrets Act. The group was then split with potential radio operators being sent to STS 52 at Thame Park near Oxford for specialist wireless training. Both groups ended their training, but no longer together, at a large group of country houses near Beaulieu in Hampshire, sometimes known as the 'Finishing School'. The four prospective organisers were housed in STS 31, The Rings. In a letter home from Beaulieu my father gives nothing away, writing on 24 June, 'I am afraid my letters are a bit dull but then nothing much is happening.'

There are many descriptions of the training given to SOE agents in other books, but I found an official version written in October 1942, which I do not think has been published previously – see Appendix 1.

On Claude de Baissac's file I found the report that Lieutenant Searle had made at the end of the course at Beaulieu. It is dated 6 July 1942 and it comments on all four of the potential organisers, although it is not very enlightening on my father, only saying, 'He has brought to this course a balanced sense of discrimination and constructive criticism.' On de Baissac he is more explicit and expansive:

He has been inclined to criticise this course and particularly the general nature of the B lectures. (Organisation in the field, Security measures, cover.) This led him first to a certain feeling of frustration since his mind, which needs to seize on a fact and consider its immediate application, is irked by generalities which can only be brought to bear concretely on his work at a later stage in his training. He has worked with extreme thoroughness. He enjoyed the scheme and gained confidence through the ease with which he managed to obtain the information he was instructed to seek.[2]

Of the four, only these two were selected to be sent into France as organisers. Indeed there was no opportunity for de Baissac to have the suggested further training as he, with Peuleve as his wireless operator (WTO), was parachuted into France only three weeks later. My father had to wait another three months.

Compared with Searle's unenlightening comment, Maurice Buckmaster was effusive in an article he wrote after the war, perhaps exaggerated with hindsight:

Prosper had the clear intellectual vision and logical perspicacity which are often found allied to Gallic features. Dark hair and clear grey eyes, combined with a classic profile, made him striking to the close observer, but it was not until he spoke that one realised the full extent of his charm and balance. It was a joy to work with a man whose brain cut like a knife into the problems we put before him. He never made the mistake of minimising the difficulties of his mission, and he took as much care over the study of his brief as if he had found it difficult to understand.[3]

Notes

1 . HS 9/1430/6, TNA.
2. HS 9/75-/76, TNA.
3. *Prosper*, Chambers Journal, January 1947.

THE CALL TO FRANCE

Finding the basic outlines of the Special Operations Executive, or SOE for short, was fairly easy as an official history – *SOE in France* – had been written by Professor Michael Foot. (The first 1966 edition was officially amended and republished by HMSO in 1968. A revised and updated edition was published by Frank Cass in 2004 and a French translation of this edition was published in 2008 by Tallandier under the title *Des Anglais dans la Résistance*.)

The origins and development of SOE have been described in great detail in the official history and many other books and so I will not repeat them here. Following the famous directive 'And now set Europe ablaze',[1] SOE was set up as a secret organisation to send specially trained agents into occupied countries to identify, train, supply and coordinate the activities of local resistance groups. Initially their main objectives were sabotage targets but ultimately to attack the enemy in concert with the eventual invasion.

Churchill and SOE were both aware from the beginning of the danger that sabotage might trigger savage reprisals if too much of it was done too soon: SOE's initial approach to armed activity in France was consequently tentative and slow.

In France two parallel organisations were set up: F Section, using mainly officers of British nationality, and RF Section, using officers of French nationality and linked to the Gaullist headquarters. By 1942, the head of F Section was Colonel

Maurice Buckmaster, an avuncular figure whom I met several times after the war, and the basic pattern of SOE activity was becoming established. At this stage only the northern part of France was occupied by the Germans.

The first agents to be sent into France by F Section, despite the recruitment rules, were two Frenchmen and an Englishman. These were Georges Bègue, a wireless operator, on 5 May 1941; Pierre de Vomecourt on 10 May; and Roger Cotton-Burnett on 13 May. Pierre de Vomecourt based himself in Paris and started the Autogiro circuit, receiving the first drop of two containers in June. Cotton-Burnett had been sent in to start a circuit in Brittany but joined de Vomecourt as his second-in-command. In July Noël Burdeyron was sent in to start a circuit in Normandy with a wireless operator but the latter was arrested soon afterwards and Burdeyron stayed quietly in Caen.

In August Jacques de Guelis was landed to reconnoitre in the south together with an agent, Georges Turck. On 6 September six more agents arrived with another wireless operator, André

Colonel Buckmaster.
(Buckmaster family)

Bloch, all to work in the south except for Ben Cowburn who was sent in to identify oil targets and then joined Autogiro in the north. A fortnight later, a third group of four arrived, this time by sea on the Mediterranean coast. A fourth group, a team of sabotage instructors, including another wireless operator, were dropped in the south on 10 October. One of them landed some way from the others and was arrested, carrying the address of Georges Turck where they were to meet. When the rest of the team arrived there, they were also captured but the compromised safe house continued to be used and the last two wireless operators were caught, first André Bloch and then Georges Bègue, leaving the remaining agents throughout France with no direct radio link with London.

Pierre de Vomecourt was now not only in desperate need of a radio link with London but he had also run out of funds. He was put in touch with a group of former Polish intelligence agents, known as Interalliée, who were in contact with British intelligence. He decided to test the reliability of this link by asking them to send a request for funds.

Pierre de Vomecourt. (SFC)

A positive response was received and also the necessary funds. What de Vomecourt did not know when he did this was that the Abwehr had just turned one of Interalliée's agents, which resulted in many arrests including the group's leader 'Armand', Captain Roman Czerniawski. One of those arrested was Mathilde Carré and she was also turned, leading to the total destruction of Interalliée and the capture of four wireless sets tuned to London, then used for radio games. The story of what happened next is extraordinary and is set out in several, not entirely reliable, books[2] but is not directly relevant to my father's story.

De Vomecourt returned to London in February 1942 and it was decided that the original structure that had been proposed should be abandoned. This had involved having 'a chief organiser for the whole of France having under his command a delegate from each zone and zone delegates controlling a certain number of organisers by Region and Department'. It was realised that in such a structure, one arrest could bring about the collapse of the whole organisation due to the multiplicity of contacts. The solution was to create watertight independent groups having their own system of communications with London; this was sometimes referred to as Plan B.[3] So when de Vomecourt returned to France at the beginning of April 1942, it was with strict orders to break up his organisation into several independent sections having no contact with each other. He spent a fortnight in the south and apparently achieved his missions there before going north to Paris.

In the south, despite the many arrests of SOE personnel, the situation initially looked more promising. Henri Frager, an architect by profession, had fought in the 1914–18 war and had joined up again in 1939. He made contact with British intelligence in North Africa and in July 1941, SOE landed him near Marseilles. Here he met the painter André Girard, known as Carte, who not only claimed to have formed several resistance groups but was also in radio contact with London. SOE were interested and sent Francis Basin to France in September 1941 to liaise with Carte and establish his own radio contact but this was no longer possible when all of the wireless operators were arrested. His task was further complicated as there were several other organisations all attempting to take overall control. Basin was arrested in August but was quickly replaced by Peter Churchill who arrived on 28 August 1942.

This was at the same time that a staff officer from F Section, Nicolas Bodington, was sent in by SOE to investigate Carte's organisation. He presented a very favourable report on his return to London in early September and this resulted in SOE taking a serious interest in Carte. The situation changed soon afterwards however when, in retaliation for the Anglo-American landings in north-west Africa on 8 November, the Germans three days later occupied the southern part of France. Also in November, a Carte courier, taking the details of over 200 members of the organisation from Marseilles to Paris, fell asleep on the train and was relieved of his briefcase, which ended up in the hands of the Abwehr.[4] Curiously the Germans do not seem to have made any immediate use of this information but Carte was beginning to fall apart for other reasons. Basin's replacement, Peter Churchill, did not get on with Girard as Basin had done and then Henri Frager, who had become Girard's deputy, also fell out with his leader, feeling that Girard was not only achieving nothing himself but was preventing other SOE agents from getting on with their missions out of jealousy. There was a final split and Frager left Carte on 2 February 1943 to start his own circuit around Montelimar.

But I must return to the second half of April 1942 with Pierre de Vomecourt reaching Paris, although he does not seem to have achieved any of his objectives there before he was arrested on 25 April. This news apparently only reached London on 26 May,[5] by which time another wireless operator, Marcel Clech, had been sent in to join Autogiro, but he was warned in time and was diverted to another circuit. Four days after de Vomecourt's arrest, Edward Wilkinson was sent in with Cowburn to take over the latter's Autogiro contacts in Paris with Denis Rake as wireless operator but they struggled to get themselves and a radio there. On 19 July Richard Heslop was sent in to try and rescue de Vomecourt from prison but on 15 August he, together with Wilkinson and Rake, were arrested trying to cross the demarcation line and SOE finally gave up on Autogiro.

Soon after de Vomecourt returned to France, SOE received its 'Charter for operations on the Continent' by way of a directive from the Chiefs of Staff dated 12 May 1942 and reiterated by them on 8 August 1942.[6] This required SOE to endeavour to build up and equip para-military organisations in the areas where invasions of the Continent might take place:

The action of such organisations will in particular be directed towards the following tasks:-

- Prevention of the arrival of enemy reinforcements by the interruption of road, rail and air transport.
- The interruption of enemy signal communications in and behind the battle area generally.
- Prevention of demolitions by the enemy.
- Attacks on enemy aircraft and air personnel.
- Disorganisation of enemy movements and rear services by the spreading of rumours.

For most of this time my father was in training, which he completed in the first week in July. On 7 July the F Section War Diary records 'Physician – The name of this agent in the field will be François Alfred DESPREZ and he will work in Occupied France. He has been allotted the number 001.F.'[7] Then there is a hiatus. On 26 July he writes home, 'I hope they find something for me to do soon.' And in another, 'I gather that the intentions of the authorities with regard to me change several times a day just now. I rather think my job will not be what I thought. I don't think I shall be away for longer at a time than a few days.' This sounds more like a Staff job in London and he is clearly marking time – 'Life is frightfully dull here and it is not warm enough to walk in the parks. So I just sit in the library quite a lot and try and do some work.'

The first mention of a date for him to go to France is a proposal to send him on 20 August to an approved ground near Vendôme with a deputy but without a wireless operator or a courier.[8] This is just after the final death throes of Autogiro on 15 August. However, it is noted that the exact date depended on my father being provided with more ration cards and safe houses. This problem is reiterated in a document on de Baissac's file dated 27 July in which he is asked to, 'Insist ... upon the great urgency of our receiving the safe houses to which we wish to send a certain number of picked organisers and W/T men this moon.'[9]

Although the period of uncertainty for my father lasted around six weeks, the debate as to what to do in northern France must have started at the end of May if not earlier. It also appears that SOE were not alone in trying to work this out as I found an intriguing reference in one of my father's letters from this summer – 'A funny thing. I passed Dansey in the street the other day. He was in civvies and recognised me. We did *not* exchange greetings.' Bearing in

Claude Dansey.

mind that the collapse of F Section's Autogiro circuit had resulted from the infiltration by the Germans of the Polish Interalliée intelligence circuit, MI6 may have felt that they should be involved in any decision about replacing Autogiro, who should lead it and whether any use should be made of previous contacts. There was a Claude Dansey who was the Assistant Chief of MI6 and served as their liaison officer with SOE and this could be the man my father had met and clearly had not got on with![10]

The fact that SOE was not in total control of this debate is recorded by Colonel Buckmaster. After the failure of Autogiro:

It became apparent that our men would derive encouragement and assistance from more precise briefing. Although it proved extremely difficult to extract a directive from the authorities (it was not even quite certain which authority was the competent one), the increase in target briefing and the more precise orders regarding the preparation for guerrilla warfare afforded some satisfaction to our officers.[11]

One positive decision that resulted from this debate was that:

The events of April and May had led the Section to abandon a 'long term economic' in favour of a 'short term semi-military' target policy. ... It had long been realised that the French character is such as to welcome the prospect of action, provided it is immediate, but becomes discouraged if action is long deferred. Consequently each agent was given one target for action as soon as circumstances permitted.

By August 1942 the plan that had been laid down for the Occupied Zone (ZO) was:

to expand our various organisations to the maximum possible without pyramiding them and to deliver at least 1500 lbs of stores immediately. W/T communications to be extended as far as was compatible with optimum safety. Insaissable sabotage to be encouraged, particularly the destruction by fire and water of factories working for the enemy.

However, 'Owing to flak and other technical difficulties, it was not possible to deliver stores to the ZO until the end of September 1942, when one small container was delivered.'

Despite these uncertainties, decisions were made during this period to send in to France all of the organisers who had by then been trained, except for my father and Michael Trotobas, who only finished his training at the end of August. Three of these – Cowburn, Wilkinson and Heslop – have already been mentioned and six others were sent in to operate in the south – Pertschuk, Le Chêne, Brooks, Frager, Churchill and John Starr. Three more had been sent into the ZO: Charles Grover-Williams[12] to organise the Chestnut sabotage circuit to the west of Paris; Raymond Flower to start the Monkeypuzzle circuit around Le Mans; and Claude de Baissac to start the Scientist circuit in the Bordeaux area. Clearly my father had been held back for some special purpose and a purpose of a scale that meant he needed a deputy, although apparently not a courier or a wireless operator as the people who would join him in these capacities were at this stage allocated to other circuits. The woman who did become my father's courier was Andrée Borrel who, having finished her training towards the end of June, was recorded as being ready to go to France on 23 July but this record does not state in what capacity or where in France she was to go.

A report in September 1942 mentions the desirability of fixing a date by which SOE plans should be ready to be put into action in the event of an invasion into the Continent. It concluded that, if the war continued to progress at its present pace, it would appear unlikely that invasion could be undertaken until the early spring of 1943. The end of February 1943 is therefore suggested as a suitable target date for these plans to be ready.[13]

Despite the evidence for a long and fierce debate as to the future activities of SOE in northern France, there is little in the files to show what was ultimately decided. The basic premise of the SOE Charter of May 1942 was reiterated three months later and Buckmaster's memories in his history of F Section only emphasise the need for the concept of Plan

B, the creation of independent circuits each with a separate communications link with HQ, and all of this to be set up and ready for action by the end of February 1943.

It appears therefore that my father was either simply the only person left to take on the job or had been picked as a possibility sometime earlier and kept in the dark until the last minute when all other options had failed.

NOTES

1. Hugh Dalton, *The Fateful Years*, Frederick Muller, 1957.
2. See, for example, M-L Carre, *La Chatte*, Four Square, 1961.
3. French Resistance and Allied Services, Sub-Section II, HS 7/133, TNA
4. Memo 19.05.1942 HS 9/1539/6, TNA.
5. The Abwehr was the German military intelligence service often in conflict with the Gestapo who were part of the Nazi state security services.
6. W. Mackenzie, *The Secret History of SOE*, St Ermins Press, 2000).
7. HS 8/275, TNA.
8. HS 7/244, TNA.
9. Operations Schedule for September/October Moon, HS 8/136, TNA.
10. HS 9/75, TNA.
11. There was another Dansey who worked with SOE's Code Section but I have not found any reason for my father to have met him.
12. History of F Section, HS 7/121, TNA.
13. Really Charles Grover but this name is never used in official records.
14. HS 8/275, TNA.

ARRIVAL

In the autumn of 1942 Monkeypuzzle was the only circuit that was able to organise and receive parachute drops north of the demarcation line as it had a radio operator. The organiser, Raymond Flower, was parachuted blind (not to a reception committee) near Tours on the night of 27 June 1942 and was supposed to set up his circuit around Le Mans, near where he had run a hotel before the war, but he damaged an ankle so badly on landing that he had to be taken to Tours for treatment. He then decided that he was too well known in the Le Mans area so he based Monkeypuzzle in Tours.

The radio operator was Marcel Clech. He had been landed in the south of France on 20 April to work for Autogiro but was diverted to Châteauroux to collect a radio left by the arrested Bègue. He was warned of Autogiro's collapse before being caught up in that disaster himself and was redirected to Tours without having recovered the radio to await the arrival of Flower. He reached Tours

Raymond Flower.
(Flower family)

Marcel Clech. (SFC)

on 23 June but only met up with Flower on 16 July. In the meantime, Edward Wilkinson, who was in Paris trying to pick up Cowburn's Autogiro contacts, sought to take Clech over. SOE initially agreed but then reversed the decision as Clech did not receive a radio until 8 August and Monkeypuzzle was intended to be the main conduit for sending agents into northern France.

The day before, they were joined by a courier, Yvonne Rudellat, who also arrived from the south where she landed on 30 July. There is some confusion concerning her orders as, in a document prepared for the official history by the then SOE Advisor, he writes, 'July 1942. By sea on a felucca, via Gibraltar, Yvonne Claire Rudellat (Suzanne, Jacqueline) was infiltrated with instructions to join the Prosper circuit as courier.'[1] Not surprisingly, Michael Foot incorporated this into his official history, writing, 'She settled down unobtrusively at Tours to establish a cover and await orders from Suttill, her organiser, whose arrival was held up for some time.' However SOE's 1942 War Diary[2] on 21 July describes her as a 'lady courier for Le Mans'. There are several mistakes in Boxshall's document and the War Diary appears to be correct. This confusion probably arises because Rudellat did ultimately become a courier in part of the Prosper circuit but initially she was to act as courier in the Monkeypuzzle circuit.[3]

Flower was not particularly pleased with Yvonne Rudellat and Clech had difficulty in finding safe locations from which to make regular transmissions as he was constantly harried by German direction-finders. Indeed one of the immediate targets given to Flower to attack were direction-finding vans, which tracked the transmissions of wireless operators. The result was that the group was not able to achieve anything and they could not even find somewhere to receive parachute drops of arms and sabotage materials. This is where Pierre Culioli came on the scene and he would later play a very large part in the Prosper–Physician circuit. He had been introduced to Clech by a mutual friend in Tours before Flower arrived. He knew the area because he had been a tax inspector in Le Mans before the

Yvonne Rudellat and her daughter. (Julie Clamp)

Pierre Culioli. (P. Guillaume)

war and had married Ginnette Dutems from Mer, 80km up the Loire from Tours. She was killed when an Italian aircraft bombed Mer in July 1940.

Culioli's father-in-law owned land on the south side of the Loire known as Bois Renard, between Nouan-sur-Loire and Crouy-sur-Cosson. A field here was chosen and approved by the RAF and Flower asked for '12 Colts with ammunition, 10kgs of plastic, 800 primers, detonators and other devices', a modest sabotage order with pistols for protection. SOE was at last able to implement its long-delayed plan to set up the Physician circuit and give the Scientist circuit another wireless operator to replace Peuleve who had been seriously injured on landing. Flower was told to expect one container and two agents. On 18 September 1942, Operation Monkeypuzzle 1/ Whitebeam/Artist was ordered. Whitebeam was the operational name of Andrée Borrel who was to be the courier in the Physician circuit. Artist was Lise de Baissac who was to base herself in Poitiers and, amongst other tasks, act as liaison between the Physician circuit and the Scientist circuit organised by her brother, Claude. They were the first women to be parachuted into Occupied France.

This operation was almost cancelled when Clech received information from Pierre de Vomecourt's brother, Philippe, that they should not trust a man called 'Culoti'. Clech believed this to be the same person as Culioli who had worked previously for an intelligence gathering organisation in the area where Philippe operated. He therefore asked Flower to cancel or reschedule the operation whilst further enquiries were made but Flower refused.

The BBC message announcing the drop, '*Les singes ne posent pas des questions*' (Monkeys do not ask questions), was first broadcast on 23 September but the attempt that night was a fiasco. When the aircraft arrived, the pilot found that the reception team led by Flower had not yet set up the lights. When he heard the aircraft, Flower rushed out and tried to organise the lights but he placed them too close to the edge of the wood and the women might have ended up in the trees. The pilot of the aircraft reported that, as the lights were incorrect and were too close to the wood, being only 20m away from the edge, the operation was abandoned and the aircraft returned to base.[4]

This was too much for the already panic-stricken Flower who is reported to have declared, 'We are betrayed. It's a German plane. Leave quickly. We are surrounded.'[5] Whereupon he fled, returned across the Loire and stayed with the Bossards who had a safe house at Avaray, a few miles from Mer. The next day he returned to his base in Tours and showed no further interest in this parachute operation. It was Culioli who heard the BBC message repeated the next day. Taking his two brothers-in-law, Guy and Jean Dutems, he reached Bois Renard in time to set up the lights. This time the pilot hesitated because the lights on the ground were white instead of red but as the flashing signal was correct, the drop went ahead. The despatcher reported that 'Agents jumped when told; everything OK'. The newly arrived agents asked for Flower as he had been specifically ordered to meet them, and were asurprised to be told that he was not there.

A few days later, on the night of 1/2 October 1942, my father at last arrived in France. The order that had been placed for him to go in August would have dropped him to an approved ground near Vendôme, some 50km from both Tours and Bois Renard, and this remained the preferred option through September.

The delays were very frustrating for all concerned and my father wrote home on Tuesday, 22 September:

> I was as you know to be going today but it has now been postponed till the 27th so as to give me time to get everything ready. Ever since Friday midday till late last night I have been talked and talked at. You say it is tiring to talk to others; I think it tires both. I am sorry if I was not too clear last night but I had completely ceased to think at all clearly. I shan't be able to phone tonight as I have to go and see somebody off officially.

This was of course Andrée Borrel, his courier. Five days later he wrote a letter that was both practical and emotional:

> Before going further I must confirm two things. First that the amount at Barclays will be credited with £500 p.a. paid quarterly in advance. Secondly my application for majority at once was not approved but in the event of my decease on this mission, my application will be confirmed and antedated so as to carry major's pension. I am sorry I could not do better but there it is. I got your letter. Don't worry – I shall have sandwiches and tea on the trip. I may incidentally pass over not very far from you as we do a circular trip to avoid opposition. I shall also have barley sugar. I do feel a bit foul, not for my sake but for yours. Anyway I know that your thoughts and good wishes

will always be with me as will mine with yours. I have a marvellous job and an excellent team under my orders and I will do all I can to make the thing a great success. Goodbye my darling and thank you a thousand times for all the happiness you have always given me. I am the luckiest of men. Goodbye darling one, Francis.

Finally on 1 October he wrote what would be the last letter home before he left for France:

If I am not going tonight I will have phoned before you get this. If I am going I can only say goodbye again. The last few days have been a queer experience – much easier than when I saw the others off last week. It is easier for oneself than for others. There is also a very pure feeling of exultation – I say pure because when one is at last facing the real thing, which is nothing more or less than a protracted 'going over the top', there is no feeling of what you would rightly call 'showing off' left. One feels like Rupert Brooke when he wrote –

'Now, God be thanked who has matched us with his hour,
And caught our youth, and wakened us from sleeping,
With hand made sure, clear eye, and sharpened power.
To turn, as swimmers into cleanness leaping,
Glad from a world grown old and cold and weary.'

But that world does not include the portion you inhabit because that is in my heart and is with me. Goodbye my love, Francis.

When he did at last take off on 1 October, in a Halifax piloted by Flying Officer Anderlé of 138 Squadron, he was to be dropped blind near La Ferté-sous-Jouarre, to the east of Paris.

Perhaps the first inklings of the problems in Monkeypuzzle had reached London and made them think it would be wiser not to drop my father to one of their receptions. With him was his deputy, Jean Amps, a jockey from Chantilly, whose operational name was Chemist and he was to be known to the team as Tomas.

Even this operation was not as simple as it might have been as there was low fog over the dropping point. The passengers were told that they might have to drop 2–3 miles from the pinpoint and at first they refused to jump. The pilot then flew in circles around a point on the river Seine and persuaded his passengers that he knew where their pinpoint was. They did then jump and the pilot estimated that he was then not more than 3 miles from the pinpoint, but my father reported that they were dropped 12km from the pinpoint and half a kilometre from each other. When they landed, my father dislocated his knee, breaking the cartilage where the muscles were already atrophied as a result of polio. The package dropped with them was not in their suitcases with all of their clothes, but a wireless set they knew nothing about.

Within a few days, he had met up with Andrée Borrel and they set off on a tour of northern France to assess possibilities. They were told to go together because there were doubts about my father's accent as he had not lived in France for ten years. One of the French men he met later commented that he had '*un très légère accent qui pourait à la rigeur passer pour belge*' (a very light accent that could pass for Belgian). He also needed some physical support to walk.

The choice of Andrée Borrel as his courier was ironic as he had hoped not to be teamed with her. He had clearly met her in England as he told one of his training companions, Louis Lee-Graham, 'that he found her attractive, so much so that the prospect of working long months with her at his side,

My father. ID card photo taken in Paris in 1943. (Author)

once they were in France, to some extent troubled him, in as much as he was a married man and might find the enforced proximity a strain'.[6] She did in fact enter into a relationship with a member of the circuit but it was not my father!

Meanwhile, back in Mer, Maurice Dutems was so concerned at the behaviour of Flower that he refused to allow him on his land again and said that any further operations would have to be received by his sons and Culioli. This was the team that received the next Monkeypuzzle operation on the night of 20/21 October, which brought four containers. The aircraft was meant to drop three packages as well containing a wireless set and the suitcases for my father and Amps but the crew thought that they were charity food parcels, known as Granthams, and dropped them over the nearby town of Marchenoir where they were handed to the Germans.

Flower had originally wanted to send Culioli to London for training but he was furious at being barred from the field and reported to London that he considered Culioli to be too dangerous because he was overly curious and wished to have everything in his own hands, being unwilling to accept any directive. Culioli was also initially thought to have stolen the suitcases and wireless set as it was not until a few days later

Andrée Borrel. (Archives SHD)

that it was realised that they had been dropped elsewhere. London replied that if Culioli was suspected, all necessary steps should be taken. Flower decided that Culioli would have to be killed and ordered a lethal pill from London.

This was brought by Gilbert Norman, a wireless operator initially intended to go to Corsica, with Operation Monkeypuzzle 3 on the night of 31 October, following the BBC message '*Les écrivisses marchent de travers*' (The crayfish walk sideways). Also dropped that night were Roger Landes, a wireless operator to replace the injured Peuleve in the Scientist circuit; an RF Section agent; four containers; and three packages to replace those lost on the previous operation. A packet for Flower included the lethal pill and, ironically, Norman had to give it to Culioli to pass on, as Flower was again barred from the DZ.

Now Flower decided that he could not do the deed himself and asked Clech and others to do it for him. When they all refused, he asked Norman, who said that Culioli would be sent to London. So the plan was abandoned and a provisional pick-up of Culioli was planned for 17 November. Not surprisingly, the plan to kill him reached the ears of Culioli who was furious. He immediately decided to leave the group and, to make it impossible for Flower to organise further operations at Bois Renard, he spread pieces of parachute over the field so that it was no longer safe to use. He also, with Norman's help, moved the material that had been parachuted and hid it in a different part of the wood where it could not be found by Flower. By this time Norman's orders had been cancelled and he had been offered to Lise de Baissac, but she said she did not need him so he was finally allocated to my father. The only problem was that his wireless had been sent to the south of France where he had been expected to collect it on his way to Corsica. Because of this uncertainty, Norman stayed with the Bossard family in Avaray for the first few weeks after his arrival, not joining my father in Paris until December.

Flower also decided to get rid of Rudellat, claiming that she was compromising the group through contacts in Tours, which included Germans. To this end, he visited her room when she was out and left there a suitcase containing a pistol, a radio with its crystals, codes, wavelengths and schedules of hours for transmitting. Luckily, Rudellat returned before anyone else saw them and got rid of them. She decided that it was time to leave with Culioli and together they moved to Étrépagny and joined my father's circuit.[7]

Flower did manage to organise one more parachute operation but to a ground a long way from Bois Renard near Saché, southeast of Tours; it was known as La Crépellière. On the night of 18/19 November, two agents and four containers were dropped

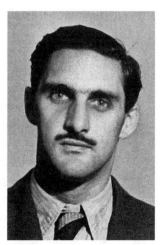

Gilbert Norman. (Guy Laurent)

there following the BBC message '*Michel monta trés haut (ou tard) dans la pommier*' (Michael climbed very high (or late) in the apple tree). The agents were Charles Hayes, who was to join the Scientist circuit as a sabotage expert, and France Antelme, who had a roving commission to establish political and financial links.

This was, however, the end of Monkeypuzzle. Damning reports from my father and others led to a cessation of activities and radio contact. Rudellat refused to give Flower back his radio and de Baissac refused to let him send messages through his wireless operator. On 17 December, Clech reported that they were *brûlé* (burnt) at Tours. He and Flower were expecting to be returned to London but because of bad weather early in the new year and lack of anyone to organise pick-up operations, it was not possible to return Flower to London until March. Clech returned a month later and was sent on another mission to France in May 1943. Flower was not sent into the field again.

After his return to London, Clech reported that he had always worked in perfect harmony with Flower but he did make certain criticisms of him:

- he lacked tact and initiative;
- he had no get-up-and-go;
- he was too talkative and indiscreet – on receipt of the poison pill, he told everyone present its purpose; and
- on receipt of a message telling him to blow up everything that was useful to the Germans, he said that nothing should be blown up because it would result in reprisals against the population.

He also gave his opinion of Culioli – 'I judge Culioli to be a very dangerous individual for our organisation because what he has done to Flower, he will do to anyone at all that stands in his way and he is only out for himself. We need to get rid of him or remove him.'[8]

Notes

1. Colonel E G Boxshall, Chronology of SOE Operations with the Resistance in France during World War II, 1960. Copy in the IWM.
2. HS 7/244, TNA.
3. Stella King's, *Jacqueline*, Arms and Armour, 1989.
4. AIR 20/8452, TNA.
5. Stella King's, *Jacqueline*.
6. J.O. Fuller, *The German Penetration of SOE*, William Kimber, 1975.
7. See 3 above.
8. Report 20.04.1943 now redacted by the Foreign Office, HS 9/379/8, TNA.

THE MISSION

There is not a copy of my father's orders on his file; like his training records, they have been lost. The orders of his planned deputy, Jean Amps, do still exist but do not say anything about the basic mission as they are based on the assumption that he has already seen the orders given to his chief. Under the heading of Broad Lines of Mission, they say only:

> You are to act as lieutenant to Prosper in the formation of a new circuit, having Paris as its centre. You have been shown and know all the details of Prosper's mission: its objects and their order of importance; policy in regard to attacking targets; and necessity for maintaining at all times your communication with London. The reason for your having been put so fully into the picture is that it will be necessary for you to take over from Prosper should anything happen to him, pending further instructions from us. It is also necessary that you should know our general policy in these matters, as at some later date you may be called upon to form an entirely separate group under your own orders.[1]

The orders for his courier, Andrée Borrel, are even less helpful, saying, 'You will act as courier for Prosper's organisation and carry out whatever instructions he may give you.'[2] The same

Claude de Baissac.
(de Baissac family)

applies to the orders of his two wireless operators who are simply told that they are to act as operators to Prosper.

I found that Claude de Baissac's orders were still on his file and, as he had been sent on a similar mission to the Bordeaux area at the end of July, I wondered whether his orders might have been similar to those given to my father. They were:

> You will recruit one first-class lieutenant, who will be able to take your place if need be. He will recruit four others who will not know you or have any contact with you. They in their turn will recruit groups of 4 to 5 men each for your various tasks. These actual figures are a suggestion and you alone can be the final judge on the cadre of your set-up. Do not forget to investigate the possibilities of the Duboue organisation which is already in existence.
>
> You will reconnoitre landing grounds and advise us of the grounds you have chosen by W/T.
>
> You will arrange for the reception of material. You will under no circumstances take part in reception committees yourself.

You will reconnoitre the specific targets which have been given you.

Remember above all that your primary task is to RECONNOITRE and REPORT; to prepare for concerted action when you receive the order; and to receive in as large quantities as possible the material which will make that action effective. With the exceptions which B.P. has indicated to you, acts of sabotage must wait orders from H.Q. before being carried out.

The sphere of your activities will, in principle, be the area from Bordeaux to the Loire in the Occupied Zone.[3]

My father's orders would almost certainly have been similar, although I do not know what area was specified. He had already been given a deputy and he must also have been asked to report on an existing organisation as Carte was still active in his area when he arrived and is mentioned in his first report

Germaine Tambour. (BDIC)

at the end of November 1942. That his orders placed an emphasis on reconnoitre and report is supported by an article that Colonel Buckmaster wrote just after the war:

> He had been extremely carefully briefed, for he was destined to become our leading man in France, with Headquarters in Paris. We wanted to find out the extent to which the French could be relied upon to use arms against the invader, if these were dropped to them by parachute, and if they could be restrained from premature action by the presence of British officers in contact with Allied Headquarters in London. We did not expect an immediate answer: we considered that it would take Prosper six months to form a reliable estimate. We realised that it would be necessary to make trial deliveries of weapons and to perform some specimen acts of sabotage, if only to keep up the morale of the patriots.[4]

Charles Grover-Williams. (Author)

Michael Trotobas.
(SFC)

Whilst still in England, my father and Borrel had made an arrangement to meet in Paris. She described to him a café that she knew in rue Caumartin, near the Gare Saint-Lazare, to which he should come between noon and five past every day from 28 September to 5 October. They made other arrangements in case either or both of them did not reach France in time but these proved unnecessary as she arrived in plenty of time on 25 September. Although there were further delays in my father's arrival, he did eventually land near Paris on 2 October and he managed to reach the arranged meeting place in time, despite the injury to his knee. Their first action was to make a tour of likely areas and contacts from information he had received in London and then from Germaine Tambour in Paris. She had been Carte's secretary and took an active part in his organisation, being his representative in Paris.

It is not known exactly where they went but they must have been warned to stay away from certain areas, such as the northern coast, where the density of Germans meant that it would not be safe to arrange parachute drops. He would also have known that other organisers were already setting up organisations or were on their way to do so. Claude de Baissac, from the same training group as my father, had already arrived at the end of July to set up the Scientist circuit in and around Bordeaux. Even before this, the racing driver, Charles Grover-Williams, had been sent in May to organise a small sabotage group in the Paris area. He enlisted the help of other racing colleagues and it was at the home of one of these, Robert Benoîst, that he established his base at Auffargis, between Rambouillet and Trappes to the west of Paris.

My father would have avoided the Lille area as close members of his family were still living there and he would probably have been told soon after his arrival that Michael Trotobas was on his way to set up the Farmer circuit between Lille and Abbeville. He obviously knew about the Monkeypuzzle circuit operating to the south and east of Tours, although he would quickly have become aware of its shortcomings and he contributed to its demise through the reports about it that he sent to London. He certainly met Pierre Culioli in October as it was he who recommended that my father should organise his first parachute operation in Étrépagny (Eure). Culioli had worked there as a tax inspector and knew a local garage owner who looked after the small aircraft that he flew from an airstrip, which still exists to the west of the town.

My father also started to train some people from groups in the north who Germaine Tambour had told him had recently left the Carte organisation. However, he was then contacted by Carte's representative in the north, André Heyermans, and he met him and his lieutenant, Pierre Geelen, in November and agreed that, although he would no longer consider them to be part of his organisation, he would continue to give them help. Unfortunately, Heyermans was arrested soon afterwards and it was some months before these contacts were picked up again.

It was clear to me from books that I had read that the main parts of my father's organisation were elsewhere and the problem was to find out exactly where he had operated. I had been told that the records of the Air Ministry included detailed records of each parachute operation and I realised that if I could plot the parachute drops to my father's groups, I would gain an understanding of where these groups were located and hence the geographical spread of his operations.

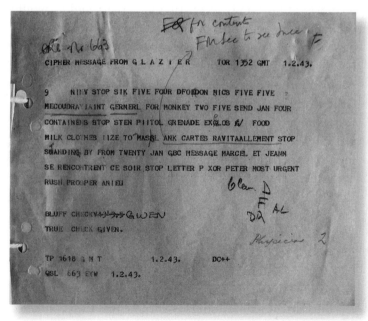

Message requesting a delivery by parachute.

This proved to be quite a complicated task as the files did not appear to be in any logical order, had unhelpful titles and were not even complete. However, the end results were amazingly revealing and ultimately took me to France to meet a few survivors from these groups and the families of others.

After the fall of France, the RAF was desperately short of aircraft and gave priority to the air defence of the United Kingdom and the bomber offensive against enemy targets in Germany and occupied Europe. Resistance groups in occupied territories had yet to prove themselves and trying to supply them with weapons and sabotage material meant keeping valuable aircraft on stand-by, and therefore idle, whilst they waited for the right conditions to operate. Senior RAF officers therefore not unnaturally opposed the diversion of scarce aircraft to supply them.

However, a first special duties flight was set up in mid-1940, 419 Flight, and this was expanded a year later to a full squadron, 138 (Special Duties) Squadron, but only comprising twelve operational aircraft. The addition of 161 Squadron in February 1942 increased the number of operational aircraft to twenty-nine and from the next month they were based at Tempsford, west of Cambridge. 138 Squadron was mainly used for SOE's parachute operations. 161 Squadron handled non-SOE operations and operations which involved landing specially adapted Lysander and Hudson aircraft in occupied territories to drop people off and pick up others, although it did carry out some SOE parachute operations when aircraft were available. The aircraft used for landings were based nearer the Continent at Tangmere to the east of Chichester.

The basic procedure for parachute operations started with an agent finding a suitable ground or Dropping Zone, known as a DZ, and sending details of its location for approval by the RAF, who allocated each DZ a reference number when approved. To these DZs were dropped agents, containers of weapons and sabotage material and packages containing such things as an agent's luggage or a radio. Containers were of two types: the C type was a single cylinder, inside which there were usually three cells; the H type comprised five cells held together by metal rods. Both were the height of an average man and weighed up to 160kg when full.

Once a DZ was agreed, the agent would send a message by radio specifying what he required, the letter to be flashed in Morse code by the reception committee and sometimes a unique coded message to be broadcast by the BBC – see below. The agent would then be given two dates during the next moon-period between which attempts would be made to deliver the material ordered. For each day of the specified period, members of the reception committee would try to tune in to the BBC and listen for the agreed message, which would be broadcast twice; once early in the evening, meaning that the operation was to take place that night, and again some two hours later to confirm this. On hearing both messages, the committee members would make their way to the DZ, put their signal lights in the correct positions to guide the aircraft and then wait. As soon as they heard the approaching aircraft, everyone took up their positions, turned on their lights in the approved pattern and started flashing the agreed letter. The pattern of the lights was set out to show the pilot the wind direction at ground level.

The message on page 62, which was received by London from Glazier (Jack Agazarian) on behalf of my father, Prosper, is typical and requests the delivery of four containers of pistols, grenades, explosives, food, milk, clothes to fit Tomas (Jean Amps) and blank Cartes Ravitaillement (for rationed food) to a DZ known to SOE as M (for Monkey), at which a reception committee would be standing by from 20 January onwards (full moon was on 21 January). The BBC message was '*Marcel et Jean se rencontrent ce soir*' (Marcel and Jean are meeting tonight) and the letter to be flashed was P for Peter. The message does not seem to have reached F Section until 1 February. This mission was known as Operation Physician 2 and, despite several attempts in February, was never successful.

In The National Archives there are two types of record available, which give the date and location of each operation, the number of containers and/or agents carried and whether the mission was successful. The first are the orders, Form A.T.F.6 Operational Instructions for Despatch of Personnel and Stores by Air, for each operation, detailing the number of containers and agents to be delivered. The location of the DZ is described by latitude and longitude; by cross-references to adjoining towns or villages; and by the number of the appropriate Michelin map. The two dates within that month's moon period during which delivery will be attempted are also given.

The second set of files contains the reports made by the captains of the aircraft after each operation. These also give the location of the DZ by latitude and longitude and confirmation of the result of the mission – see example on next page.

It seemed at first that I was going to be able to obtain the details of all of the drops labelled 'Operation Physician' as I found a file[5] that gave a summary of the success or failure of all operations day by day, and for the successes, what had been dropped. The records in this file were not always accurate but I later found files containing summaries for each of the two squadrons involved, which allowed me to cross-check for accuracy.[6]

MOST SECRET

Date. 2.ⁿᵈ Oct. 1942   Copy No................

REPORT ON OPERATIONS UNDERTAKEN BY 138

SQUADRON on night.... 1/2 . Oct. 1942

1. Name of Operation: PHYSICIAN / CHEMIST
     Result: completed   (continued with CRAB 3)

2. Aircraft: HALIFAX   No: 9613......
     Crew: 1st Pilot F/O ANDERLE.   F/Gunner
         2nd Pilot   R/Gunner
         Navigator   Despatcher
         W/Operator   F/Engineer

3. Personnel & Equipment carried:

    (a) Personnel   2   (c) Containers   —   (e) Leaflets 3F97
    (b) Packages   1   (d) Pigeons 15 to Scatter   (f) Bombs

4. Instructions to Captain of A/C:

    (a) Area: FRANCE.
    (b) Pin point: 48° 56' 40" N. 03° 10' 25" E.
    (c) Alternative Pin point: NONE
    (d) Action if Pin point not located: suitable spot within 2 or 3 Kms.
    (e) Reception arrangements: —
    (f) A/Cs Recognition Signal to Reception:

5. Times:

    (a) Take-off:
    (b) Over target: 0136
    (c) Landing: 0435 at ?? ????
    (d) Action taken on landing away from base: Phoned base to report result of operation.

6. Captain's Report:

    (a) Was exact Pin point found? Yes.

    (b) Estimated dropping point: just N of road from La Selé to Montmirail, alt 3 mls E of pinpoint.

    (c) Description by Capt. of target Pin point: difficult to see owing fog, but broken by river.

    (d) recommended for further use:

    (e) Category recommended (A,B or C): B.

    (f) Reception Lights: Report by Captain indicating suggested improvements if necessary:

    (g) Number of 'chutes seen to open: 3.

    (h) Bombs } dropped N of Paris   at 0200 hrs.
        Leaflets }

Pilots' report of my father's drop.

7. Report by Despatcher: Jumped when told.

8. Enemy Opposition: Ran into 20 Miles. S. 1000' 2 large flam
fire up ~~~~ ~~~~ which exploded at 1000' with Verey fire
flak, followed by innumerable ~~~~ which floated to ground

9. Meteorological Conditions: low fog in target area, with
no cloud above.

10. Report by Captain: S/e from Cabot II straight to
pinpoint, pinpointing on Bourges & Chateauroux.
From Bourges ground was covered by fog, but
identified target by bend in R. Seine. Told passengers
owing fog might have to drop them 2/3 miles from
pinpoint, so at first refused jump. Then made to
circule pinpointing on R. Seine, and ~~~~ ~~~~
passengers were in target area, so they jumped,
impossible say exact position of jump but not more than
3 miles from pinpoint. Then set for French Coast which
and ~~~~ crossed at ~~~~ S.W of Le Treport 0229
50½', and English Coast at Selsey Bill at 0508 200',
~~~~ Start Point and landed at ~~~~ at 0435.

11. Remarks by Officer Commanding No.138 Squadron:

W/Cdr.
Officer Commanding,
No.138 Squadron.

Distribution: Copy No:

Pilots' report of my father's drop.

The files containing the captains' reports were many, bulky and fragile, so the summary meant that I did not have to go through every report but only find those that concerned Physician operations. I thought at first that there had been seventy-nine Physician operations as I found operations with numbers between one and seventy-nine but not all of these numbers had been used. In fact the summaries revealed that there were sixty-eight planned Physician operations, of which fifty-four were successful, although not always at the first attempt. There were times when the number of operations requested exceeded the capacity of the RAF to deliver and this may explain the eleven missing numbers.

I started with the files containing the orders but was disappointed to find that the orders for May and June 1943 were missing. This meant that the only hope of finding the location details for the DZs used in these months lay in the captains' reports but there was a second problem; the captains' reports for June for one of the squadrons was also missing. This was the busiest month, for which thirty-eight operations had been ordered, but only three of these had been carried by 161 Squadron; the rest had been carried by 138 Squadron and it was their captains' reports that were lost, with the result that I could not find the location of over half of the DZs used by Physician groups from this source – see Appendix 2.

Despite this setback, I plotted on a map all of the DZs that I had found, which revealed that my father's circuit had extended over a much wider area than I expected. There was a DZ in the Ardennes in Belgium, one near Falaise (the birthplace of William the Conqueror) in Normandy, three around Le Mans and two around Troyes. However, there were two clusters: one in the Vernon/Beauvais/Meru triangle

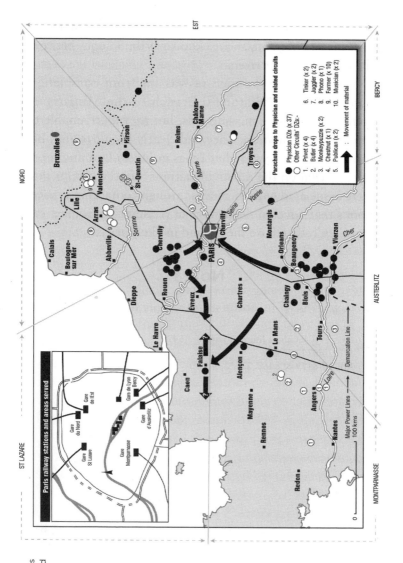

Parachute drops to Physician and related circuits.

to the north-west of Paris and the other between Tours, Orléans and Vierzon, an area known as the Sologne between the Loire and Cher rivers.

Knowing that the picture was far from complete, I approached the Historical Branch of the Ministry of Defence about the missing files, but they were unable to offer any explanation. They had clearly been irretrievably lost and the only way that I was going to find any more information on the missing locations and the groups that were associated with them was through contacts in France, books that covered the history of resistance in some areas and then research on the ground in likely areas.

Notes

1. HS 9/30/2, TNA.
2. HS 9/183, TNA.
3. HS 9/75, TNA.
4. *Prosper*, Chambers Journal, January 1947.
5. AIR 20/8252, TNA.
6. AIR 20/8459 & 8460, TNA.

FIRST STEPS

The first parachute drop that my father organised, Operation Physician 1, was for the middle of November 1942. Details of the ground were sent to London through Clech on 4 November and approval received two days later. This was fast work bearing in mind that he had only been in France for a month, most of which had been spent on the tour. Claude de Baissac, who had dropped into France two months before my father, only received his first drop on 20 November. The Dropping Zone (DZ) was just outside the small town of Étrépagny some 75km north-west of Paris in the Eure at the eastern end of Normandy.

The documents prepared by Colonel Boxshall for the official historian in the 1960s stated that the circuit chief in this area had been Georges Darling and this was repeated in the only French article that I could find.[1] But neither of these documents suggested how my father and Darling had been introduced. On the other hand there was a claim by Pierre Culioli[2] that he and Yvonne Rudellat had started the circuit in the Eure. He and Rudellat did not break with Flower until he found out about the lethal pill brought in on 1 November but he must have met my father before then and worked with him to find the ground at Étrépagny. My father and Borrel would have gone to the Loire valley during their tour to find out what Monkeypuzzle had achieved and must have met Culioli then.

All this speculation ended when I finally met someone who had been in the reception team at Étrépagny. I had tried to find contacts here in 2007 but failed due to a misunderstanding with the *mairie* (town hall). I wrote again before a visit in 2010 and this almost failed as well as I learnt later that my letter was waiting to be filed when it was spotted by an interested councillor. This led to a meeting in 2011 with Robert Artaud, a very alert 84-year-old. His father, Raymond, had been a mechanic who owned a garage in Étrépagny but also serviced aircraft, which is how he met Culioli. Artaud introduced Culioli to the gamekeeper of an estate just to the north of Étrépagny, Gustave Tiercelin, and my father stayed at his house in the hamlet of St Martin. Tiercelin recommended a field alongside a wood, le bois de Génétray, as a DZ. There was a convenient ditch on the edge of the wood where the containers could be rolled and hidden temporarily. The final member of the team was Jules Villegas who ran a hotel and restaurant between Étrépagny and Gisors, which gave him many contacts in the area including Culioli and Artaud.[3]

It was this team together with my father, Gilbert Norman, Andrée Borrel and Yvonne Rudellat that received the first drop of four containers on the night of 17/18 November, the pilot reporting that he had not seen any reception lights when he had flown the operation the previous night. The contents of the containers were '88lbs of Plastic Explosive, 24 Sten guns, 34 revolvers, 46 grenades, 15 Clam mines and 50 Incendiaries'.[4] The material was picked up from the ditch by Artaud in his lorry, taken to his garage and hidden in a barn. Later most of it was packed into a honey wagon belonging to Robert Menessier, which he and his son drove to Les Andelys on the river Seine and put onto a barge going towards Paris. I have not discovered to whom these arms were sent, but it is clear that my father had very quickly

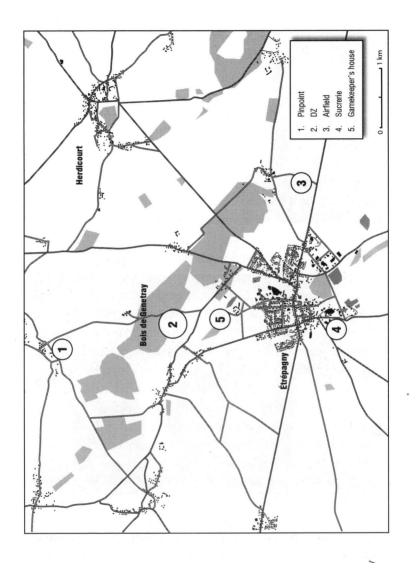

Étrépagny
DZ.

Robert Artaud. (Libre
Résistance)

Pierre Culioli with his aircraft.
(P. Guillaume)

found people ready to take them and they appear to have
been used almost immediately as there is a record that, 'By
January 1943, Physician was attacking his electrical targets
and the results were extremely satisfactory.' This followed
a change in policy as a reaction to the total occupation of
France by the Germans in November when 'it was decided

Robert Artaud showing author the DZ. A typical DZ location – open fields adjoining woodland where the containers could be quickly hidden. (F. Dury)

to call for sabotage immediately and on as large a scale as possible …' This policy was set out formally in a directive received by F Section on 22 January 1943.[5]

Sometime in December, my father met Jacques Weil, a wealthy Swiss industrialist, who ran an intelligence gathering organisation passing information to London via contacts in Switzerland, and through him, met Albert Forcinal of Gisors, the local chief of Cohors Asturies, who was referred to by SOE as Colonel Chandon. One of his men was Georges Darling, whose parents were English but who had lived in Neufles-Saint-Martin where his father had been the steward of a stud farm. Darling had also worked for the Deuxieme Bureau and was recruited to organise groups in the eastern Eure and western Oise from his home in Trie-Château.

Following the first successful operation at Etrepagny, a second was organised to the same DZ for the December moon period to drop another four containers, Physician 2,

Jack Agazarian. (SFC)

Georges Darling. (G. Harny)

and Jack Agazarian who was to be a second wireless operator for the circuit. A first attempt was made on Christmas Eve but failed due to bad weather. Agazarian and another agent were dropped successfully a few nights later on 29/30 December, without any containers but with his wireless set.

Pierre and Anne-Marie de
Bernard. (Julie Clamp)

By this time Culioli and Rudellat had returned to the
Loire as my father had decided, in view of the recruitment
of Darling, that it was more important for them to start
organising reception teams by following up contacts they had
made while working for Monkeypuzzle. They had just started
work in Meung-sur-Loire when their landlord died suddenly
of a heart attack on New Year's Eve and they decided to leave
quickly as their activities might have been discovered if they
were involved in an inquiry. They moved to Pontlevoy to the
south of Blois and started organising groups in the triangle
between Orléans, Tours and Vierzon, leaving Maurice
Lequeux to take over their contacts in Meung-sur-Loire.

Meanwhile, Gilbert Norman had also been busy. Just before
he joined the circuit as a wireless operator in December, he
had visited the de Bernard family. Comte Pierre and Anne-
Marie de Bernard lived in a small château at Nanteuil, just
across the Loire from Blois. She organised Red Cross parcels

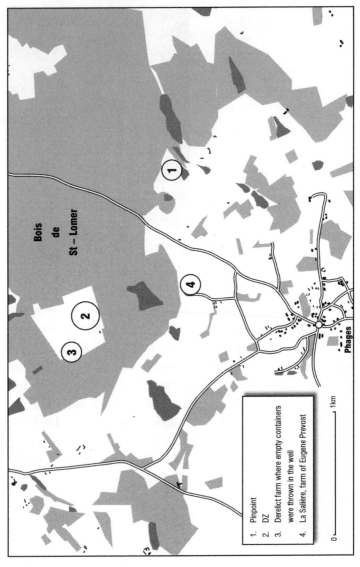

Bois de St
Lomer DZ.

from rooms in the château de Blois and so had no trouble in crossing the heavily guarded Loire. She had also helped several Allied escapees to cross the demarcation line a little further south.

Norman had no hesitation in asking for her help and she willingly gave it. She contacted an old friend, Captain Marcel Buhler, a veteran of the First World War with a limp to prove it. In 1940, when the Germans invaded France, he had been acting as a military governor in Blois. Together they immediately set off south to see the Comte de Vibray, who owned a large estate with its centrepiece the château de Cheverny, one of the great Loire châteaux. The Comte considered that he had too much to lose to take such a risk as allowing part of the estate to be used for parachute drops and he declined.

Despite this setback, sometime in January a ground was found some 12km to the north of Blois, near Hameau-Mézières. I found a reference to this being called 'Malakof' and a detailed map revealed Malakoff just to the south of Hameau-Mézières. I have not yet been able to find out who owned the land and what their connection with the de Bernards was. Gilbert Norman returned on 29 January and he and Marcel Buhler prepared for the first reception there.

At the same time, Pierre Culioli and Yvonne Rudellat recruited the hotelier and chef in Pontlevoy who had given them shelter, Marcel Thénot, but they were not able to stay for long as the hotel was frequented by Germans. They moved to a cottage in the hamlet of Sassay, south of nearby Contres where they stayed until the end of April. At Contres, Culioli was introduced to Julien Nadau, who was the manager of the local electricity supply network, which gave him useful contacts over a very large area as his responsibilities covered around fifty-two communes. Soon after this, a DZ was found in the Bois de St Lomer, halfway between Contres and Pontlevoy.

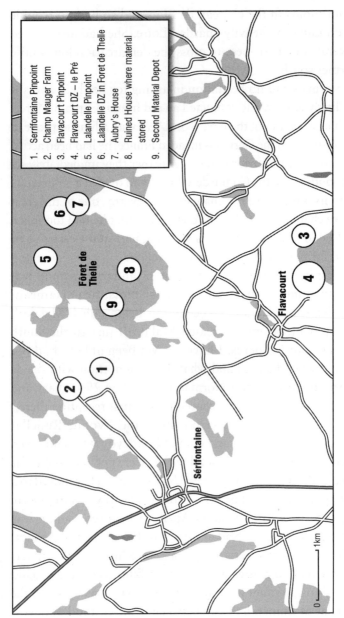

1. Serrifontaine Pinpoint
2. Champ Mauger Farm
3. Flavacourt Pinpoint
4. Flavacourt DZ – le Pré
5. Lalandelle Pinpoint
6. Lalandelle DZ in Foret de Thelle
7. Aubry's House
8. Ruined House where material stored
9. Second Material Depot

Flavacourt and Sérifontaine DZs.

People in this area were aware that arms could be parachuted from England as there had been a drop to an RF Section team on 22/23 January 1943 between Meusnes and Lucy-le-Mâle on the opposite side of the Cher. Unfortunately, the team were betrayed but the potential had been demonstrated.

It was originally intended that Operation Physician 2 should be tried again at Étrépagny in January but for reasons that remain unknown, this DZ was abandoned and the drop moved to a farm called Champ Mauger outside the village of Sérifontaine, just to the north of Gisors. The farmer, Alexandre Barbier, had been visited by his friend Jules Villegas at Christmas and agreed to join the circuit. This is the DZ referred to in the message sent by Agazarian (see p. 62). As at Étrépagny, it was intended that the material parachuted should not be kept locally but be taken to groups

Alexandre Barbier (seated) and family, including his son-in-law Raymond Hérisset. (Barbier family)

Jules Villegas. (Libre Résistance)

in Paris and this time a team from Paris was sent to help at the reception. On 23 January a communist member of the FTP in Paris called René Fortier was ordered to meet 'Jean' at the Gare Saint-Lazare and go with him to the farm to receive arms and money. The BBC message for this operation was '*Marcel et Jean se recontrent ce soir*'. When it was realised that there would not be a drop that moon, they left the farm on 1 February and it was arranged that they should return later in the month.[6]

Although no containers were dropped in January, two agents arrived whose activities were to be closely linked with those of my father. During the night of 22/23 January, Jean

Worms and Henri Déricourt were parachuted blind near Pithiviers, Loiret. Worms was the director of an insurance company in Paris and became involved with Jacques Weil. One of his couriers was caught in the middle of 1942 and forced to reveal the involvement of Worms. His office

Jean Worms. (Worms family)

was confiscated, his secretary was arrested and he fled to the south of France. Through SOE contacts in Marseille he was sent to London in October to be trained as an organiser. Although his training had in most respects been successful, there were serious doubts about his security as he was very inquisitive and liked to gossip about what he found out. It was recommended that he only be sent back if there was a 'lone wolf' mission in which he would be self-contained. In the event, and presumably after consultation with my father, it was decided to take advantage of the fact that he knew the railway chief in Châlons-sur-Marne, now Châlons-en-Champagne. This was a major railway centre and Worms was given the task of organising sabotage teams. This became a sub-circuit of Prosper–Physician called Juggler.

Henri Déricourt was a French pilot who came to England and joined SOE at the end of November 1942. A fortnight later, an order was placed for him to be flown to France so he must have been seen as so vital that he was not put through the usual SOE training. It had been realised that it was necessary to have a specialist agent in France whose sole responsibility was to arrange the landing in France of suitable aircraft to take in agents who could not be parachuted and to pick up agents who needed to return to England. His orders were:

> to choose suitable landing grounds and to supervise the resulting infiltration and exfiltration operations. He was to commence

Henri Déricourt. (J.O. Fuller)

his activities in the Poitiers, Tours and Anger regions, moving northwards to Le Mans and Rouen, thence via Compiègne to Châlons, Troyes and Auxerre. After this he was to explore the Bordeaux area finishing in the Correze, Cantal and Lot departments.[7]

In the event the landing grounds that he found were all in the Poitiers, Tours and Anger areas. There is a widely held view that his role as Air Movements Officer meant that he was to arrange all air operations, both landings and parachute drops; this is not correct as can be seen from his orders. He was only responsible for pick-ups and had no knowledge of, or involvement with, parachute drops that were arranged directly by circuit organisers through their wireless operators. The original intention was that his circuit, Farrier, should be another sub-circuit of Prosper–Physician but he was soon involved at SOE's request with agents from all parts of the French Section and all parts of France as well as bringing out political figures. So he operated as independently as he could whilst still relying on Prosper–Physician wireless

operators, mainly Agazarian, to communicate with London. As soon as he arrived he moved his wife from Marseille to Paris and asked an old friend, Julienne Aisner, to work with him as his courier.

Julienne Aisner. (Aisner family)

When Raymond Flower decided to base his Monkeypuzzle circuit in Tours rather than Le Mans, he asked Henri Garry to take over in the Sarthe but he was not able to do much without further help from SOE. My father was so busy establishing the northern and southern areas that he did not have time to follow up this contact. He therefore asked France Antelme to do this on his behalf as he had already met Garry through Flower. Henri Garry was an engineer and had worked with Philippe de Vomecourt before the collapse of his brother's Autogiro circuit, which caused Garry and Octave Simon, a sculptor, to move elsewhere. When they were contacted by Antelme, Simon offered to make use of connections that his wife had amongst the landed gentry in this area. Simon's first contacts were with two landowners who were related to his wife and to each other and had adjoining estates to the west of Le Mans. The château d'Eporce, near the village of La Quinte, was the home of the Celier family. Comte Pierre Celier was not always there as he worked as an Inspecteur des Finances but his brother Jean lived there full-time for health reasons. Their cousin, the Marquis Antoine du Mascureau, lived at the château de Renaudiére,

near the village of Saint Julien-en-Champagne. A DZ was found between the two châteaux near a farm called Champ Failly.[8]

A first operation (Physician 7) was attempted here in early February but the pilot could

France Antelme.
(Antelme family)

not find the reception; those waiting on the ground said that they heard the aircraft but that it was too far north to have seen them.[9] However, it was successful on the night of 15/16 February following the BBC message '*La baleine aime les eaux froides*' (The whale likes the cold waters), when four containers were dropped.

Elsewhere the groups were struggling. The most unlucky was the group near Hameau-Mézières where Operation Physician 6 was attempted four times before being abandoned. They should have received five containers as should the group waiting at the DZ along the edge of the Bois de St Lomer. At the first attempt on the night of 9/10 February no reception was seen at Mézières because Norman had not heard the BBC message – '*Les sauterelles arrivent par milliards*' (The locusts arrive in their billions). The pilot thought that he had found a reception at Bois de St Lomer, but he was not sure of it and so decided not to drop the containers. The RAF tried again on the night of 13/14 February but found no reception at either location.

Henri Garry. (Garry family)

Octave Simon. (SFC)

Jean Celier. (Celier family)

After this the weather deteriorated to such an extent that a further attempt on the night of 24/25 February also failed at both DZs. Despite continued bad weather, a final attempt was made at Mézières a few days later but no reception was found. This was not surprising as, although a team had been sent from Paris to help, they refused to let the operation go ahead, claiming that a German observation post had been set up only 20m from the ground. Both operations were then abandoned but the de Bernards later collected material from Culioli and took it to Blois. It was never found by the Germans and was used in the liberation of Blois.[10] The groups in the north were not faring much better. Another attempt was made to drop containers to the DZ near Sérifontaine on 9/10 February. The pilot reported that although no reception was seen, there were a number of flashing lights. It was also too dark to see ground detail. It was much the same six nights later. This time the pilot was able to identify the woods alongside the target but he did not see any reception lights, only a number of other lights. This operation was combined with Operation Physician 8, attempting to drop three containers and a package to a new DZ a few kilometres further east between the villages of Flavacourt and Boutencourt. The DZ was again alongside a wood in the grounds of an estate belonging to the Domet family and included a pond into which the empty containers could be jettisoned. The same combined operation was flown again ten days later. The pilot identified both targets by their ground detail and made several runs over them, even spending over half an hour circling in the Sérifontaine area, but in neither case was there any sign of a reception committee.

What the pilot did not know of course was that the reason for nobody turning up was the arrest of René Fortier, the communist, on 9 February. He had been persuaded to talk and had revealed the planned drop.[11] My father reported this to London in March, 'Terrain D (Sérifontaine) denounced in Paris. Superintendent and four inspectors sent. 24 February. That's why the drops failed at D and I on the 25th. I was there on the 26th and we blagged it with the police.' (*'Terrain*

Flavacourt DZ and pond. (F Dury)

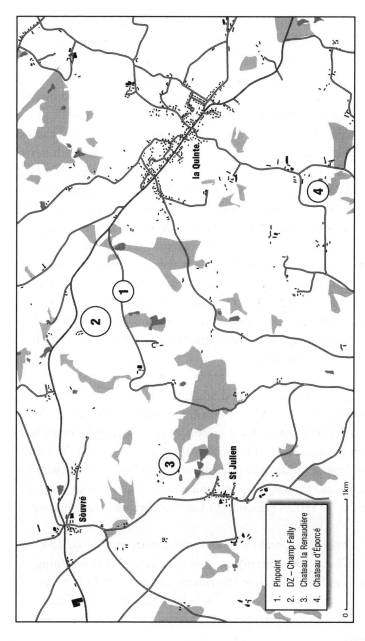

1. Pinpoint
2. DZ – Champ Failly
3. Chateau la Renaudière
4. Chateau d'Éporcé

0 _____ 1km

Champ Failly DZ.

D (Sérifontaine) denonce a Paris. Un commissaire et quatre inspecteurs envoyés. 24 Fevrier. C'est pourquoi les receptions ont ratees a D et I le 25. J'y etais la le 26 et on a bluffe la police.'[12]) So despite the presence of the police only 5km away at Sérifontaine, the team at Flavacourt (*Terrain I*) led by my father calmly received the expected four parachutes.

I met Michel Domet, who then owned the estate that in 1943 belonged to his father, Georges. They had both been part of the reception committee. He remembered that the BBC message had been '*Le laitier passera demain* à *onze heures.*' (The milkman will pass tomorrow at 11 a.m.) He told me that there had been no Englishmen at the reception so my father's accent must have improved by this time. Another member of the reception team was Raymond Hérisset, a farmer from Boutencourt and married to one of Alexandre Barbier's daughters, so the activities of the groups here and at Sérifontaine were linked. This probably explains why, although there was only a problem at Sérifontaine, neither ground was used again.

The package dropped at Flavacourt was (probably) a W/T set for Norman. SOE had originally planned to send Norman to Corsica to establish communication with Carte. These orders were cancelled a couple of days before Norman left for France but by this time his set had been sent to the south of France on the basis that he would collect it on his way to Corsica. My father sent someone to Marseilles in January to try to retrieve the set but Carte had refused to give it up.

Progress Report to SOE Executive Committee – 15.03.1943
Glazier (Agazarian) has come on air and is functioning regularly. Butcher (Norman) has now made contact. Contact established with Sebastien (Grover-Williams) through Prosper; attempting to send own WTO. Explosives

Author with Michel Domet. (F. Dury)

delivered to Physician have been used but the results are not yet known. He hopes to neutralise the Paris, Chartres and Orléans electric line soon. He is well established and hopes to attack allotted targets as soon as possible. Gaspard (Flower) is forced to lie low but hopes to start again soon.

Notes

1. C. Menard, *Les Cahiers de la Société Historique et Geographique du Bassin de l'Epte*, No. 25, 1990.
2. Report 28.04.1945, HS 9/379/8, TNA.
3. There was a separate French intelligence gathering organisation in the area known as Cohors-Asturias led at this time by Albert Forcinal of Gisors. He has been suggested as a candidate for the introduction of Georges Darling as Forcinal and Culioli were from the same political grouping. Robert Artaud was certain that Albert Forcinal had no links with Culioli's activities and that Georges Darling was not involved with the Étrépagny group at that time.
4. War Diary November 1942, HS 7/245, TNA.
5. HS 7/121, TNA.
6. BS2 carton 41, Archives de la Prefecture de Police de Paris .
7. HS 9/421-425, TNA.
8. After the collapse of the circuit Octave Simon reached England and was trained as an SOE agent. In March 1944 he was parachuted back to France with orders to set up a circuit to be called Satirist around Beauvais but was captured on landing. Many writers refer to his groups in the Sarthe and Orne in 1943 as Satirist; this is not correct. At that time his groups were a sub-circuit of Prosper/Physician with no unique name.
9. Report 25.03.1943, HS 9/42, TNA.
10. 1221 W18 6727, Archives départmentales, Blois.
11. See 6 above..
12. Report 09.03.1943, HS 9/183, TNA.

SLOW GOING

Progress Report to SOE Executive Committee – 15.03.1943
Physician operation against Chaigny Transformer Station, one of the major power links on the Paris/Orléans railway near Tours, has been completed. No details yet. He reports that he can receive an Airborne Division in Normandy and Touraine and has given 9 landing grounds for this purpose. Glazier (Agazarian) and Butcher (Norman) coming up regularly.

Antelme gave London full details of the sabotage carried out by the Prosper organisation:

CHAIGNY – The sequence of events seems to have been as follows:

The RAF bombed but missed. They cut one or two lines only and lost three or four planes. The Germans left the bodies of the aviators for four days which caused intense anger in the neighbourhood.

(Norman) took up the hunt and made a reduced scale model on which practise charges were laid.

(Norman) and (Suttill) blew up the transformers. This took 20 odd charges and caused an eleven hour delay in the supply.

A train taking foodstuffs (wheat, hay, etc.) to Germany was set on fire and destroyed on leaving Paris.

Three troop trains were derailed near Blois. These appear to have been entirely German and 43 Germans were killed and 110 wounded. As a result, sentinels were placed on the line but these were shot up over a period of ten days. It is interesting to note that the only reprisals carried out for these acts were the imposition in Blois of a curfew from Friday to Monday from 19.00 hrs to 8.00 hrs and the closing of the cinemas.

Bombs were released in the Ministère de la Marine, Place Vendôme. Although this was not probably done by our own people, it was certainly done with our materials since no one else has any. This had the curious result that, next day, the German sentries were replaced by French. A bomb was also released in a hotel in the rue d'Alger, used by the Ministère de la Marine.

Incendiaries have also been given to a Police Official to be introduced into the HQ Archives in the rue François 1er.

Germans are killed daily in the streets of Paris and, although once again, this is not done by our people, 90% of these attacks are made with arms provided by us, e.g. to the Communists.[1]

Apart from these sabotage operations, March appears to have been a relatively quiet month for deliveries and the only successful operation, Physician 11, was a second drop of another four containers to the Champ Failly DZ in the Sarthe. A third followed, Physician 19, dropping five containers and a Eureka on 12/13 April. This was the last drop to this DZ as it was felt its continued use would be too risky.

The lack of operations in February and March was not unique to my father's circuit. At the beginning of February my father and Claude de Baissac had sent a joint warning – 'United opinion of the only two active circuits of your section that our possibilities are practically umlimited subject only to the help you can send us.'[2] Throughout these months, increasingly frustrated messages were being sent to London from all over France complaining that they were losing recruits due to their inability to provide the arms and sabotage material they had been promised. One organiser wrote on 26 March, 'If no operations, impossible to carry on. Teams losing confidence. Am receiving no help from you. The people here have lost faith in me as you have left me five months without operations.' Two days later my father writes, 'Rush all orders. Need material urgently. Every night of March was perfect reception night. Every one very disappointed. Owing to no receptions February March security and morale of teams falling rapidly. Rely on your cooperation at once. Disappointed. Prosper.'

Antoine du Mascureau, in a letter from 1964,[3] lists some of the other things that were in the containers: Sten guns and pistols with ammunition; mills hand grenades; plastic explosive; time fuses; battery chargers and reception torches; first aid kits and dressings; and chocolate, tobacco and cigarettes for the helpers.

The Eureka was an improved radar device for aircraft to locate landing grounds; it worked in two halves. One half was a beacon transmitter, which emitted an individual call sign from the ground as well as a constant (or intermittent) signal; this weighed nearly a hundredweight, but was just portable in a large suitcase and if well enough packed could be parachuted to the field and set up on a dropping zone. Rebecca, the receiving half, also an elaborate piece of wireless equipment, could be fitted in the navigator's cabin of a bomber. In the best conditions it could pick up the beacon from 70 miles away, and a skilled navigator could

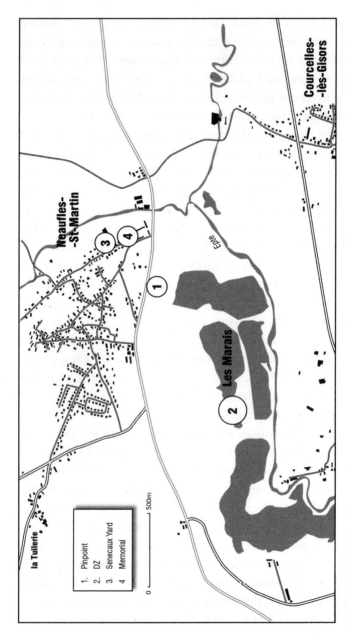

Neaufles-Saint-Martin DZ.

get within a few yards of the beacon with its assistance.[4] I did not find any mention of these actually being used by my father's groups.

Having abandoned the Sérifontaine and Flavacourt DZs because of the police interest, four new ones were found around Trie-Château. One was further north in the la Landelle and forêt de Thelle area; one to the east of Trie-Château; one at Neaufles-Saint-Martin to the west and the fourth at Bois-Jérôme-Saint-Ouen some way to the south-west and just north-east of Vernon. The team in the north was headed by Maxime Aubry who lived in the middle of the forest of which he was in charge. He was helped by two men from La Landelle, André Anselme and Camille Bigot, a mechanic.

Neaufles-Saint-Martin was the village where Georges Darling's father had been the steward in a stud farm and Georges grew up in the village before moving to Trie-Château. It was also home to Jules Villegas whose restaurant was in the hamlet of Les Bosquets just across the river Lévrière from Neaufles-Saint-Martin and joined to it by a road now named after him. Darling chose a retired gendarme, Alexandre Laurent, to be the leader here. Others involved were Sylvain Sénécaux, a charcoal merchant, and Raymond Ridard, a postman. A DZ was found on the poor land next to the Epte river, which was a convenient place to jettison the empty containers.

The DZ to the east of Trie-Château was known as les Groux and was next to the Bois d'Etoile where the forest guard, Pierre Perret, had been recruited. Two other members of this team were Kleber Harny and his nephew, Gilbert, who were refugees from Compiègne.

There were many Perrets related to Pierre who were farmers and foresters in the village of Bois-Jérôme-Saint-Ouen and he took Gilbert Norman there to meet them. The oldest cousin, Lucien Perret, became the leader and a DZ was found initially in le Petit Bois where areas large enough for further receptions were regularly cut for firewood and charcoal. A successful operation, Physician 20, dropped five containers here on the night of 11/12 April. The empty containers were thrown into a pond in the woods and the arms hidden in an abandoned tile kiln. On a visit to the village I was taken to the woods by two descendants, Claude and Robert Perret. They told me that on two occasions one of the parachutes had become entangled in one of the few uncut trees. The first time it was low enough for someone to be able to climb up and retrieve it but the other was caught so high that the tree had to be felled.

The first operation to the other three DZs a few days later did not go so easily. On the night of 14/15 April an aircraft carrying fifteen containers was meant to drop five at each. The pilot reported that Physician 15 to Neaufles-Saint-Martin was dropped at 1.35 a.m. and Physician 10 at Trie-Château ten minutes later, but that he saw no reception at La Landelle where he was supposed to drop Physician 14.

My father's report dated 18 April tells a different story. He writes:

Ground Huts received 2 receptions – the second due to the fact that the plane persisted in flashing the letter George. The first had also dropped on *receiving* the letter George. The light signal was operated by Archambaud (Norman) himself for both receptions so the mistake for the first reception was the fault of the pilot. I was at Ground Monkey and clearly heard three planes successively low over me at which I signalled the letter Zebra. All three continued straight on and did not attempt to re-pass.

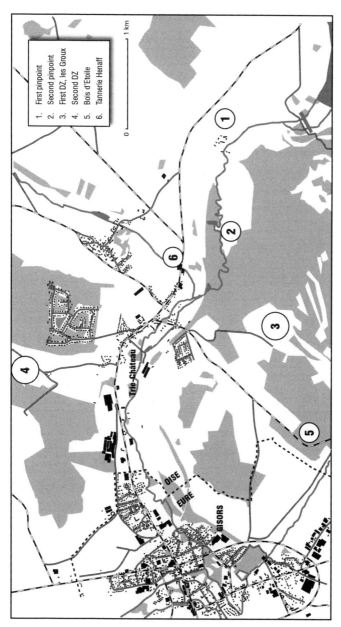

Trie-Château DZs.

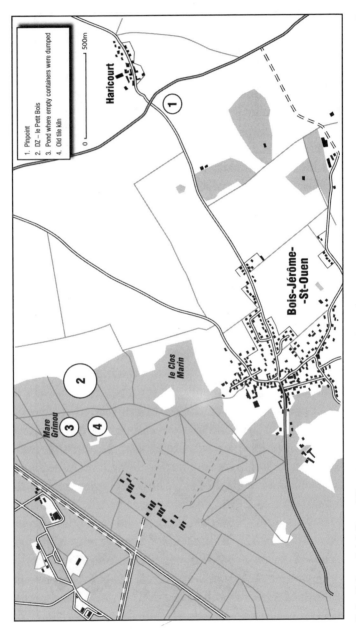

1. Pinpoint
2. DZ – le Petit Bois
3. Pond where empty containers were dumped
4. Old tile kiln

0   500m

Haricourt

Bois-Jérôme--St-Ouen

le Clos Marin

Mare Grimou

Bois-Jérôme–Saint-Ouen DZ.

One plane passed straight over Ground Johnnie and was signalled at. All three of us were using car headlights with 6 volt batteries. I suggest you warn the RAF of the existence of neighbouring grounds with different light signals. All three of us were sending the signal letter at 25 letters a minute.[5]

It took me a little time to identify the grounds in this report but as Physician 10 was re-ordered and was flown to the DZ at Trie-Château in May, it must have been the DZ at Neaufles-Saint-Martin that received the two drops ten minutes apart. My father at Trie-Château must have wondered what was happening. It should be noted that the two DZs are only 10km apart, which may explain the confusion for the crew. Ground Johnnie would have been Lalandelle and the pilot noted that whilst they were circling over the target between 1.51 and 1.58 a.m. without finding the reception, 'an unidentified aircraft passed underneath us'. Operation Physician 14 was successful there six nights later and the pilot reported, 'After load dropped, reception flashed V at aircraft'.

Georges Darling, now firmly established as the leader of the groups operating in the western part of the Oise and the eastern part of the Eure, had also started a group near St Quentin. A land surveyor from Fonsommes, Eugene Cordelette, had served under Darling when they were both called up in 1939 and they became good friends. By chance, they met again in January 1943 and Darling immediately asked Cordelette to recruit people in his area who would in due course be commanded by a British officer. This would have initially been my father but the nascent group was given to Guy Bieler who had been parachuted into France with Trotobas in mid-November. He hit a rock on landing and badly damaged his back so he was taken to Paris for treatment and lodged with Marié-Louise Monnet and her daughter, Léoné, in one of my father's safe houses.

Bieler's original orders were twofold: to act as SOE representative with the Carte organisation in the Lille district and to give instruction; and to keep in contact with Trotobas' Farmer circuit.[6] When the Carte organisation collapsed in January 1943, Bieler's main mission was no longer relevant even if he had been physically capable of carrying it out. It was not until the end of March that his condition improved sufficiently for him to be ready for a new mission. This was when he was asked to take over the St Quentin area from my father and he moved there on 7 April, giving the circuit his operational name Musician, known in France as Tell. Cordelette had by this time found a suitable DZ near Fonsommes and a drop had already been organised through the Physician wireless operators before Bieler left Paris. Musician 1 was flown on 13/14 April but no reception was seen. By coincidence, the aircraft was also carrying five containers for Trotobas' first successful operation, Farmer 1, which had been tried five times before without success. After this time, Trotobas no longer had to rely on others for arms and sabotage material but he was still reliant on the Physician wireless operators.

In the Sologne, there were also no drops in March but the teams were busy with sabotage. The material that had been dropped to the Monkeypuzzle circuit in 1942 on the Bois Renard DZ was moved again. Maurice Lequeux brought a lorry from Meung-sur-Loire and he and Gilbert Norman took the material to Paris. Some of it may then have been passed on to Trotobas and the rest passed to the communists. My father is credited with destroying a train carrying requisitioned food to Germany and bombing government buildings. I suspect this was the work of the communist groups using either

Eugene Cordelette. (Libre Résistance)

some of the sabotage material from Bois Renard or the first Physician drop at Étrépagny in the Eure. Chaigny was attacked again in April and three goods trains derailed.

Two new DZs were also found. Marcel Thénot, who was looking after Pierre Culioli and Yvonne Rudellat for a short time at Pontlevoy, introduced them to his 70-year-old father, Alfred, who lived off the land near Chaumont-sur-Tharonne. A local author describes Alfred as, 'This old Solognot – crafty say his friends; yes but crafty like a poacher say his enemies, if he has any.' Although he naturally liked to work alone, he was persuaded to accept the help of his 17-year-old nephew, Georges Beauvais, to deal with the five containers of Physician 17 that arrived on the night of 11/12 April at a DZ known as Miraillon.[7] The BBC message was a special for the Thénot family, '*Marcel souhait le bonjour à Marcel*' (Marcel wishes Marcel a good morning). On the same night, the team at St Lomer heard their message, '*Les petits cochons seront farcis*' (The piglets will be stuffed) and received not only the five containers of Physician 12 but also two agents, Tinker and Innkeeper. The operation almost failed, the pilot reporting that whilst the recognition letter was flashed as the aircraft approached, the reception lights were slow in coming on and he had to make three circuits before they were lit.

Guy Bieler. (Bieler family)

Tinker was Ben Cowburn, who was to take over the Physician groups already started around Troyes, and Innkeeper was his radio operator, Denis Barrett. Cowburn gives a description of their reception:

When I had removed my harness, I rolled up my parachute and carried it back along the line of flight. I soon saw two dark figures coming to meet me. I caused them some alarm by dropping to the ground to see them against the skyline, quite a routine precaution. They hoarsely whispered – No, no don't shoot, we are friends. I got up and a second later we were warmly shaking hands.

They led me to Barrett and the third receptionist, Prosper's lieutenant, Pierre Culioli. Barrett was unhurt, the containers were well grouped on the ground but the two packages had landed some distance away in the trees. We wanted those packages badly as they contained our personal

Benjamin Cowburn. (SFC)

luggage and Barrett's precious wireless sets. As there were only three of them, the leader asked whether Barrett and I were too tired to give a hand with the containers. All five of us set to work. The empty shells and cells were carried some distance away and thrown down a disused well (in the farm of St Lomer). They made quite a din as they banged against the sides and finally crashed at the bottom, but our hosts said it did not matter. We moved the sacks of supplies to a safe hiding place.

Our hard night's work was enlivened by a political argument between the two farmers. They were friends but one was a democrat and the other a communist. It was funny to watch them lifting a container together and hoarsely gasping doctrinaire broadsides at each other.

Theo (Bertin), the democratic farmer, and I happened to be carrying a heavy canister between us. He asked me if I would not mind changing sides as one of his hands was not so good. I thus found out that he had been wounded in the 1914–1919 war. There was a lump in my throat as I reflected that this man was again serving his country by partaking in this new, weird warfare.

At dawn we went to the communist's farm (Eugene Prevost at la Saliere). His wife was waiting and gave us a huge breakfast. When the sun was fully risen we went to beat the woods along the line of flight and finally located the missing packages hanging in the trees.[8]

Cowburn says in his book that he planned to keep completely clear of other circuits but that he was ordered to meet my father to give him some new quartzes to be used to change the wavelengths of the circuit's wireless sets. When he did so, he reports the following conversation in his book, starting with my father saying, 'Thanks. Is there anything I can do for you?'

To which Cowburn replied, 'I don't think so. I have my own W/T operator and I'll soon be on my way to Troyes.' 'I'm glad to meet someone who believes in the self-contained unit!' responded my father. 'Nevertheless I'd like to put you in touch with someone who has a friend in Troyes. He might be useful.' This was Henri Garry whom Cowburn was already expecting to contact and Garry in turn introduced him to Pierre Mulsant who had started a group there the previous year. Cowburn completed several missions for SOE, so it is not surprising that his memory is faulty. He was clearly not sent to start a new circuit from scratch but to take over and expand an existing organisation. Another organiser, John Hamilton, had been dropped at the same time as Agazarian to organise this area but he had been arrested a few days later. In fact my father, with the help of Antelme and Garry, had already organised two groups that had been ready to receive drops on two DZs, one some 20km north-east of Troyes and the other some 60km south-east. Operations Physician 9 and 23 were flown to these DZs on 13/14 April and again two nights later but neither was successful as no reception was seen. Cowburn added another DZ to the west of Troyes near Verlaines where Mulsant had a factory but despite this, by the time he returned to London five months later, he had only received two drops delivering a total of ten containers.

Four nights after the arrival of Cowburn, the same team received another drop of five containers, Physician 13, at St Lomer whilst a further five, Physician 21, were dropped to a new DZ found by the same group to the north-west of Pontlevoy in a field known as les Motteux on the edge of the bois de Sudais. The BBC message was, '*Il y a des lunettes à la suite*' (There are spectacles to follow).

My father did not initially plan to organise any groups along the Belgian border after he had met André Heyermans,

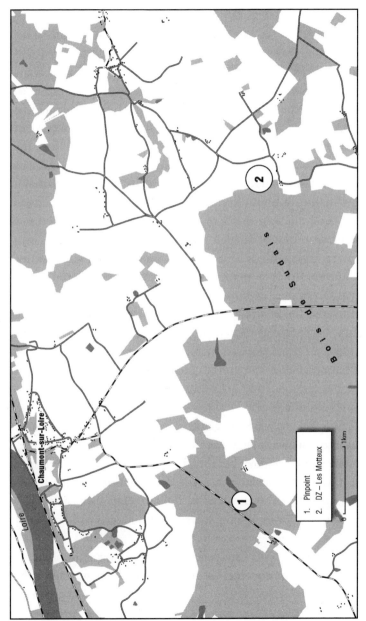

Les Motteux DZ.

the Carte representative for northern France and Belgium, in November 1942. After talking to Heyermans, and a Belgian colleague, Pierre Geelen, he decided that as Carte was active in this area, he would leave it alone. However, Heyermans was arrested almost immediately and at the beginning of January 1943 Carte finally broke up. Geelen decided to transfer to the Prosper organisation and my father asked him and his friend Walther Marly to go to Hirson and the Ardennes and organise groups there with Armel Guerne as liaison. Guerne had met my father earlier in the year through Germaine Tambour and it was he whom my father blamed for the failure of the operation near Hameau-Mézières in February. Indeed Geelen reported that my father was still quarrelling with Guerne about this in March and did not want him to go with Geelen to Hirson. Geelen noted that it was Germaine Tambour who made the peace, telling him that my father had bad days when he was difficult to get on with and 'had nothing good to say about any Frenchman'.[9] They found a DZ to the east of Hirson, just outside Origny-en-Thiérache where a team was formed, and Physician 18 was attempted there on 12/13 March. The pilot reported:

> Several runs were made over target but no reception seen. A red and white light was seen flashing intermittently in the area of the pinpoint but they did not flash any characteristic and it was decided it was too uncertain to drop load. A large white V sign was picked out in white lights about a mile northwest of pinpoint, sides 50ft long.

This operation was successful a month later, dropping five containers, the contents of which were hidden in a mill in the centre of the town.

Andre Heyermans
(Libre Résistance)

Meanwhile, Heslop and Wilkinson, two of those arrested in Lyons in August 1942, escaped in November and were eager to contact London for new instructions. Wilkinson decided to return to his home in Angers and to see if he could contact London through Charles Grover-Williams whom he knew had arrived in France in May before Wilkinson's arrest. The Chestnut circuit still did not have a wireless operator of their own so Wilkinson was introduced to my father, who had arrived while Wilkinson was still in prison and had two wireless operators. Heslop went to the south and contacted Peter Churchill who also contacted London and told Heslop to go to Toulouse where he would receive instructions in March. He went to Toulouse but no one contacted him, so he went on to Angers as by this time Wilkinson had received instructions from my father to organise a circuit there, using his operational name of Privet, with the help of Heslop, until such time as the latter received further instructions to go to Dijon as an organiser.

Wilkinson had already found a DZ but Heslop was not impressed with his choice:

It was two small fields with some tall trees at one end and it was only three miles from the centre of town which was teeming with Germans who would be on the scene in minutes. And it was bordered on two sides by rivers,

Pierre Geelen. (Geelen family)

the Mayenne and the Loire, which formed two sides of a trap if the reception committee was raided.[10]

Their first drop (Privet 1) on 11/12 April was to the DZ that Wilkinson had chosen in Angers but which Heslop did not like. The reception described by Heslop was very different from that of Cowburn. Heslop had managed to convince Wilkinson that they should use instead another DZ that he had found some 30km outside Angers and Wilkinson had gone to Paris to see if my father could get a message to London with details of the new DZ before the first drop took place, but it was too late.

> One night I heard on the BBC – Jim and Vic are two fine retrievers.[11] The RAF was coming that night. I decided the drop should go ahead, even though it meant using the old DZ, because this was the first to be attempted in the area, which meant that the Germans would not be perturbed at low-flying aircraft.

Heslop tried to find Henri, Wilkinson's deputy, as he was the only person around who knew the people who had been recruited as a reception team, but he was out of town. With some help from Wilkinson's wife, he managed to recruit two men, Monsieur Bruges and Boris Tourganief. Four containers landed where intended but the fifth landed in a tree.

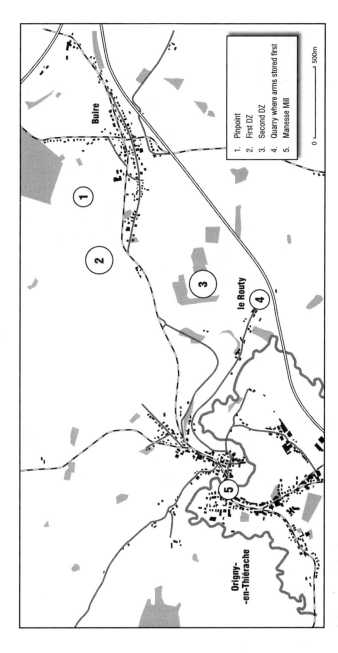

Origny-en-Thiérache DZ.

Edward Wilkinson. (Guy Laurent)   Richard Heslop. (SFC)

I ordered the men into the trees for twenty minutes just in case some nosy farmer had seen the torches, the aircraft and the parachutes. After a while the all clear sounded and once again all was quiet except for the night noises. I waved my helpers on and we walked into the middle of the field where I showed them how to lever open the containers, which was a noisy business, and remove the cells. After each one was opened, we lay still and listened for a minute or two in case we had been heard, straining for the sounds of patrols on motorbikes or afoot. But everything remained quiet and we rolled the silk parachutes and stuffed them into the containers. Then I took the containers to a small pond and sank them.

Boris did very well, for he was a big man and broad, but poor Monsieur Bruges found the work of carrying the separate cells to the hiding of a near-by hedge a tiring one and I watched him stagger as he carted one off. We stored all the cells away in their temporary place and I went to check on the container that had fallen into the tree. I saw it was hopeless to get it down without a ladder and an axe and unfortunately the only white parachute in the group was now folded completely over the tree like a white counterpane on a newly made bed. It would show up for miles around in the morning and the Germans would be sure to start a search for the other goods as soon as it was reported. So I was forced to move the twelve cells from the hedge right away if I was to stop the Germans from seizing the lot.

I told my helpers that we would have to carry them more than a kilometre to an estate. They were not very enthusiastic and I could not blame them for each cell weighed 40 lbs and was shaped like a drum with sharp edges which cut into the shoulders. I was glad when I reached the estate, as my cell seemed to weigh 400 lbs, and poor Monsieur Bruges collapsed on the ground after a few minutes' walk with his and said he was going home and to hell with it. Boris and I left him and trudged the kilometre to the wall which Boris climbed to report that, although there were many trees, all the undergrowth had been cleared and there was nowhere to hide our goods. Worse, the grounds were in full view of a large house. This was a serious setback and I wondered what was the best thing to do. In the end, I decided to hide the stores under the shrubs and blackberry bushes which grew thickly at the base of the wall. We tucked the first two cells away and walked back to see if we could help Monsieur Bruges. Luckily, I had brought a flask of brandy with me and, after a few nips, he felt much better. Boris and I managed to make him laugh a couple of times and persuaded him to complete the journey with his load. In fact he made two more journeys by sheer willpower rather than the strength of the brandy flask, which he emptied on his own.

I was trembling and my knees were knocking by the time I had carried my fourth load and hidden it away. Monsieur Bruges was worse off than I was and I thanked God for the tall, tough Russian who, not only carried his four cells, but also managed to walk more than half a kilometre with Monsieur Bruges's fourth. But at least we had stored them and, unless the search was very thorough, I felt the Germans would not stumble on our cache. By now it was five o'clock in the morning so we set off, very tired but very pleased, back to the house to find both Wilkinson's wife and Madame Bruges exhausted with worry. They had heard the sirens and the aircraft and waited for hours, boosting each other's morale by saying that we were too careful to be caught. But a bottle of wine, an omelette, bread and cheese restored us all. Monsieur was exhausted and, after his meal, he went straight to bed – where he stayed for nearly a week.

To the west of Angers in Nantes, Armel Guerne's brother-in-law, Charles Berruet, formed a network along the coast to the east of St Nazaire and, in April, my father asked Wilkinson to take this over as he was having security problems in Angers where Heslop was left in charge.

Jean Worms, who had parachuted back into France with Déricourt at the end of January, tried to persuade Weil to follow his example and go to London for training but he refused and joined Worms in forming the Juggler circuit to organise sabotage groups around Châlons-sur-Marne. They linked their activities to those of my father as they had lost their own link with London, but Weil also continued his

intelligence work. There is not much information about their
activities in official records except that ten sabotage groups
were organised in the Châlons area. More information is
given in a book[12] but the author confuses the characters of
Worms and Weil, calling both Robin, and some of the actions
claimed for Weil were in fact those of Worms, and in some
cases even those of my father. One significant success claimed
was the copying of the timetables for German troop and
supply trains, which enabled the RAF to attack these targets.
They also found two DZs, one on farmland near Thibié
known as la Cugna to the south-south-west of Châlons and
the other at Humbauville to the south of Châlons and south-
west of Vitry-le-François. Operation Juggler 1 delivered
five containers to the Thibié DZ on 14/15 April, the pilot
commenting, 'Reception not at all good. Completed only
because of clear definition of ground details.'

In the middle of March Henri Déricourt arranged his first
landing operation through the Physician wireless operators.
Operation Trainer on 17/18 March brought four agents to
France and took another four back to England. Francine
Agazarian was brought in to assist her husband in coding and
decoding messages and to act as his courier. Robert Dowlen
was to be the wireless operator for the Chestnut circuit of
Charles Grover-Williams, freeing him from his dependence
on the operators of the Physician circuit. The other two
passengers were Pierre Lejeune and John Goldsmith whose
task was to organise the French military groups under the
control of General Girard to receive arms. Lejeune was not
impressed by Dowlen who I think must have been putting on
an act to avoid talking to Lejeune:

*J'avais pour compagnon de voyage un maltais dote
d'énormes moustaches noires, qui parlait mal l'Anglais,*

> *pas du tout le Français, pelait de peur et ne voulait pas*
> *porter sa valise contenant so poste emetteur. C'était un*
> *agent de SOE!* (For a travelling companion I had a Maltese
> endowed with an enormous black moustache who did not
> speak English well, had no French at all and did not wish
> to carry his case containing a wireless set. It was an agent
> of SOE!)[13]

This operation also took four agents to England. Raymond
Flower was at last returned to London and was not used
again as an agent whilst Claude de Baissac and France
Antelme were returning to report (and had been asked by
my father to write to my mother). The fourth passenger was
André Dubois who had been recruited by Marcel Clech as he
had been a wireless operator in the French Army. A set had
been sent out for him but he was not able to use it, so he was
going to England for the necessary additional training.

At the end of March, three more agents arrived: Jean
Bouguennec was to establish the Butler circuit in Brittany with
Marcel Rousset as his wireless operator. SOE had been trying
to get them into France since the end of 1942 and had tried
again in February but weather and lack of aircraft resulted in
a three months' delay. They finally arrived on 23/24 March,
parachuting blind near Château-du-Loir in the Sarthe, halfway
between Le Mans and Tours. But the drop was a disaster.
Bouguennec broke his ankle, Rousset landed in some electric
wires and they could not find any of their luggage, which
included Rousset's wireless set. Leaving Bouguennec in the
care of the local doctor in Château-du-Loir, Rousset went to
Paris to find my father to report back to London through the
Physician wireless sets and request a new one for himself. He
had to continue to rely on the Physician sets for another month
before he received a replacement of his own.

Jean Bouguennec.
(Bouguennec family)

Bouguennec's orders were to establish a circuit in Brittany and to deny the enemy the possibility of withdrawing rail rolling stock from Brittany and of reinforcing troops there.[14] This did not happen as he was not capable of travelling to Brittany. Following the failure of Raymond Flower's Monkeypuzzle circuit, which should have been based in Le Mans but had been based instead in Tours, there was a gap between these two towns. This is where Bouguennec decided to organise his Butler circuit as Henri Goude, the doctor who had treated his leg, was willing to lead a local team and had contacts. Another group was formed further west around Sablé-sur-Sarthe under Michel Lemore.

The third agent dropped with Bouguennec and Rousset on 23/24 March was Marcel Fox and he landed unharmed. His orders were to form the Publican circuit in the region of Meaux on the Marne to the east of Paris. He went to Paris

Marcel Rousset. (SFC)

with Rousset and my father introduced him to Maurice Braun who knew the forest of Fontainebleau well and persuaded Fox to use contacts there to form a second group, where a DZ was found and cleared.

All of these agents would have no doubt been given the same briefing as that given to Claude de Baissac on 1 April:

> At the present stage of the war, our orders are to cause the maximum damage and confusion in the shortest possible time. This will continue to apply even if France is not the scene of actual hostilities during the next few months, since we have been and must still be successful in pinning down a large number of troops who would otherwise be available for other sectors.[15]

In the middle of April, Déricourt organised two operations on consecutive nights. The first was on 14/15 April to a field outside Amboise and brought in four agents, but the first aircraft ran into a tree and had to be extricated, causing the second aircraft to circle for a quarter of an hour before it could land. The usual turn-around time on the ground was just two or three minutes. One aircraft carried Philippe Liewer and his lieutenant Joseph Chartrand, whose mission was to organise a new circuit in the Rouen-Le Havre area to be known as Salesman.

The other aircraft returned Henri Frager to France, now authorised to gather up some of the remains of the Carte organisation and proceed with his own contacts. It had been decided during his stay in London to split the old Carte area into three: the area along the south-east border of France would become the Jockey circuit; the areas around the Savoie and up to the old demarcation line would remain as Spindle; and Frager would take over the eastern frontier of France

Marcel Fox. (Fox family)

west of Nancy, Châlons-sur-Saône and the Paris region. Spindle, Peter Churchill, who parachuted back to France on the same day, was arrested two days later so Frager took on his areas as well. In the event, he organised groups in the Dordogne, Jura, Lorraine, Mantes, Paris, Montauban, Normandy and the Yonne valley, the circuit being called Donkeyman and known in France as Jean-Marie.

The fourth passenger was André Dubois, now a fully trained wireless operator. The only passenger back to England was the man who had recruited Dubois, Marcel Clech, who after the collapse of the Monkeypuzzle circuit had worked with my father, who had no operator until Agazarian arrived at the very end of 1942. Although Norman had arrived before Agazarian, he did not have a wireless set until February and even then, he did not send his first message until March for some reason, so Clech had been filling in.

Once the aircraft had departed, there was another problem. Déricourt and his lieutenant Marc Clement had only brought four bicycles. Déricourt took Frager and Dubois and they cycled to Tours. The others had to hide most of their luggage, only taking one case of clothes balanced on the other bicycle whilst they walked the 15km to the nearest station, from where they caught a train to Tours. Here Dubois was waiting for them and took them to his mother-in-law's flat in the grounds of a girls' school. Shortly after their arrival, they were warned that German officers had just entered the grounds. Chartrand describes what happened next:

> Needless to say we did not lose time and we rushed out by a back door and made our way, with Dubois, to his mother-in-law's cottage about 5 kilometres out of the city, somewhat worried as to why our German friends were visiting so close to us and so soon after our arrival. We had the answer later on in the day. It was merely a commission visiting schools' libraries and examining the text books in the hands of children to make sure that only the right kind of history should be taught![16]

The Salesman circuit was slow to get started as Liewer was unable to find somewhere safe to stay in Rouen, and Dubois came to his rescue again. Through a friend, Ben Bossard, whose house in Avaray had been used by Flower and many others, he introduced Liewer to 'Micheline' who ran a dressmaker's shop in Paris and had another in Rouen with a manager who agreed to help and a flat where he could stay. Even so it was not until June that Liewer felt it was safe to move there. Neither Frager nor Liewer had wireless operators so they used Dubois, although he remained in Tours.

The next night Déricourt received two more agents at a different landing ground 50km away to the north of Tours. Although neither was from F Section, one does play a major part in the story. This was Pierre Natzler who was being sent in to test the Lasalle escape line and collect 'all information about clandestine travel under present conditions'.[17] He had been waiting since the end of 1942 and an attempt was made to drop him on Christmas Eve with Agazarian. This failed and they ended up spending

Christmas at Tangmere where they met Déricourt who was training there at the time. The only passenger back to England was Julienne Aisner, whom Déricourt was sending to be trained as his official courier.

There were no incidents with the aircraft this time, but instead of crossing the demarcation line and travelling straight to Lyons, Natzler turned up a few days later in Paris, having apparently decided that it was too dangerous for him to cross the demarcation line into the southern part of France. He was not of course expected but had been given the address of one of my father's safe houses for use in an emergency. Unfortunately, this was where Ben Cowburn had been placed by my father, and he and Natzler had to share a bed until Cowburn moved on to Troyes. Another agent who was in Paris at this time reported that Natzler 'did Prosper a good deal of harm'.

The RAF were so concerned about the aircraft running into a tree that an empty aircraft was sent just before Easter on the night of 22/23 April to bring Déricourt back to England to explain.

There was also trouble in Paris on 22 April; Germaine Tambour and her sister Madeleine were arrested together with other people from the now defunct Carte organisation. This was the result of one of its couriers, carrying a list of 200 members, falling asleep on a train the previous November and having his briefcase stolen, but why it took the Germans six months to react is not known.

Progress Report to SOE Executive Committee – 12.04.1943
Physician and Butcher report that the Chevilly transformer station has been successfully attacked; the Paris-Le mans railway has been reconnoitred; and stores are available provided further deliveries are made. They are prepared to attack five other lines at five days' notice.

The problem of lack of material at this time is emphasised in a note on a March report on de Baissac's file:

> This is in some ways a very sad document. The record of achievement and of possibilities is so great but the record of assistance from this side – particularly in the matter of supply – is so small. It is obvious that the stake is big and it is to be hoped that the effort in the next few months will be sufficient to make up the leeway before it is too late.[18]

Progress Report to SOE Executive Committee – 26.04.1943
Physician and Butcher carried out a further attack on the Chaigny Transformer Station on 5 April resulting in all high tension lines out except that to Paris. Three German goods trains were derailed between Orléans and Vierzon, Vierzon and Tours and Blois and Villefranche. They will repeat their attacks when repairs are effected. A further report gives news of attacks on German goods and oil trains followed by attacks on repair cranes and equipment.

Juggler has 10 groups at Chalons-sur-Marne plus 5 railway sabotage groups and one coup-de-main party.

Notes

1. Report 09.03.1943, HS 9/43, TNA.
2. Annexe of telegrams, undated, HS 6/33, TNA.
3. 9 J 46, Archives départmentales, Sarthe.
4. M R D Foot, *SOE in France*. The first edition published by HMSO in 1966 is not now used as it was officially amended and republished in 1968. A revised and updated edition was published by Frank Cass in 2004 and a French translation of this edition was published in 2008 by Tallandier under the title Des Anglais dans la Résistance.
5. HS 9/11/1, TNA.
6. HS 9/147/5, TNA.
7. P. Guillaume, *La Sologne au temps de la trahaison et de l'heroisme*, 1949.
8. B. Cowburn, *No Cloak, No Dagger*, Frontline Books, 2009.
9. Interrogation 13.10.1943, HS 9/570/6, TNA.

10. R. Heslop, *Xavier*, Rupert Hart-Davis, 1970.
11. In the Circuit Liquidation file, 17P 5, the message is given as 'Il faut rattraper le temps perdu', which is in the BBC list of April messages so either Heslop's memory failed him or this was an earlier personal message to assure the locals that Heslop did have direct contact with London.
12. C. Wighton, *Pin-Stripe Saboteur*, Odhams, 1959.
13. Temoinage 07.06.1986, 72 AJ 40 II, Archives Nationales, Paris.
14. HS 9/189/8.
15. HS 9/75, TNA.
16. Report 04.12.1943, HS 9/299/10, TNA.
17. Executive Committee Report fortnight ending 26.04.1943, HS 8/220, TNA.
18. HS 9/75, TNA.

PROGRESS AT LAST

Progress Report to SOE Executive Committee – 10.05.1943
Physician confirms that all of his targets have been
reconnoitred and that stores are available.

Déricourt returned to France on the night of 5/6 May,
parachuted blind near Mer on the Loire. This was before the
start of that month's moon period on 10 May, presumably
to give him time to organise his next operation, for which
he had been ordered to stand by from 12 May, although he
and my father are reported to have left Paris for Amboise
the day before. Bad weather prevented the RAF from flying
any operations at the start of this moon period and this
operation finally took place on 14/15 May. It was a double
Lysander operation bringing in four passengers, including
Julienne Aisner, now fully trained to be Déricourt's courier,
and picking up my father.[1]

There is no official record of the reason for his visit but
Buckmaster wrote:

As early as April 1943, the rumour ran like wildfire that the
Allies were about to land in France. The patriotic upsurge
of enthusiasm was dangerous. It had to be quelled ... We
decided that we must bring Prosper back to London ... The
fires of enthusiasm would have to be damped down. Only

a first class man like Prosper could convey that message successfully.[2]

The only person he is known to have met apart from Buckmaster was someone called Colquhoun whose identity I have not been able to trace. A possibility is that Colquhoun was from Air Liaison or Air Intelligence, taking advantage of the opportunity to exchange views with an active agent. I know from my mother that she came up to London to see him but apart from that he seems to have been busy with Buckmaster as the latter records in his diary:

15th Saturday. Prosper arrived. Lunch in the canteen.
16th Sunday. Lunched at Carletta's with Prosper.
17th Monday. Prosper and Colquhoun to dinner at Pelham Court. (Buckmaster's flat)
18th Tuesday. Lunch with Prosper at Park Lane Hotel.
19th Wednesday. 1000 hours meeting with Prosper. Lunch with Prosper in canteen.
20th Thursday. Prosper and Renaud (Antelme) left.

He and Antelme parachuted back to a Culioli reception at the Miraillon DZ near Chaumont-sur-Tharonne together with two containers and three packages, following the BBC message, 'Les bicyclettes du châtelain ne valent rien' (The bicycles of the lord of the manor are worth nothing).

The others to arrive on 14/15 May were Sydney Jones with Vera Leigh as a courier and Marcel Clech, returning for his second mission, as their wireless operator. Their orders were to organise a circuit in the Troyes/Nancy area, part of the area allocated to Frager after he split from Carte. Although independent of Frager, they were ordered to maintain contact with him as he had to use Clech for communication with London. They went first to Paris and stayed with Julienne Aisner. Here they met Agazarian who suggested that they await my father's return, as he had sent a report through Agazarian expressing doubts about Frager, which he intended to pursue in London. The message was part of a report that my father sent on 18 April:

> Please, please, please avoid all contact between me and (Frager). I have had reliable reports which induce me to distrust him or at least his methods. I can, if necessary, give you chapter and verse for this.[3]

They did wait and met my father but, whatever the problem was, he must have been reassured whilst in London because they did proceed with their mission, although Clech was not able to transmit. He had left a suitcase containing his codes and signals in the care of Déricourt's number two, Marc Clement, when they landed but when he went back to collect the case he found that they were missing. I found later that they had been stolen on the orders of Déricourt. This was revealed by an Abwehr agent, Hugo Bleicher, who had made friends with Frager. He was annoyed as he had intended to steal them himself.[4]

As it had been decided that a fourth drop to the DZ between the two châteaux to the west of Le Mans would be too risky, a new DZ was found to the north-east in the grounds of the château de l'Hermitière, near Le Theil and just over the border in the Orne. This belonged to the de Courson family who were also cousins of the Celiers of château l'Eporce who had recommended them. Simon and Garry attended the first reception with help from Aymard and Guillaume de Courson, another relation Arthur de Montalembert, a neighbour M. de

Guillaume de Courson.
(Libre Résistance)

la Vigne-Bernard, the estate farmer Gilbert Plessis and his son and a valet de ferme, Jean Reiss. The first operation here was Physician 27 on 13/14 May but it did not go too well as the containers dropped 750m from the designated spot. As the ground was wooded and crossed by ditches, it was difficult to retrieve the containers but before dawn they managed to find the five they had counted in the air and the contents were transported to a sand pit nearer the château and buried. Unfortunately there was a sixth parachute, which they had not seen, bringing a Eureka; this was found by a farmer some distance away and they were not able to retrieve it without drawing unwanted attention to their activities. The de Courson family remember the message as *'L'amateur de rose et de porcelaine'* which is not in the official BBC list so it must have been selected by those in the reception team.[5]

The aircraft that delivered Physician 27 also delivered Physician 45 to a DZ near Falaise in Calvados. This was the nearest to the channel coast of all of the Physician drops. One of the Prosper couriers in Paris was Yvonne de la Rochefoucauld, whose husband, Count Bernard, lived at Versainville just to the east of Falaise, where he was mayor. Early in 1943, my father asked Bernard de la Rochefoucauld to find a ground suitable for parachute operations and a team

Aymard de Courson. (Libre Résistance)

Jean-Michel Cauchy. (Cauchy family)

to help, and he in turn recruited a cloth merchant in Falaise, Jean-Michel Cauchy.

My father went to Falaise to make arrangements with Cauchy who had found what he thought was a suitable ground, but when my father came to inspect it on 1 May, he found that a German post had been set up nearby. A DZ was then found on the farm of Georges Bertin near Martigny-sur-l'Ante to the west of Falaise. Following the BBC message '*Le serpent chauve devient zazou*' (The bald snake became hip), five containers and a wireless transmitter were dropped. Cauchy collected the material over the following days and hid them in a granary next to his house in Falaise.

Also on the night of 13/14 May, two operations were flown to Darling's groups by 138 Squadron. Physician 23 brought ten containers and a package in a second successful operation at Lalandelle and there was an operation further south to replace the load that had been destined for Trie-Château a month earlier but had been delivered by mistake to Neaufles-Saint-Martin. The earlier mistake was recognised in the order for this operation, which was called Physician 10, 2nd sortie. The aircraft crashed near Le Havre and it is not known whether this happened before or after completing its mission. Curiously 161 Squadron's Rough Diary also claims this operation but claims that ten containers and a package were successfully dropped. However, the report that the pilot would have completed confirms that the aircraft was from 138 Squadron. It would seem therefore that the 161 Squadron record is faulty in this instance and the mystery of whether it was successful or not will only be resolved if a record is found in Trie-Château.

The night's activities were completed by a sabotage attack on the Sucrerie Sayat, an alcohol factory in Étrépagny (Eure), in which 6 million litres of alcohol were reported to have been destroyed. Darling's courier, Renée Guepin, brought the explosives from Trie-Château on her bicycle. The saboteurs were the Alavoine brothers, Gaston and Guy, who came to Gisors from Beaumont-sur-Oise and were driven to and from Étrépagny by Georges Darling. The Artauds had watched the plant in advance and knew that the guard made his rounds at night every hour on the hour, so the charges were set for the half hour when the guard was safely in his hut. However, the time pencils were not as accurate as hoped and the charges exploded some two hours later than intended and only a couple of minutes after the guard had made a round. The operation was not as successful as planned, or later claimed, as one of the silos had just been emptied and the other contained acid at that time, not the expected and more valuable alcohol.

Sometimes acts of sabotage were carried out when it was known that there would be aerial activity in the area, so that the Germans would think that the damage was caused by bombing and would not take local reprisals. There were attempted drops that night at Lalandelle and Trie-Château, some 20km to the east, but if it was hoped that they would be blamed for the attack at Étrépagny, the Germans knew immediately that it was a ground attack as they found part of one of the time fuses. The investigation found that two vehicles had been seen in the area at the time of the explosions but one turned out to be a patrol and the other was the local vet called out to a sick horse. Ironically the vet, Maurice Daviaud, was involved in resistance but with an intelligence gathering network known as Cohors-Asturias. Fortunately Daviaud's alibi was found to be sound and his resistance activities remained undiscovered.[6]

Sabotage at the Sucrerie at Étrépagny. (P. Guillaume)

Robert Artaud remembers the moment the explosions went off. (F. Dury)

The aircraft that delivered Physician 32 to Lalandelle was also carrying five containers to a Roach reception just to the north-north-west of Beauvais. Roach was a French resistance organisation and in February 1943, Michel Sailly was appointed chief of their operations in the Oise. Sometime in April, and before he had been able to organise any drops, Sailly met my father who already had successful groups in the Oise. Sailly did not want to join a circuit not organised by the French but he and my father made a gentleman's agreement that Sailly would organise drops in the west of the Oise helped by my father's links to London. The material from the first such drop, Roach 8, was taken to Berneuil-en-Bray to the south of Beauvais where Georges Darling's involvement is commemorated on the war memorial. Sailly organised nine other drops before his arrest in November, all of which were further east than the first around Senlis and Noyon.[7] Colonel Boxshall referred to Sailly as being a circuit chief in the Prosper organisation; this is not correct.

The night of 14/15 May saw two more drops. Operation Physician 25 delivered ten containers and a package in the second operation to the group at Bois-Jérôme-Saint-Ouen, this time to a clearing inside the wood, and the same amount was dropped by Operation Physician 22 to a new DZ south-west of Neuf-Marché. Two nights later there was a third drop to the Lalandelle DZ. Operation Physician 24 was meant to deliver a package and ten containers but one of the containers 'hung up and could not be released', so only nine arrived.

There is a record in Air Ministry files that on 23/24 May, the very end of the moon period, an attempt was made (Physician 38) to drop containers to a DZ much further north of the others, some 40km from Trie-Château. The pinpoint is just south of Crèvecoeur-le-Grand. I have not managed to find any names of people involved in this area and have no idea where the actual DZ was. The pilot reported that he had been able to identify the location by the bend in the railway but had found no reception.

There is also another mystery. At the very beginning of this moon period on 12/13 May an attempt was made (Physician 33) to drop ten containers to a DZ between La Ferté-sous-Jouarre and Château-Thierry, not far from where my father had first landed in France the year before. This may be linked to a report that Norman and Claude de Baissac were arrested in March or April whilst looking for suitable grounds in the La Ferté-sous-Jouarre area but released.[8] The pilot reported that he could not positively identify the ground. Physician 33 was flown again the next night. but this time to a DZ in the Sologne where it was also not successful. I then noticed that a week later Roach 33 was flown with the same pinpoint, but still with Physician involvement. Norman sent a message the following day saying that the reception had not gone out as the BBC message had been mutilated. It appears that this was another example of co-operation between my father and a French organised group in Saulchery.

By the time that the May moon period started, the de Bernards and Culioli had each made many more contacts. Anne-Marie de Bernard knew a vet in Bracieux, François

Cortambert, and he willingly recruited a team with his friend Albert Lemeur and found a DZ near Neuvy. Meanwhile, Julien Nadau introduced Culioli and Rudellat to two groups that had already been formed but were looking for a role. André Gatignon was a wine merchant in Noyers-sur-Cher who regularly crossed the demarcation line with wine casks. He found a DZ in the bois de Juchepie on the other side of the Cher. The other group was to be the biggest of all of the groups in the Prosper organisation. Roger Couffrant, an electrician, and his friend André Brasseur were both based in Romorantin. They organised teams in Selles, Villefranche and Châtres along the Cher and in Villeny, deep in the Sologne to the north of Romorantin. They found DZs near Châtillon just to the east of Selles; at Langon, west of Châtres; near Maray across the Cher from Châtres; at Rére between Theillay and La Ferté-Imbault; in the forest to the north-west of Villeny; at Gy-en-Sologne to the west of Romorantin and two around Courmemin. Three of these were used in May.

There were four operations attempted in the Sologne on the night of 13/14 May, of which two were successful but not without problems. Two of the loads were in the same aircraft that was meant to deliver the five containers and a package of Physician 36 to the new DZ at Neuvy, following the BBC message '*Quatre gangsters*

André Gatignon. (Gatignon family)

Roger Couffrant. (Couffrant family)

assis sur l'herbe' (Four gangsters sitting on the grass), and then the ten containers and a package of Physician 35 to one of Couffrant's new DZs south of Courmemin, following the message '*La surprise est au fond de la boîte*' (The surprise is at the bottom of the box).

The operation did not go smoothly either in the air or on the ground. The pilot reported:

Only four containers came away on first run. A second run was made but the container still hung up and it was not possible to jettison because Physician 35 load was still on board. After the completion of Physician 35, we returned to Physician 36 and attempted without success to jettison the container.

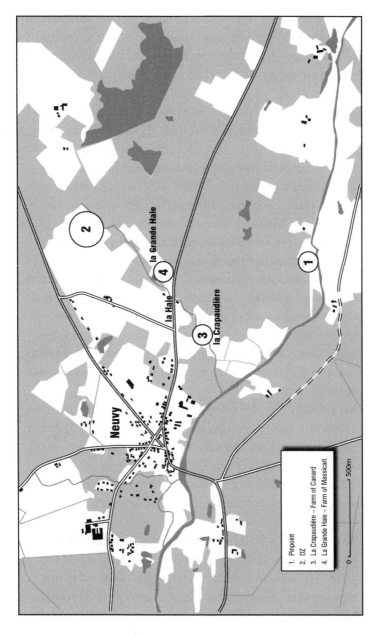

1. Pinpoint
2. DZ
3. La Crapaudière – Farm of Canard
4. La Grande Haie – Farm of Massicart

Neuvy DZ.

On the ground at Neuvy, a kilometre along the road to Neung-sur-Beuvron, the team thought that the aircraft had fired a machine gun at them and then had problems finding all of the containers that had been dropped:

> The next day, the occupants of the neighbouring farms recounted that there had been an air battle during the night. Then, three parachutes had got tangled in the fir trees; to get them down they [the members of the section] had to cut down the trees, in the dark, without arousing the attention of the neighbouring farmers who lived just 300m away. Although they were novices, the members of the section rescued all the containers and provisionally stowed them at the abandoned and deserted Haies farm. The next morning, however, another parachute was discovered and the containers were put in a safe place before farmers noticed them.[9]

It must have been the noise made by the crews' attempts to release the last container that the team on the ground mistook for gunfire.

Meanwhile, at the ground just to the south-west of Courmemin, they were also having problems. The DZ was surrounded on three sides by woods and by a lake on the fourth. The reception team from Romorantin, and Culioli and Rudellat who had recently moved to nearby Veillens, saw eleven parachutes descending but at the last minute:

> The wind, which has suddenly picked up, inflates the parachutes, carrying their precious cargo off towards the pond. The resistance members hear plop, plop, plop, one after another. All of the parachuted cargo is in the water, except for one container which has landed at the edge.

Without hesitating the men get into the water and among the reeds, wading in the mud. They find five containers, one containing a 'suitcase radio' with a transmitter. The parachutes are rolled up and the containers, which weigh 150 kilos, are pulled with difficulty onto the bank to be inventoried. The arms and munitions, which are susceptible to water, are carried by hand to the nearest road, put into a car and stored in a safe place. A warning interrupts the work. A large dog, let out by the Riou farmers, who believed there were marauders around, comes running up but is soon called off by his mistress. The day is already dawning. The men hurry back to Romorantin to resume their professional occupations and avoid arousing attention, despite the tiring work they have been doing during the night. Two of them go to visit the Riou farmers to find out whether they have become aware of the parachute drop. The first introduces his friend as an English parachutist who has been dropped with military supplies that have fallen in the pond. The farmers, who are patriots, immediately offer their services to the Resistance and put an old boat out onto the water, so that the five containers that had to be abandoned during the night can be fished out. On the final outing, the boat, too heavily loaded, sinks to the bottom with all its crew, but all the supplies saved, the containers opened on the spot and the contents put into hiding.[10]

Of the other two operations on 13/14 May, Physician 32 was to a new DZ near Mur-de-Sologne south-west of Courmemin, but was not successful as the crew lost sight of the reception committee whilst making a circuit. Physician 33 to a new DZ in the south-east of the Sologne between Theillay and La Ferté-Imbault, was also not successful as the pilot could not positively identify the ground. They tried

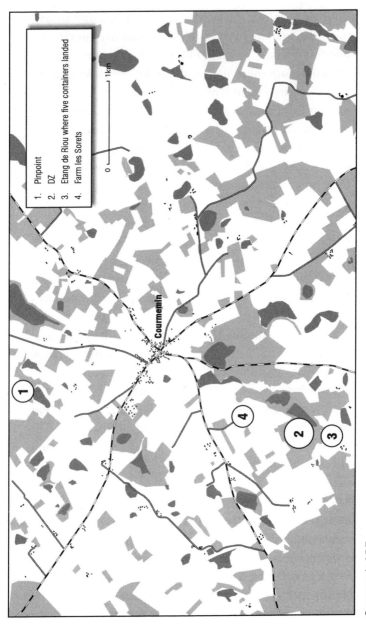

Courmemin 1 DZ.

again the next night, 13/14 May, but this time they found no reception. It was finally successful, dropping ten containers on the night of 23/24 May (Physician 33). In 2009 I met Robert Courtois who in 1943 worked on the railways and had been part of the reception team that was led by Roger Couffrant with the help of André Daguet and Georges Brault. The parachuted material was later taken to Selles-sur-Cher where Pierre Chassagne had a depot. Unfortunately he was too ill to take me to the DZ but he did remember that the message was '*N'oubliez pas la pince*' (Don't forget the pliers). When I checked the official list of BBC messages for May, I found '*N'oubliez pas l'Alsace*', which must have been the actual message. This was one of several occasions when I was given a message as someone had remembered it that had changed over time – not surprising after 70 years. In 2013 I was able to visit the area and found a farmer who remembered that it was his uncle Desire Lambert who had been on the farm in the war and had helped Couffrant with the drop, which was between his farm and the woods to the south.

The next night, 14/15 May, there was a second drop (Physician 28) to Les Motteux south of Chaumont-sur-Loire of ten containers and a package following the BBC message '*Les cornichons sont marinés*' (The gherkins are pickled). This was followed on the night of 15/16 May by a drop (Physician 34) to the new DZ in the bois de Juchepie when ten containers of light arms, explosives and '*crayons incendaires*' were delivered. The BBC message was '*La main microscopique amorce l'opération*' (The microscopic hand starts the operation). The pinpoint for the operation was just to the north-west of this wood but in papers from the archives in Blois the location was given as les Bûcherons, which is to the south of the woods, whilst a display in

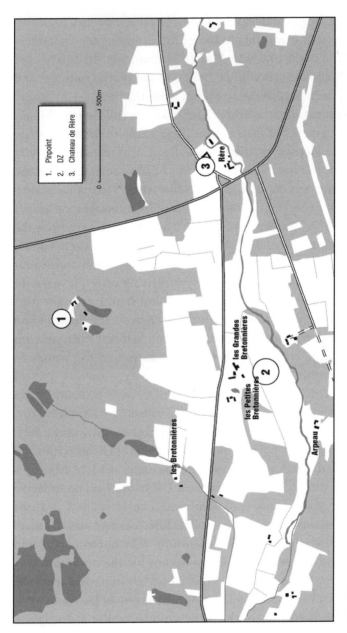

Rére DZ.

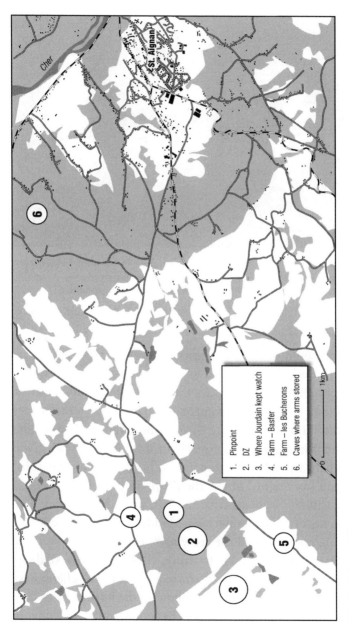

1. Pinpoint
2. DZ
3. Where Jourdain kept watch
4. Farm – Basfer
5. Farm – les Bucherons
6. Caves where arms stored

Bois de Juchepie DZs.

Christian Jourdain and I being shown the caves where the material from the
Bois de Juchepie was stored. Christian's father was Gatignon's deputy and
took part in the reception and transport of the containers dropped.
(Y Ribrioux)

the museum in Blois suggests la Boulaie, which is to the
north. I was lucky to find a local historian from Mareuil,
the commune that includes the bois de Juchepie. Yannick
Ribrioux kindly found someone who had known the farmer
of the land used for the drops who lived at Basfer. The
farmer threatened to denounce the team if he was not given
compensation for the damage to his crops but was told,
'If you say a word about the drop, do not be surprised if
an accident happens in your farm, probably by fire.' The
contents of the containers were hidden in the galleries of an
old quarry now used for growing mushrooms.[11]

On the night of 18/19 May, there was a first drop
(Physician 37) of five containers to a DZ at Langlochère, west
of Meung-sur-Loire (Loiret), following the BBC message '*Les
genets ardennais sont fleuris*' (The broom in the Ardennes is

Maurice Lequeux. (Libre Résistance)

in flower). This was the group that had just been started at the end of 1942 by Culioli and Rudellat when their landlord died suddenly and they left hurriedly. Maurice Lequeux took over the group and a DZ was found on the land of Jean Bordier. Lequeux suffered from a heart condition and so was happy to rely on Jean Flamencourt, an engineer, to lead the reception team. Jean's brother Edouard, a chicken farmer, allowed his house to be used to lodge agents and to keep a radio for Norman and Agazarian to use. I tried to find this DZ in 2007 and was just about to give up because the geography of the area has been altered by industrial development and a motorway, when I saw an old man picking fruit. When I told him what I was looking for, he asked me who I was and when I told him, he almost embraced me with delight – he was Jacques Bordier and had helped his father with all three of this group's receptions. The DZ is now lost to the motorway but was near the Moulin des Troussets, which is still visible just outside the service area, and the containers were stored overnight in an old quarry before being taken to Paris.[12]

The reports to the SOE Executive Committee had mentioned that landing grounds had been found in Normandy and the Touraine for up to four divisions ready for an imminent invasion. In the latter area, the plan was to land some 40,000 men in April or May between Mer and

Jean Bordier. (Bordier family)

The Moulin des Troussets. (Author)

Meung-sur-Loire to attack the airfield at Bricy, to the north-west of Orléans. Lequeux and his men were to listen between the 10th and 15th of these two months for the BBC message *'Les sports d'hiver ne se pratiquent pas en Russie'* (Winter sports do not take place in Russia). The Philbée family in

Jacques Bordier showing the author one of the cells from a container. Jacques later presented me with this container as a souvenir. (Author)

Orléans were recruited to organise the supply of food and fuel for this force.[13]

They and many others in France also lent money to my father against promissory notes signed by him giving an agreed rate of exchange and backed up by a unique BBC message. In Orléans various people lent a total of over 1 million francs and a similar sum was raised through France Antelme's banking contacts in Paris, of which a quarter was given to my father. Amounts from individuals varied, ranging from 30,000 francs lent to my father by Charlotte Suard of Trie-Château in April 1943, worth £150 at 200 francs to the pound, to 300,000 francs lent to Norman by Robert Beline of Neuilly six weeks later, worth £1,000 at 300 francs to the pound.

On 21/22 May, the night after my father and Antelme parachuted back from their visits to London, another twelve containers were delivered to the Miraillon DZ but this time Alfred Thénot was helped by François Cortambert and Albert Lemeur. A team from the village of Villeny also attended to be shown what to do when their turn came in June.

In the north of France, a second operation (Physician 30) of ten containers was flown to Origny-en-Thiérache. The pinpoint was the same but Geelen had changed the location of the DZ to avoid German patrols and the pilot took some

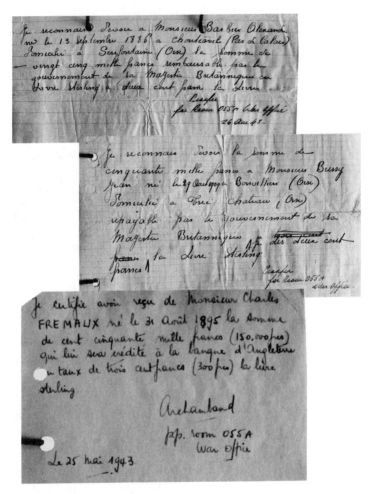

Examples of notes agreeing loans.

time to find it. Geelen had also started groups each side of the
border with Belgium in the Ardennes at Muno in Belgium and
Carignon in France. He asked his friend and fellow refugee
from the failure of Carte, Walther Marly, to be the leader
here. A DZ was found on a ridge right on the border where

Belgians farmed on French fields. It was known as le Monty and Physician 29 dropped another ten containers here also on 21/22 May and the material was distributed to local resistance groups.

> **Progress Report to SOE Executive Committee – 24.05.1943**
> The Physician organisation has made excellent progress particularly during the last two months. Physician's short visit to this country has been of immense value.

In the related circuits, Cowburn had organised Tinker 1 to drop five containers on 16/17 May to a new DZ he had found with the help of Mulsant near Verlaines, but Worms was less successful. Both Juggler 2 on 16/17 to the same DZ as Juggler 1 in April and Juggler 3 two nights later to another DZ near Vitry-le-François failed. Wilkinson, now in Nantes, was also unlucky when his first operation there on 23/24 May (Privet 2) was defeated by the weather. Heslop, however, managed to organise two successful drops around Angers.

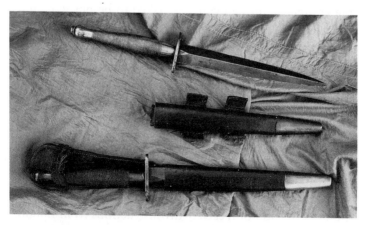

Daggers and parachute from one of the drops on le Monty.

Privet 3 on 19/20 May delivered five containers to a new DZ to the south of the town as well as two wireless sets for Grover-Williams' Chestnut circuit. In a French file[14] I found the message recorded as '*Quant il fait beau, il ne pleut pas.*' (When the weather is fine, it does not rain). This is another example of memories distorting the real message as when I looked at the list of BBC messages for May I found '*Lorsqu'il ne pleut pas, il fait beau temps*' (When it's not raining, it is fine). Three nights later Privet 4 brought five containers to a new DZ, this time some way to the north of Angers and with a new team under Jules Duval. The BBC message here was '*Après la soupe, une verre du vin*' (After the soup, a glass of wine).[15] Wilkinson made a good start in Nantes, finding two DZs to the north of the town, but he had no drops in May because of bad weather.

My father missed not only all of the parachute operations in May but also a curious incident in Paris that has led to much speculation. Two agents apparently from SOE's Dutch Section, calling themselves Adrien and Arnaud, arrived in Paris sometime in the second week of May. Arnaud went to a contact point in a café and asked to be put in contact with 'Gilbert'. He wanted to contact Déricourt, code named Gilbert, to arrange for Adrien to be flown to London, but he was instead sent to Gilbert Norman who happened to be playing cards nearby with Agazarian. Once the confusion over names had been sorted out, Agazarian offered to make the necessary arrangements with the required 'Gilbert' as he was acting as wireless operator for Déricourt. He and Arnaud agreed to meet again on 17 May. This all happened at the same time that my father and Déricourt were waiting for the pick-up, which finally took place on 14 May. Déricourt said that he had not received any instructions from London about another pick-up in May and he refused to organise one unless another passenger could be found to justify it. This was not possible so Adrien and Arnaud were told to return on 9 June, where they would be met in the café Capucines. One of them asked if he could borrow a 'poste radio' and some writers have translated this as a wireless transmitter, accusing Agazarian of carelessness, but in fact it is simply a receiver for listening out for BBC messages.

Progress Report to SOE Executive Committee – 24.05.1943
A Dutch general, whose presence in this country is urgently required, has reached Paris after travelling on a line from Holland to France arranged by Stromboli. It is hoped to exfiltrate this officer by Lysander as soon as possible.

Notes

1. In 161 Squadron's Operational Records Book, AIR 27/1068, the date is given as 13/14 May; this is an error.
2. M. Buckmaster, *Specially Employed*, Batchworth, 1952.
3. HS 9/11/1, TNA.
4. H Bleicher, Colonel Henri's Story, edited by Ian Colvin, William Kimber, 1954.
5. *L'Hermitière*, Cahiers Percherons, No. 75, 1983.
6. 26 R2 50 B, Archives départementales, Évreux.
7. 16 P 530436, SHD archives, Paris.
8. 1221 W11, Archives départmentales, Orléans.
9. P. Guillaume, *La Sologne au Temps de l'Héröisme et de la Trahaison.*
10. P. Guillaume, *La Résistance en Sologne*, Orléans, 1946
11. Information from local historian, Yannick Ribrioux.
12. See 8 above.
13. P. Guillaume, *L'Abbe Pasty: Prêtre et Soldat*, Loiret, 1946.
14. 17 P 5 Alexandre, SHD.
15. In Heslop's book, *Xavier*, he remembers these two operations in reverse order and he also remembers twelve containers to the new DZ whereas RAF records show five.

FAST FORWARD

On 9 June Adrien and Arnaud duly arrived at the café Capucines followed by Agazarian but not Déricourt. What happened next is best left to Agazarian to tell:

> Only about five tables were in use inside the café, the rest of the café being roped off for cleaning, and at one of the tables on the terrasse outside the café was a civilian in a grey hat and mackintosh, with nothing on the table in front of him. Arnaud afterwards said he did not think this man was there when they arrived: up to about a minute before (Agazarian) arrived, the café was empty and then suddenly it was full of people. They had been there a little time and (Agazarian) was in conversation with Arnaud, when he noticed Arnaud looking over his shoulder at two German officers dressed in green uniform (they might have been Feld Gendarmerie) questioning other people. Immediately Adrien got up and with his hands in his pockets, walked out: not fast enough to be in a hurry and not slow enough to be quite natural. The German officer looked up, watched Adrien go out and went on with the examination. Arnaud, who saw Adrien being taken across the road by a civilian said to (Agazarian): 'They have arrested Adrien'; (Agazarian) told him to be quiet, and they proceeded to discuss their cover story. The German officer then asked for their papers, which he examined thoroughly, but took

no further action. (Agazarian) and Arnaud left the café separately and (Agazarian) joined (Borrel) and (Lejeune) at the Napolitain.[1]

Lejeune was there because he was also hoping to be picked up in the next operation. Agazarian reported Adrien's arrest to Déricourt and to London.

The Air Ministry files show that up to the end of May, Physician operations had delivered just under 100 containers. The records also show that attempts were made to drop another 300 in June in thirty-eight separate operations, a huge increase, of which 205 were actually delivered, twenty-seven of the operations being successful. Unfortunately for me, thirty-five of these thirty-eight operations had been flown by 138 Squadron for which the pilot's reports for June had been lost, so there was no record of the intended location or target for these thirty-five, of which twenty-five had been successful.

The pilot's reports for 161 Squadron did exist so I thought I had the necessary information on at least three operations but I immediately ran into problems. On 11/12 June a combined operation, Physician 32/Charlotte, was flown intending to drop ten containers to a Physician DZ between Trie-Château and Beauvais and four packages to a location further west for an SIS group called Charlotte. The aircraft did not return and was officially recorded as having crashed in the Channel on its return journey. There is of course no report by the pilot but in the Operation Record Book of 161 Squadron[2] is written:

Aircraft took off at 11.20 a.m. but no further news received. Reported missing. Later news received from a secret source to the effect that an aircraft answering the description of D G 406 was seen to be shot down in flames by ground flak at a position in the vicinity of Beauvais which was near his second pinpoint. Reported that first operation had been carried out successfully.

This suggests that the Physician operation was not successful and in another file I found a note saying, 'No reception on this ground. Aircraft believed shot down Beauvais.' A message from Norman on 16 June confirmed that the load had not been received.[3]

When the French started to release some of their files in 2010, I found lists of people who were awarded pensions because of their involvement with my father's circuit.[4] Amongst these I found the names of three people from the village of La Houssoye in the Oise, all of whom had died in Germany, and one from the nearby hamlet of Jouy-la-Grange. These were the nearest to the pinpoint for Physician 32 so I went to La Houssoye with a French friend to ask in the *mairie* whether there was anyone living locally who might have known these people. The *maire* and two others were in the *mairie* but as soon as I started to ask my question, the *maire* told us that the *mairie* was not open and asked us to leave. Whilst my friend and the *maire* crossed swords loudly and volubly, the other two had a whispered consultation and discreetly slipped a name and address to me.

This is how we met Pierre Lenglet, who was very angry when we told him what had happened at the *mairie*; he said that this *maire* ignored the memory of those who had died because they had worked with the British. Once he had calmed down, he told us that containers had been dropped on land farmed by Leon Vandendaele of Jouy-la-Grange. He had not been part of the reception team but had helped to transfer the material on more than one occasion from the

farm to the fôret de Thelle. This had been done by a chain of
three teams and he had been part of the middle one so he did
not know exactly where the material had been dropped or
where it was hidden in the forest. Unfortunately he could not
remember any dates. So containers were definitely dropped
near Jouy-la-Grange in an operation that must have followed
Physician 32 as there were no earlier attempts in this area.

161 Squadron was also flying Déricourt's operations and
on 16/17 June four agents were landed and another four
picked up, including Lejeune returning to report and Jack
Agazarian. The incident with Adrien and Arnaud seems to
have brought to a head a simmering conflict between my
father and Agazarian. My father had written a letter setting
out his views on the Agazarians, which is lost, but Jack
Agazarian responded to it in the report he made when he
reached London:

Pierre Lenglet. (F. Dury)

I was going to make a lengthy report on the letter from Prosper but feel this is unnecessary and I will limit myself to the following remarks:-

'I am sending back (Agazarian).' Prosper did not send me back. I insisted on returning. Adrien arrested, I told him there was a spare place on the plane and he had no reasonable excuse for continuing to prevent me from returning.

'He is not being very useful'. My report on my activities, as well as my file here, during this period show this to be incorrect.

'He is imminently (sic) unfit for our work in the field'. Why then did he keep me for six months, prevent me from working with (Déricourt) and do his damnedest to prevent me from returning?

'His nervousness has a bad effect on those he contacts'. Why did he send me to contact people if he thought this? This statement is definitely not in accordance with other people's opinions.

'He has not the slightest organising ability'. How does he know never having tried me out.

'I don't want him to work for anyone else, he knows too much'. 'Don't show him my June report, he knows too little'!

'(Francine – Agazarian's wife) is ill and cannot work here'. A medical examination will prove this untrue.

'She has not been able to fit into the picture'. She (and I) were never invited into it.

'She considers herself outside my authority'. It was not (Francine) but I who refused to allow her to be anybody's courier.

'Adrien behaved throughout with complete lack of security'. I dealt entirely with Adrien. Prosper never even met him or his guide.

Prosper's first words to me on my arrival when he asked me for whom and for what I had come were, in answer to my reply for him as his (wireless operator), 'I don't want you and I never asked for a (wireless operator)'. His attitude never really changed the whole time I was out there.'[5]

Later in this report he mentions my father's plans for the invasion:

Prosper has two main operational centres where good contacts have been made and where there are a great number of patriots willing and capable to work for him. As is the case with contacts, they are continually on the increase. His main centre is in the vicinity of Gisors and the second near Orléans. I believe the intention is that when matters are at a head, (Norman) will take charge of the Orléans area and Prosper will make his headquarters in the Gisors area.

Three of the passengers arriving in France in the aircraft that collected the Agazarians were going to organise or join circuits in the south of France: Skepper to organise Monk; Cecily Lefort to be a courier in Cammaerts' Jockey circuit; and Diana Rowden to be a courier with the Acrobat circuit. The fourth was the first female wireless operator to be sent to France – Noor Inayat Khan – and her mission was to join Emile Garry in the Le Mans area. Once he had his own wireless operator, his groups in the Sarthe and Orne could become the independent Phono circuit. I was surprised to see in her file that her Conducting Officer for her initial training at Wanborough Manor was Lieutenant Tongue. This was my uncle Jack, married to my father's oldest sister. He had once told me that he spent some of the war with SOE but this was before I started my research and so I did not think to ask him about it. Inayat Khan was selected for wireless training but she was sent to France before her training was complete, the urgency perhaps the result of the recall of Agazarian. There had been doubts about her suitability as set out in her finishing report dated 21 May: 'Not overburdened with brains but has worked hard and shown keenness, apart from some dislike of the security side of the course. She has an unstable and temperamental personality and it is very doubtful whether she is really suited to work in the field.' Against this comment, Colonel Buckmaster has written, 'Nonsense. Makes me cross.'[6]

The second parachute operation by 161 Squadron (Physician 49) took place the next night, 17/18 June, and dropped an agent and ten containers to the DZ found by Culioli and Rudellat at les Motteux following the BBC message '*Mon vieux Julien, quelle aventure*' (Well, what an adventure, my old Julian). The agent was Pierre Raynaud on his way to join the Jockey circuit in the south of France. He described his arrival:

Good jump, landed smoothly in the undergrowth some 400 metres from the lights. Immediate contact with the reception committee, whose organisers, Jacqueline (British agent) and Pierre, were present

Noor Inayat Khan. (J.O. Fuller)

Jack Tongue – my uncle. (Author)

... A group of German officers were in the neighbouring woods, around 1½ km away, hunting wild boar and weren't particularly visible.

After the war he claimed that he had to throw himself to the ground because the Halifax was followed by a Messerschmitt night fighter that flew so low that it was not so much hedge-hopping as ground-hopping. The Halifax returned to base safely, the pilot saying, 'No incidents to report.'[7]

Inayat Khan had not been sent in with a wireless set so her first transmission was from one of Norman's sets. Her sets arrived on 21/22 June in the third successful drop by 161 Squadron, Physician 67, to a DZ in the forêt des Alluets in the commune of Bazémont, south of Maule.

This had been found by staff and students of the National Agricultural College some 15km south at Grignon-Thiverval, to the west of Versailles. This group was started at the end of April when Germaine Tambour introduced one of the teachers there, Professor Serge Balachowsky, to my father. The college quickly became an informal country HQ. The drop on 21/22 June, announced by the BBC message '*La commissaire deviant agent de change*', was to deliver an agent, ten containers and two packages or parcels, one of which contained the wireless sets for Inayat Khan. The drop was scattered and initially only the containers were collected and there was no sign of the agent or the packages. Antelme described the story as it had been told to him:

The drop had been a very bad one as far as personnel and parcels were concerned. Some members of the Reception Committee thought they had seen one parcel, some two, some none for they were dropped at a very great distance from the ground itself. Prosper thought he saw two in the distance. As they were expecting Jacquot who could not be found, (Guerne) was left in charge of the Committee to carry out re-searches. Meantime, (Norman) had remained at Grignon for a sked early on Tuesday morning. He received a message giving him the number of parcels (RAF records show two) and confirming Jacquot's arrival. He immediately proceeded to the reception ground to make sure that everything was in order. He met (Guerne) and the Committee who had given up the re-searches. They all set out again on re-searches and at 10 am (Guerne) came across Jacquot's stripties and parachute which were lying neatly folded on the ground. Later still he found

Farm at le Roncey where arms were stored. (F. Dury)

Alfred Balachowsky.
(Libre Résistance)

Jacquot's suitcases and at noon
(Norman) found (Inayat Khan's)
two wireless sets. Everything was
removed and hidden at Grignon.
Had it not been for the message
which (Norman) received in
time, such extensive re-searches
would not have been carried out.

My father had also left as soon as the containers were found
as he had an early appointment in Paris.[8] Jacquot was George
Connerade on a reconnaissance mission to prepare an attack
on the canal lock-gates at Lesdain near St Quentin. One of
the reception team reported that someone in the team had
accidentally let off a burst of Sten gun fire, which might
have frightened Jacquot, but when he returned to London
Connerade admitted that he had misunderstood the order and
jumped late so that he landed outside the clearing in a tree.[9]

As that was all the information about Physician operations
available in Air Ministry records, I next went through the
SOE files to see what I could find in the reports of the people
involved. In 1960 the SOE files were not yet available to the
public and were looked after by Colonel Boxshall. When it
was decided that there should be an official history, Boxshall
prepared a document giving many details of the French Section
circuits.[10] This was the document that stated incorrectly that
when my father had been dropped into France in October
1942, it was near Vendôme, a mistake that has been widely
quoted. There were other mistakes so I decided that it would

be wise to accept statements from this document only if they were supported by information from other sources. By the time I found Boxshall's document, the files of SOE agents were at last becoming available but only for those who were known to have died in the war; those whose death since the war could be proved; or if it could be proved that 100 years had passed since an agent was born. But even for those like my father who were known to have died during the war, it was not that easy at first. When the files were transferred to the Public Record Office, now The National Archives, it was decided that as there were thousands of files, they should be filed in alphabetical batches. So my father's papers were in a file that also held the papers of other agents from all over the world and I was told initially that it would only be possible to open my father's papers if I could provide evidence to show that all of the other agents in the file were dead! My father's papers were in a file with the papers of eight other agents, none of them from French Section – an impossible task. Luckily common sense soon prevailed and it was agreed that people could apply for the papers of individual agents to be released and given a unique file reference, but even this process initially took three months.

There were two references to June Physician operations in Boxshall's document. The first was supported by an agent's report[11] in which I found that there had been problems on the Grignon DZ earlier in the month on 13 June when my father was expecting to receive not only ten containers, but a wireless operator to join Juggler so that it would no longer be dependent on the Prosper organisation. This was Gaston Cohen, operational name Watchmaker, and he jumped successfully, landing 'about a yard from the first light', but the bomb door in the aircraft jammed and the ten containers of Physician 60 could not be released. Curiously the Squadron records do not mention this and claim that the whole operation was a success. I discovered a Physician 60 (2nd) recorded on the night of 16/17 June and this time the ten containers were dropped successfully. Some of the material was destined for the communists who came with a lorry from nearby Mantes; the rest was hidden for the group to use in the expected invasion.

The second operation recorded by Boxshall was the dropping of two agents to a reception organised by Culioli on the Cher on the night of 15/16 June. This fitted with an Air Ministry record for that night of operation Archdeacon/Plumber/Physician 55. The agents were two Canadians, Frank Pickersgill and Ken Macalister, a wireless operator, who were to take over and expand the activities already started by my father in the Aisne and Ardennes to be named the Archdeacon circuit. The museum in Romorantin helped me here by sending me a map showing the location of a farm called les Arrachis just across the Cher on the boundary of the communes of Châtillon-sur-Cher and Meusnes, where the drop had taken place in the surrounding fields.

Culioli noticed that their papers were out of date. There had just been a change requiring photos to be attached to ID cards with rivets rather than staples. While Culioli went to Paris to organise the new cards for them, Pickersgill and Macalister were lodged with Jean Charmaison who owned a large estate conveniently situated halfway between Châtillon and Romorantin. After three days they were moved to the cottage where Culioli and Rudellat were based, la Cercle near Veillens. Here they found Raynaud, whom Culioli had installed there while he went again to Paris to organise new papers for him and to collect those for Pickersgill and Macalister.

In a report by one of the agents already working in the Aisne, Pierre Geelen, I found a reference to a drop at his Hirson

Gaston Cohen. (SFC)

DZ on 14 June at which a wireless for Macalister had been 'smashed to pieces owing to the parachute failing to open'.[12] I later accounted for the location of five of the six Physician operations flown on 13/14 and 14/15 June leaving Physician 56, which must therefore have been the drop of ten containers and two packages at Origny-en-Thiérache. Three of the team involved at Muno in the Ardennes left testimonies that they had received one of the last two successful Physician operations on 21/22 June – Physician 58 with five containers.[13]

Having exhausted the information available from files in The National Archives, I turned to French sources. The French are only just beginning to open their wartime files but for the southern groups, quite a lot of information was available in four books written by a local abbé, Paul Guillaume, between 1946 and 1950. He had been a friend of the abbé Pasty of Baule who had belonged to the Lequeux group. He mentions nine other operations in this area in June, four of them to DZs that had not been used before and five to DZs already used. I found references to two more drops to another new DZ near Montrichard in a book by Jack Vivier and some documents sent to me by the archives department in Blois suggested another two new DZs and another operation to one that had been used in earlier months. Roger Couffrant, the leader in Romorantin, had also assembled some information about the location of parachute drops and the names of those involved. The information varied in quality so I made two trips to the area in 2007 and 2008. One of my visits was to the Resistance Museum in Blois where there is a long list of parachute operations but less evidence to support the dates than I already possessed and the Monkeypuzzle operations had been mixed up with those of Physician. I had hoped that there would be more information there but I was told that no one was interested anymore! My subsequent route was not orderly so I will start at the most westerly of the DZs.

I knew that there was a group at Montrichard started by Marcel Buhler and led by Georges Fermé. Jack Vivier mentioned two successful drops to this group, one on 20/21 of June and the other at the end of May with the BBC messages *'Le marc se vend au poids'* (The brandy is sold by weight) for the earlier drop and *'Venez quand méme, en s'arrangera'* (Come anyway, we'll sort things out) for the latter.[14] There could not have been a drop here in May as the records for this month were complete so the second drop would also have to have been in June. I was able to contact Jack Vivier and he sent me a map showing the location of the DZ, a field on the edge of a wood called la Prénauterie to the north-west of Montrichard on the road to Amboise. The dates remained a problem so I wrote to the *maire* twice

Frank Pickersgill. (SFC)

Ken Macalister. (SFC)

saying I would be visiting and asking him to put me in touch with anyone who might be able to help. Although I received no reply, I called in at the *mairie* and mentioned my letters. I was told bluntly that if the *maire* had not replied, then he was certainly not interested in meeting me. I was somewhat shocked and saddened at this response to those trying to record the stories of the people who had fought to liberate them. Luckily I had spotted that a Mme Fermé was listed in the telephone directory. She turned out to be the daughter of Georges Fermé and was not only able to confirm that there had been two drops there but she also knew the dates – 16/17 and 20/21 June. She was sure of this because in each case the aircraft had also made drops to the Mistral circuit set up by the SOE wireless operator, André Dubois, with which her father had also been involved. The Air Ministry records showed that Mistral 1 on 16/17 June was flown with Physician 72, which dropped ten containers. Mistral 2 on 20/21 June was flown with two Physician operations, Physician 73 of ten containers and Physician 79 of five. The material was hidden in a cave behind the house that Fermé used to store goods for his grocery business. One side chamber had a large hole high in the wall leading to another space. After the arms had been stored there, the hole was bricked up, plastered and painted to look like stone. The Germans found out that there was a store there and tapped round all of the walls but the new piece was just out of their reach.

My reception at the *mairie* in Noyers-sur-Cher, the next DZ up the river, was the complete opposite of that at Montrichard; the staff competed to give me the names and addresses of people who might be able to help. I only had time to visit one of them, Geova Denis, who had helped his father with the containers but unfortunately he could not remember the date of the June operation. Guillaume had given the BBC message for the June drop here as *'Il reviendra à la Trinité'* (He will return on Trinity Sunday) and the location of the DZ as the bois de Juchepie. I did find evidence in a report by Culioli that this group had received twenty containers, which confirms that there was a second drop here in June.[15] When I visited this area with the local historian and Christian Jourdain, whose father had been in the group, Christian showed us a photograph of his father standing on the edge of a field not far from the DZ where he had acted as the look-out.

The next DZ along the river was at Châtillon-sur-Cher where Pickersgill and Macalister had dropped. As I was passing, I went to the farm buildings known as les Arrachis and was lucky to find the farmer there. He confirmed the drop of two agents and told me that the fields had been used before the war for flying displays. The BBC message was *'Les dieux*

Georges Fermé. (Fermé family)

Monique Fermé showing author where the arms were hidden. (Author)

s'installent au balcon' (The Gods are settling down on the balcony).[16]

I had success again at Maray where the *maire*, Antoine Heurteau, took me to a farm called Doulcay. In the papers from the Blois archives[17] I had seen a reference to a letter from one of his predecessors who in 1968 had confirmed that there had been a drop of containers here on 10/11 June. We met the wife of Henri Trochet who had farmed there in 1943. She told me that the terrain had not been found by the Germans when the circuit collapsed and was later used by another SOE agent, Pearl Cornioley, who also stayed at the farm. The reason the family had survived the collapse of my father's circuit was that the Germans came looking for the 'Trochou' family and, when they stopped and asked the local milkman for directions, he told them that there was no such family in this area. The material was hidden in a well.

There was another successful drop, as far as the pilot was concerned, on the night of 10/11 June to the previously used DZ near Neuvy. Guillaume and others give the date of 13 June for the drop here but Dr Segelle, the nephew of one of the reception team, is quite clear, '*Le jeudi avant la Pentecôte, le 10 juin 1943, vers une heure du matin ...*' (The Thursday before Pentecost, the 10th June, towards 1 a.m. in the morning ...)[18] Culioli had invited the people recruited by Gilbert Norman – the de Bernards, Maurice Buhler and Georges Fermé from Montrichard – so that they could organise receptions on their DZs. The BBC message was '*Le chien eternu dans les drapes*' (The dog sneezed on the curtains) but it was not to be a good demonstration as two of the descending containers, like the dog in the message, misbehaved and exploded. Guillaume describes what happened:

Several seconds after the containers had landed a blinding glare came up from the ground, as if a phosphorus bomb had been substituted for a container, and it was followed

The farm Doulcay showing the well where the arms were hidden. (Author)

by a deafening bang. Thrity seconds later a second, even more violent, bang shook the air again, mildly injuring Mme Caillard and Deck. Albert Le Meur immediately gave the order to evacuate the terrain and everyone returned to their homes, thinking that the German base at Fontaine-en-Sologne, which was three kilometres away as the crow flies, had been alerted by the explosions. The next day, the neighbouring farmer, M. Massicart, having discovered in the field the exploded containers, and three others which he took for bombs, alerted the Bracieux police, who were required to inform the German police. The *Feldgendarmerie* arrived and had the pyrotechnists blow up the munitions, but they did not find all of the containers. In fact, two days after the explosion, M. Canard who lived close by, noticed that a large part of the parachute drop had landed in a copse. With the help of M. Cortambert, whom he had notified, he transported, to a few hundred metres away, twelve or thirteen rescued containers, which, moreover, had already been searched by curious passers-by.[19]

A local resistance chief from another organisation decided that M. Massicart should be executed for reporting the incident to the police but Dr Segelle persuaded him that this would be unjust as the police would have found where the incident had taken place even if M. Massicart had not told them and, indeed, he might have got into trouble himself for not reporting it as his house was the nearest, being only 240m away.[20]

In a different book, Guillaume had mentioned another operation near Mennetou on the Cher on 20/21 June and I thought this might also have been at Doulcay.[21] Mme Trochet remembered that there had been more than one but was not sure whether the others were organised by my father's people or those of Pearl Cornioley. I later found a deposition by André Trochet, her son, who was quite clear that there was only one operation in 1943 with the message '*LEBLANC va au marche noir*' (Leblanc goes to the black market).[22] Other documents suggested that this operation on 20/21 June was either at a place called le Coteau just to the north of Mennetou or at Préjeux in the neighbouring commune of Langon. By chance I found someone who claimed to have known about the involvement of one of the team, Prosper Legourd, and he was able to give me the exact location, a farm called Le Pereux in the commune of Langon, just to the north-west of the château de Préjeux.[23] The material was taken to a depot held by Legourd in a transformer station in the hamlet of Tourpinay in the commune of Selles-sur-Cher.

Another of the four operations on the night of 20/21 June was said to have been at Villeny. When I contacted the *maire*, M. Alain Blanche, he invited me to meet several people who had been teenagers during the war but had been told about the events of the night of 20 June 1943. They took me deep into a forest where we could hear wild boar all around us and finally came to the ruins of a farm surrounded by a few small fields. The farm was called le Bout du Monde, some 3km north-west of the village. The reception team was from Romorantin, led by Roger Couffrant, but included a local team led by the schoolmaster, Georges Marlot, who had helped at a reception near Chaumont-sur-Tharonne in May so as to be prepared for one on their own ground. The material was taken in a cart to another abandoned farm and, whilst the local team returned to their homes, the Romorantin team stayed until the morning when a lorry was due to take them and the arms to Culioli's HQ at le Cercle, a journey that they would never complete. A reporter from a local newspaper also joined the meeting and his report was published a few days later.[24]

I did not have time to visit the DZs around Courmemin labelled 1, 2 and 3 by Couffrant. Indeed at that time I had only managed to work out the location of the one where some containers had fallen in a lake in May, known as Courmemin 1, although I had the pinpoint of another, which was further to the south-west of Courmemin and where an unsuccessful attempt had also been made in May, known as Courmemin 2. One of the drops on 20/21 June was recorded as being to the DZ where containers had earlier fallen into a lake, so this meant it had to be Courmemin 1. There were problems again as one of the team, Georges Duchet, describes:

> At 5h30 all the containers were hidden in the wood; but several, carried by the wind, had fallen into a vineyard which had suffered as a result; and as an informer often passed this way, it was necessary to remove the evidence as soon as possible

Duchet went to see the owner of the vineyard, whom he was happy to find was a good Frenchman, and asked him, 'Did you hear planes last night?' 'No, I didn't hear anything' 'In your vineyard there are tracks to be removed. I hope that no one sees you putting it in order.' As the owner still did not want to admit to having heard anything, Duchet took him into the neighbouring wood and showed him the hidden containers and said to him '*Ce ne sont pas les Galeries Lafayette qui ont fait cette livraison!*' (This is not a delivery from the Galleries Lafayette). The owner now agreed to make the necessary repairs and Duchet slipped him a 1,000 franc note.[25]

According to Roger Couffrant, the Courmemin 3 DZ had been used, not by his Romorantin groups, but by the

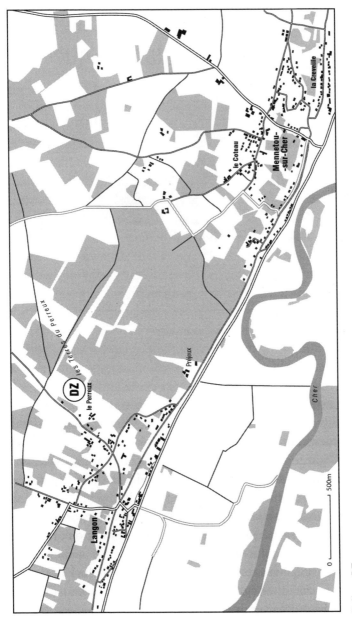

Préjeux DZ.

Un Anglais sur les traces de son père pendant la guerre

Francis Suttill est un touriste britannique peu commun. Durant ses congés d'été, il s'est fixé pour objectif de retrouver en Sologne des zones de largage d'armements et de munitions pour la résistance locale pendant l'été 1943, sur les pas de son père.

Francis Suttill Junior découvre la zone de largage, ici accompagné de Mme Brossard, arrière-cousine du capitaine Marlot.

Francis Suttill a 67 ans et réside en Grande-Bretagne. Son père, qui se nommait également Francis Suttill était commandant durant la Seconde Guerre mondiale et appartenait au SOE (Service opérations exécutive), basé en Grande-Bretagne. Son rôle était de localiser des zones de largage d'armements et munitions pour la résistance en région Centre, ainsi que de préparer et former le personnel au sol chargé de la réception des parachutages.

La commune de Villeny fut l'un des sites choisis pour ce genre de mission. C'est pour cette raison que le fils Suttill a envoyé à Alain Blanche, maire de Villeny, un mail pour l'informer de sa venue afin de recueillir des témoignages.

Alain Blanche s'est donc fait un devoir d'accueillir comme il se doit Francis Suttill. Pour ce faire, des anciens Niovilliens furent conviés afin qu'ils apportent des témoignages.

En 43, ces anciens étaient des enfants, mais ils se souviennent de leurs aînés chargés de cette opération, aînés qui aujourd'hui ont tous disparu. Parmi eux se trouvaient Louis Duchesne, instituteur qui devint maire de la commune et dont tout le monde se souvient, tout comme le capitaine Georges Marlot, également instituteur, et que personne n'a oublié. Même le curé du village fut de la partie.

Les anciens se sont donc replongés dans le passé, au grand bonheur de Francis. Il a ainsi appris que les armes et les munitions furent transportées dans un tombereau dont les roues étaient entourées de sacs afin de réduire le bruit du roulement. « J'utilisais les parachutes pour en faire des chemisiers », se souvient encore Mme Brossard parmi de multiples anecdotes.

A la découverte de la zone de largage

Les anciens ont ensuite amené Francis sur la zone de largage aujourd'hui joliment nommée « le Bout du monde »...

Après avoir laissé les voitures dans une allée de forêt, puis une bonne demi-heure de marche, guidés par les anciens dans un labyrinthe d'allées la zone s'est enfin dévoilée devant Francis.

Terrain vague en 1943, c'est aujourd'hui un terrain de buissons épineux, devenu le paradis des sangliers. Le lieu, difficile d'accès permettait d'accomplir dans un contexte de guerre ce type de mission.

Ému et peu disert, Francis Suttill Junior n'a eu cesse de remercier la commune et tous ces gens qui l'ont si bien reçu. Francis s'en est allé pour découvrir dans la région d'autres sites, avec le désir de mettre un jour sur papier ses pèlerinages.

Correspondant NR, Daniel Duretz, tél. 06.14.25.24.40.

Article about my visit to Villeny, 21 September 2007.

Chambord group. This linked to a statement in one of Guillaume's books that, after the incident of the exploding containers, Lemeur and Cortambert looked for another DZ and found one on the road to Romorantin owned by Amand Goleau, who willingly placed it at their disposal. A team of five men was recruited locally, led by Maxime Bigot, a blacksmith, and they received ten containers on 18 June. There was no precise information as to the location of the DZ and the *mairie* were not helpful but I found the name Claude Goleau in a local telephone directory. I was in luck as he was related and although he could not remember where the land was, he did remember that it was called Chassenais.

Again the museum in Romorantin came to my rescue, sending me a map showing a property called Chassenais on the road between Courmemin and Romorantin and just north of the village of Veillens. The other side of Veillens was the cottage in the woods, le Cercle, where Culioli and Rudellat had their HQ and Couffrant had referred to a possible drop there. The material from Chassenais was taken to le Cercle so this must all have been one operation and, as there was only one other successful drop on 18 June, this must have been Physician 43, which had been tried without success on 16/17 June, after an earlier attempt on 14/15 June had been cancelled even before take-off when the 'rear turret' was found to be useless.

When I met Jacques Bordier whilst looking for the DZ at Langlochère, he told me that there had been two parachutages there in June and that one was on a Sunday because he was still in his Sunday clothes when the BBC message was heard, whilst the other was very soon afterwards. This ruled out Sunday 20 June as there were no further operations in this area after that date, so the drop at Langlochère must have been on the night of 13/14 June and was therefore Physician 44 dropping ten containers and a package, as this was the only successful Physician operation that night. The next night, eight

Jean Deck with signalling lamp he invented. (Blois musée)

Physician operations were due to be flown but one aircraft, due to carry Physician 41 and 43, was found at the last minute to have a useless rear gun turret and so could not fly. A decision was then made to drop Physician 46, being carried in another aircraft, to the DZ for Physician 41. This ties in with Jacques Bordier's memory that he had heard that the second June drop was originally destined for another group. As it was considered very risky to have a second drop so soon after the first, they set out the lights nearer the farm so that the material could be retrieved and hidden more quickly than bringing it from the official DZ, which was over 2km away by road. André Raimbault buried some of the material from these drops under a vat in his cellar. The rest was taken to the presbytery where the abbé Pasty sorted it into sacks, each containing the equipment that might be needed by one man – Sten gun with magazines, grenades and explosives. In this way he hoped that some fifty men could be armed quickly when the time came.[26]

Although he did not mention any drops near Montargis, to the east of Orléans, Colonel Boxshall did identify a group there organised by Jean Baudin. I happened to mention this to the son of Colonel Buckmaster and he offered to try and find a contact as his father had lived at Crowhurst, which had been twinned with Montargis. This did produce a contact so I made a visit and met Christiane Carmignac. She had married Luce Carmignac whose father Lucien had been the leader of a reception team at Chuelles, a village some 20km to the east of Montargis. She referred me to a book by Paul Guillaume[27] that I was not aware of at that time and had a very similar title to another of his books. This described a group that had been started in Montargis under the leadership of Jean Vessière, a garage owner. Guillaume was not very complimentary about Vessière: 'Very active, dynamic even, a bit boastful and unfortunately too much of a chatterbox', although he gives no evidence to support these allegations. He recruited several mechanics in Montargis and Lucien Carmignac in Chuelles. Three tonnes of arms and ammunition were dropped between two woods to the south of the village on 16 June following the BBC message '*L'ersatz est superflu*' (The ersatz coffee is unnecessary). This could be either Physician 64 on 15/16 June or Physician 46 on 16/17 June, both of which dropped the amount remembered.

Some of the material was hidden by another farmer on the other side of the village, Kleber Gauthier; some was stored by the Carmignacs who lived in the middle of the village; and the rest was taken by Albert Guellemin, another garage owner from the village of Chantecoq, 5km north of Chuelles. Guillaume said that this organisation was part of Prosper but he did not say anything about how it was linked. The only other mention of this group was in a letter written by Lequeux in which he said that Vessière had been due to meet my father in Paris on 28 June but had failed to do so as my father had been arrested four days earlier. Christiane Carmignac had heard of a Jean Baudin who had been in the resistance locally but she did not think that he had anything to do with Prosper. I later found records[28] of some sixty people claiming to have belonged to the Prosper circuit but, even after a closer examination of their claims had reduced this by a

Jean Vessière. (Guillaume)

third, it was clear that my father had a significant organisation in this area, which seems to have left very little trace. Amongst these forty people, there were about sixteen who claimed to have taken part in parachute receptions and three claimed to have had lodged agents: the Carmignac family in Chuelles; another in Montargis; and the third in Châlette-sur-Loing, just to the north of Montargis. I hope to be able to find more information on this elusive group. I also noticed that the leader of the group had the same address as that given for Jean Baudin and it occurred to me that Baudin was probably a pseudonym used by Vessière. I also noted that in an obscure part of Montargis there had once been a Chemin Prosper but the sign has disappeared!

Despite the drop near Falaise in Normandy in May being a success, my father decided that it was too dangerous to have further drops there as there were too many Germans. The problem was that this area behind the Normandy coast was one of the areas where arms were most needed to support an invasion. His solution was to order more drops further south where it was safer and to buy a lorry for Cauchy to transport

the material from these drops to Falaise. The DZ at the château de l'Hermitière had already been used in May and another was found in the commune of Ancinnes, just outside the town of Alençon in the Sarthe. Here Simon was put in touch with Arthur de Montalembert whose

Arthur de Montalembert

family owned a farm called Vaubezon. A descendant of the de Courson family, Richard, had told me that he had been told by his father that June drops to these two DZs had been flown on the same night, possibly 10 June. The family remembered the BBC message as '*L'amateur des roses et de porcelaine*' (A lover of roses and china), which is not in the BBC list. As the material was to be taken to Falaise it was simply hidden under branches. Simon therefore went to Ancinnes to organise the first drop there whilst Garry went to l'Hermitière.

Unfortunately Simon did not give any indication of the location of the DZ nor the date of the drops. I then discovered from a colleague that the parachute operations in the Sarthe had been researched in the 1960s by a schoolmaster, André Pioger, and that his papers were now in the archives in Le Mans. The archivists were very helpful and told me that Pioger had recorded a drop at Ancinnes on 14 June at a place known as Valitourne. He had also recorded the May drop in the bois de Gemmages at l'Hermitière (although with an incorrect date) and another there in June at an unspecified date with the BBC message '*Mieux vaut voler que de nager*' (It is better to fly than to swim), which was number 27 in the BBC's June list.[29] As this was likely to have been a double operation, the only date on which there had been such a Physician operation that was not already accounted for was 14/15 June.

On one of my visits to France I thought I had better stop at Ancinnes to see what I could find out locally. I was in luck. I found a chambre d'hôte in the village called La Basse Cour run by an English couple, Phil and Jude Graham. Phil was so interested in my story that he asked around in the village and found Bernard Ruel, who knew where the DZ was as his family had farmed the land and also knew roughly where the arms were stored. He also contacted a local historian, Jacques

Paganet, who knew that the drop had taken place at 11 p.m. on 14 June following the BBC message '*Elle est bleu aux fleurs rouge*' (It is blue with red flowers) which is number 67 in the BBC's June list. As well as Simon and de Montalembert, the team comprised three local men – André Malo, a gendarme; Paul Lottin, a garage owner; and Paul Drecq, a postman. Jean Celier came over from l'Eporce to help.

Bernard Ruel showed us the field where the ten containers had dropped before being temporarily hidden in a large ditch adjoining the land known as Valitourne. From here they were taken over the next few nights in a 'vachère' some 4km east and hidden in a cave known as la Garenne in a wood. (According to my dictionary 'vachère' meant a milkmaid and I had a mental picture of a strapping country girl striding along with a yoke on her shoulders from which were suspended buckets full of grenades and pistols! I was disillusioned to be told that at that time 'vachère' was also the name given to a type of horse-drawn cart for taking cattle to market.) The fact that ten containers were dropped here indicates that this was Physician 61 and the drop at l'Hermitière must therefore have been Physician 45.

As we stood by the side of the land known as Valitourne we could see a grass track leading to the top of the escarpment at the eastern end of which was the bois de Vaubezon. We followed this much to the surprise of Phil who, thinking we were simply going for a drive, was still in his slippers, and when we reached the wood, we spread out along the slope. It was Bernard who found the remains of the cave near the top of the wood. Jacques Paganet told us that it might have been one of the tunnels reputedly dug during the One Hundred Years' War to enable the French to pass under the English lines.

In Darling's area around Trie-Château, none of those who survived had left a record so the only known June operation

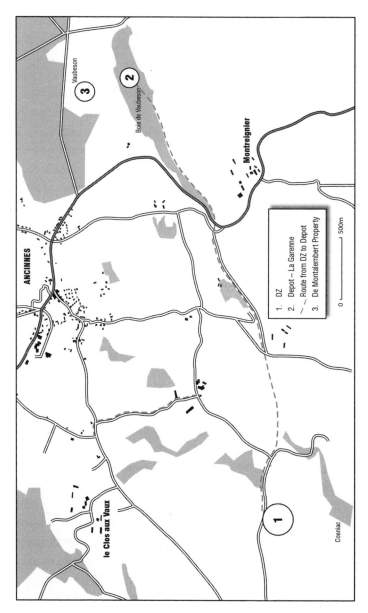

Ancinnes DZ.

The de Montalembert property, Vaubezon, showing the tower where it was planned to install a radio for Noor Inayat Khan. (J. Paganet)

The old tunnel where the arms were stored at Ancinnes. (P. Graham)

was Physician 32, which, as was noted earlier, was not successful. I did find one article written in 1990 but the author had not been able to discover how the local organisation had started or developed and gave only vague information about the number, dates and locations of parachute operations.[30] I contacted the society thinking that they might know someone who could help me, but they were not interested.

I was put in touch with a local historian in the Oise, Jean-Pierre Besse, who told me that 'according to SOE archives' there had been a drop of ten containers to a DZ in the Oise on the night of 14/15 June but he was not willing to give me a reference to his source for this information. He also told me that he had heard about a drop near the village of Haillancourt but he did not know the date or location. I wrote to the *mairie* and received a reply from a retired army officer, Gaston Lievens. He invited me to visit him and at a hospitable welcome in the *mairie*, I was introduced to Mme Marie-Louise Hebert whose father-in-law, Gaston, had owned the land where the containers had been dropped '*peu après la Pentecôte*'. One of the group, Marcel Ponléve, had written down all the details of the history and fate of the group, making it clear that they depended on Georges Darling of Trie-Château. I was given a copy and found that there were more conflicting memories of a BBC message. Mme Hebert remembered '*La dent du Midi sera plombée ce soir*' (The dent du Midi will have a filling tonight) which is probably message 29 in the BBC list for June '*On plombe la dent du midi*' (The dent du Midi will get a filling). Ponléve recorded '*La gare du Nord est encombrée*' (The Gare du Nord is crowded), which may be a false memory of message 35, '*Congestion à la gare de Lyon*'(Congestion at the Gare de Lyon).

The leader was René Davesne who was the director of the local electricity company and he recruited his foreman, Gabriel

René Davesne. (Libre
Résistance)

Lhomme; Victor Lucas who
worked in the *mairie* of the nearby
town of Meru; and Marcel Ponléve
who was a butcher in Meru. The
DZ along the northern edge of
the bois du Crochet had been
approved by an English officer
but no one knew who he was as
he kept his identity secret. The
team comprised fifteen men, one
for each container, three for the lights and two as look-outs.
Marcel Ponléve's memoir describes what happened.[31]

By 10.30 a.m. all of the men had arrived either with Marcel
Ponléve in his van or on foot. The aircraft appeared. It
circled the field, no signal was given, everyone knew
what to do. When the aircraft flew over the second time,
two white lights and a red indicated the drop point. The
third fly-over was the confirmation. On the fourth the ten
containers began their slow descent to the ground. The
total amount of 1,500 kilos was immediately hidden in a
heap of manure a few meters away in the farm of Gaston
Hebert. In the days that followed, André Carrier, the
youngest of the team at 16 years old, transported all the
grenades, Colts and machine guns to Meru hidden under
straw in a horse drawn cart.

He made several journeys, placing the arms in a granary,
which meant that he had to carry everything up a ladder in

plain view. As the feast of Pentecost fell on 13 June, I thought that this might be the operation which Besse mentioned had taken place on 14/15 June 'according to SOE archives'. However, there were only two possible operations to groups in the north after that Sunday, on 16/17 or 20/21 and the former fits with the description of just after Pentecost.

Sylviane Maurouard, the daughter of the leader of the group at Neaufles-Saint-Martin, told me that she remembered an operation in June with the message: '*Pierrette regarde la feuille à l'envers*' (Pierrette looks at the sheet of paper the other way around) , which is number 59 in the BBC list of May messages. Physician 26 was attempted twice in May and once on 11/12 June but without success and was not attempted again. The reception committee must therefore have heard the message three times, which would make it memorable but not guarantee its success.

I also visited the village at the other end of Darling's area, Bois-Jérôme-Saint-Ouen, where I had earlier found drops in April in May. This was not far from the town of Évreux where Boxshall stated that there was a group under Marcel Gouju. I had not found any record of drops to this group but wondered if they were linked to Bois-Jérôme-Saint-Ouen. I wrote to the *maire* a couple of times without response but I had noticed in the local telephone directory that there were several people called Perret living in the village who might be related to

Marcel Gouju. (Libre Résistance)

the leader of the reception team, Lucien Perret. I tried first the house of Alfred Perret as a man with this name had been part of the team but there was no answer. There was also no answer from the next house that I tried but at the third I found a great-grandson of Lucien. He laughed when I told of my house calls as the first house was indeed that of Alfred but said that there was no point in knocking as he was very deaf! He was just about to visit his grandfather so he took me along and also gave me a copy of an interview his daughter had recorded with Alfred. There were two things I wanted to know – was there a link with Marcel Gouju and had there been drops to his group in June? To my surprise he said that there had been seven drops in total, which I knew was not possible. He remembered a message '*Ils sont toujours vert*' (They are always green), which was number 24 in the June list of BBC messages, but not the June date. In another book I found a record of a second June message associated with this group – '*Halte la qu'on vous rattrappe*' (Stop where you are so we can catch up) – which is number 42 in the BBC list for June.

As regards the role of Marcel Gouju, Perret said that the team only took orders from Georges Darling but that in June they had been asked to receive drops of material that could be transported westwards by Marcel Gouju where the number of Germans made it unsafe to have parachute operations, as was the case at Falaise at the other end of Normandy. The material was collected in a lorry provided by the director of a distillery in Évreux and taken to the village of Le Plessis-Grohan where it was hidden by the *maire*, Oscar Legras, and a retired railway worker, M. Callery. I found the home of his daughter but she was away and I never received replies to subsequent letters. I did find a report that my father had visited the depot here on 17 June, so the drop for Gouju must have been earlier in the month than this date and the only operation likely to have been to a northern group was Physician 42 on 12/13 June, which was flown in the same aircraft that dropped Cohen to the Grignon group. One of Gouju's group, Robert Lainey, recorded that he had been trained by my father to use the explosives for rail sabotage and had lodged my father, Norman, Agazarian and Borrel at his home in Évreux.[32]

I thought the archives department in Évreux might be able to help and made an appointment with the secrétaire-assistante to the Director. When I arrived a few days later, I was surprised to find that she had no idea who I was or what I wanted, despite my being quite specific about this when arranging our meeting. I was made to wait for over two hours before any documents were produced, only to find that they were the ones I already knew about and had said I did not wish to see. This fiasco continued for another hour and, although my hopes were raised at one stage by the appearance of someone I was told was their Second World War expert, when I spoke to him, he simply walked away. I left the archives in disgust as it was clear that they knew very little about Gouju and did not appear, to me, to care.

I thought for a time that this was as far as I was going to get in finding information on the June drops to Darling's groups but then a colleague found some documents in the Beauvais archives, which suggested that in the Oise part of the area there had been two more drops to the La Landelle DZ and one at Trie-Château. Curiously there was no mention of the drop at Haillancourt. There had certainly been one unsuccessful operation in this area – Physician 32 on 11/12 June – and another aircraft that night failed to deliver containers to one of the previously used DZs near Trie-Château (Physician 16) as well as that at Neaufles-Saint-Martin (Physician 26) because of bad weather, but neither of these was attempted again. However, another of the documents recorded a June drop at Trie-Château taking place at a DZ north of the town. Then another colleague, quite by chance, was introduced to Gilbert Harny. He and his uncle, Kleber, had been recruited by Darling and he remembered three drops around Trie-Château at monthly intervals, of which the first and third had been successful, and the message for the third had been *'Le cabestan se déroulera ce soir'* (The capstan will unwind tonight), which is not in the BBC list. The DZ was between two woods to the north of the town and the material was taken to the bois d'Etoile in a cart drawn by the mare Javotte, which Darling had bought for this purpose. Gilbert Harny particularly remembered that Pierre Perret had made sackcloth boots to muffle the sound of Javotte's hooves when crossing the main road in the town. Another of the Trie-Château group, Marcel Hitou, mentions a drop there on 15/16 June. Every other date he mentions is incorrect so his accuracy must be doubted, but this does add to the evidence for a June drop here.

A final find was a box of membership cards of people from the Buckmaster circuits who had joined an *amicale* called Libre Résistance after the war. Two of the members were Henri Thibout and his son André from Martagny who had been part of the reception team for the drops in the Neuf Marché area. They both remembered a second drop in June to a DZ they knew as 'J' but not the date and in another document I found the BBC message *'La garde* à *vous est impeccable'* (The line-up is faultless) attributed to a drop here, which is in the list of BBC messages for June.

So near to finding all the answers but still some way to go! I have put detailed information about the relevant operations up to the end of May in Appendix 2 together with the information that I have gathered on the operations in June.

Pierre Perret and Kleber Harny with the mare Javotte and the cart used to transport the arms. (G. Harny)

Of the twenty-six successful operations in June, I have found the location of sixteen. Of the remaining ten, I have found the dates and locations of five that I have not been able to match to operation numbers – Haillancourt, Langon, Villeny, Montrichard and Courmemin 1. Three others are likely to have been flown to southern groups, as they were flown with other operations known to have been to that area, and similarly one would have been to a northern group. There is no evidence for the location of the last one.

In the southern area, there were definitely drops in June to the Saint Aignan group and to the group at Montargis and a possible drop on 14/15 June to the Courmemin 2 DZ is mentioned, without evidence, in the papers in the Blois archives. In the northern area, there are strong claims for drops at Trie-Château and Jouay-la-Grange whilst the claim for a June drop to the Neuf-Marché group may have been flown but not succeeded.

In the related circuits in June, Jean Worms had received three drops: Juggler 2 to the previously used DZ near Thibié on 11/12 June; Juggler 4 to a new DZ called les Hauts Champs slightly further from Thibié on 17/18 June; and Juggler 3 to another new DZ to south-west of Vitry-le-François. Wilkinson organised the first drop to the Nantes group, Privet 2 on 17/18 June, but he was not there to receive it himself as he fell into a trap and was arrested on 6 June. Cowburn organised a second drop to the group he had taken over from my father, Tinker 2, on 17/18 June, at a DZ very near that arranged for Physician 23 in April. Beiler did not manage his first drop until July. Bouguennec and Fox, now with a replacement radio for Rousset, organised their first drops: Butler 1 on 13/14 and Publican 1 on 21/22 June.

Déricourt had a third June pick-up at the end of the moon period. This was meant to have taken place on 20/21 June but the aircraft found no reception and Déricourt only collected the two passengers for London on 21 June. The reason for Déricourt's absence is still not explained. He took them to Amboise the same day but the Lysander did not arrive until the night of 23/24 June, having suffered a generator failure the previous night. The two passengers leaving France were a downed RAF officer, Taylor, and Richard Heslop, leaving Privet who was felt to be compromised by the arrest of Wilkinson.

Notes

1. Interrogation 05.07.1943, HS 9/11/1, TNA.
2. AIR 27/1068, TNA.
3. HS 8/225, TNA.
4. 17 P 3 and 17 P 41, SHD.
5. General Report 23.06.1943, HS 9/11/1, TNA.
6. HS 9/836/5, TNA. Foot, commenting on the arrival of Inayat Khan, says – 'Madeleine was to have gone to France a month earlier; she had had the discomfort and anxiety of a flight from Tangmere to Compiègne and back in May – no reception had been ready for her.' There had

been an unsuccessful operation called Madeleine on 21/22 May. There is confusion here between Field names and Operational names. Inayat Khan's Field name was indeed Madeleine but her Operational name was Nurse and this would have been the name used by the RAF. Operational names that were girls' names such as Madeleine referred to SIS groups and this operation was intended to drop four packages to such a group. Just to be absolutely sure, I checked Inayat Khan's training records and she was on a training exercise from 19 to 23 May.

7. Compte Rendu undated, HS 6/578, TNA.
8. HS 1235/6, TNA.
9. Supplementary Report, 09.08.1943, HS 9/42, TNA.
10. Interrogation 08.10.1943, HS 6/350, TNA.
11. E.G. Boxshall, Chronicle of SOE Operations with the Resistance in France during WWII, 1960. ImperialWarMuseum.
12. Interrogation 11.10.1943, HS 6/568, TNA.
13. Interrogation 13.10.1943, HS 9/570/6, TNA.
14. G. Lefèvre, SHD; Arthur Dacremont in A Dubru, Pages d'histoire de la résistance dans la region de Florenville, Arlon, 1987; Gaston Biazot in papers held by his daughter, Annette.
15. J. Vivier, Montrichard, Ville occupée, cite liberée 1939-1945, Editions CLD, Chambray-les-Tours, 1984.
16. Rapport 28.04.1945, HS 9/379/8, TNA.
17. 55 J 3, Archives départementales, Blois.
18. 56 3 44, Archives départementales, Blois.
19. La Republique du Centre, 13/14 September 1947.
20. P. Guillaume, La Solonge au Temps de l'Héröisme et de la Trahaison.
21. Some authors have claimed that containers exploding here was so unique that it must have been deliberate sabotage by the British. It was not unique and several other similar incidents are recorded in the files. Report fortnight ending 05.07.1943, HS 7/135, TNA.
22. P. Guillaume, Au Temps de l'Héröisme et de la Trahaison.
23. 72 AJ 39/II, Archives Nationales.
24. E-mail from Roger Taillibert.
25. La Nouvelle Republique, 21 September 2007.
26. 1 J 104/2, Archives départmentales, Blois.
27. P. Guillaume, L'Abbé Pasty: Prêtre et Soldat.
28. P .Guillaume, Au Temps de l'Héröisme et de la Trahaison.
29. 17 P 41, SHD.
30. 9 J 36, Archives départementale, Le Mans.
31. Memoir of Marcel Ponléve given to author.
32. C. Menard, Les Cahier de la Société Historique et Geographique de la Basin de l'Epte, No 25, 1990.
33. 16P 331651, SHD.

DISASTER

One of the first things that my father did on his return from London on 21 May was to visit Trotobas in Lille to pass on instructions. These confirmed that everyone was still anticipating an imminent invasion as the instructions are remembered as 'Attack in June, July, August, as quickly as possible in view of the events which can take place at any moment'.[1] Norman and Agazarian also went to Lille with him so they must have discussed Trotobas' continued reliance on Physician radios, as he was still waiting for a wireless operator of his own.

The material dropped to Darling's groups was not only being taken west into Normandy by Gouju but was also being distributed to other groups. Despite the setback in February when the arrest of one of the communists from Paris led the police to the operation intended for Sérifontaine, it was decided to try again in June. On 1 June a lorry full of 1,500 boxes of jam was stolen from the Petitjean works in rue Séguin in Paris and driven to Mériel in the L'Isle Adam, lower down the Seine. A few days later two members of a Paris communist group, Georges Bauce and Auguste Eude, were ordered to go there for an evening rendezvous with two other men and they were all to travel to the bois d'Etoile south of Trie-Château. Here they were joined by a local man who put his bicycle into the lorry and guided them to a farmhouse (Champ Mauger at Sérifontaine) some kilometres away, where he left them. Next two men from the farm guided them to the edge of a nearby forest (forêt de Thelle) where they waited for some time while the two locals went to find the forest guard (Aubry). It was an hour before they were allowed to enter the forest and drive to a wooden shed in the middle of the forest, arriving around 3 a.m. The locals left on their bicycles and the four men loaded all of the material from the shed into the lorry, some 800 kilos. Where the material was still in containers, they took those as well but the material in sacks was taken out and the sacks were left in the shed. The lorry was then driven by a different and shorter route back towards Paris. Bauce and Eude were dropped off at a station and the lorry returned to Mériel and hidden in a disused underground mushroom farm.[2]

It appears that my father had instituted a system of 'promissory notes' that he could give to appropriate groups which, when presented, would enable that group to take arms away. A report following the arrest of another local leader in Falaise, Calvados, describes my father telling him 'If a man with a certificate signed by me shows up, don't be surprised.'[3] Not only were arms being brought to Falaise from the DZs in the Sarthe and Orne but this meant that there were plans to move them even further into Normandy, although I have found no mention of where they might have been taken.

As well as organising the movement of parachuted material into Normandy and to communist groups in Paris, my father's other main concern in June was maintaining the supply of material to his groups. He must have received Culioli's request to suspend drops in the Sologne following the explosions at Neuvy on 10/11 June just before he went to Bazémont to receive Gaston Cohen on 12/13 June, as he went straight to meet Culioli afterwards. My father refused Culioli's request as he had already told him that he did not want to waste time, feeling that the invasion was imminent, and he was so serious about this that he gave Culioli the order to continue with receptions in writing.[4] After leaving Culioli, my father stayed the night with the Bossards at Avaray. Their son Alain, then 14, told me that he remembers helping my father set up the aerial for his wireless receiver over the Breton wellhead in the garden so that he could listen out for the BBC messages. He also cycled with my father the next morning to the station at Mer with my father's suitcase on his handlebars as children were less likely to be stopped.

Culioli claimed after the war that he was told by my father on his return in May that he was from that moment officially considered to have a separate circuit, with Yvonne Rudellat as his lieutenant, and with a wireless operator called Barnabé who would arrive in June. There is no record of such a role in SOE files nor of any Barnabé and it conflicts with Agazarian's report that it would be Norman who would be the leader in this area and he would not have needed a wireless operator.[5]

Antelme, who returned in May with my father to a Culioli reception, does not report this but he does record problems with Culioli at this time, which suggests that my father planned to rein Culioli in rather than give him more power:

> Pierre is a very energetic man and certainly has done good sabotage work, but he has a foul temper and had not been making things easy for Prosper lately. As a matter of fact there had been numerous complaints from his men that he did not share the comforts equally and he had even been accused, which I do not believe, of carrying on black market with them. We had discussed the matter … and had come to the conclusion that it would be far the best to request London to cancel the sending of comforts to that particular circuit. Events did not give us time to carry out this decision.[6]

Another problem for my father was the arrest of the Tambour sisters on 22 April by the Abwehr. My father was keen to rescue them from Fresnes prison and Jacques Weil suggested contacting a French police inspector whom he knew who negotiated a price with the Germans holding the sisters to have them brought into Paris as though they were being taken to court. My father went to a rendezvous at the château de Vincennes but two other women had been brought by mistake. The police inspector was told by his German contacts that it would be too dangerous to try again but, after much negotiation, they were persuaded to do so for 1 million francs. To avoid being tricked, the notes were cut in half with one set of halves being handed to the inspector in advance and the other to be paid when the women were released. The inspector did not turn up at the next rendezvous and then said that he had been instructed by the Germans to make another rendezvous in a café. Weil was suspicious so while my father and Norman waited in the café, he and his men watched the surrounding streets and saw police arrive, some of them driving past the café.[7] The group dispersed and my father went to meet Mme Balachowsky who was waiting to receive the sisters. She reported that he had told her that they had been 'photographed' in the café by Germans in a passing car, although this French expression can also be interpreted as they had been stared at, in English perhaps 'clocked', rather than actually photographed.[8] The police inspector did return the halved notes, which took three days to tape together again. After the war, Weil claimed that he alone had been responsible for the attempted rescues and that the payment of 1 million francs had been agreed by London.[9] One of my father's liaison agents in Paris, Berthe Gervoise, reported that she was told by Armel Guerne that he had received 1,500,000 francs from London for this rescue.[10]

There was also trouble in the Privet circuit, now divided between Wilkinson in Nantes and Heslop in Angers. They had both reported:

considerable possibilities in these areas. In Nantes in particular, one of our contacts had a most comprehensive plan for taking possession of the Port on Invasion Day while in Angers, plans were afoot for the cutting of railway communications and the destruction of the telephone exchange on the receipt of orders from London.

These plans were compromised by the arrest of Wilkinson on 6 June and the ensuing German raids led to the recall of Heslop two weeks later. Wilkinson's wife tried to continue but a potential replacement was warned:

It is essential that you avoid the wife of one of our organisers whom we understand to be attempting to continue on the same lines but who is most talkative and a danger on security grounds. This lady is known as Mme Wilkinson.[11]

She was arrested on 20 August, survived deportation to Ravensbrück and later married Charles Lehmann, one of the survivors from the group at Montargis. Heslop had arranged another drop for July for his group at Châteauneuf-sur-Sarthe and asked Antelme to take it over. So it became Operation Bricklayer 1, dropping eight containers on 15/16 July. SOE were able to recover from this setback very quickly as another agent, Ernest Floege, was sent in to this area on 13/14 June to 'make a reconnaissance between Nantes, Laval and Le Mans, to form groups for the reception of material and to prepare targets for D-Day'.[12] He had lived in Angers before the war and so was able to create an organisation there from his own contacts rather than those compromised by the arrests and using Dubois in Tours for communication with London. His first reception was on 15/16 July.

There are stories that around 15–18 June my father made a tour of the depots at the eastern end of Normandy. He had visited that in Falaise at the other end of Normandy at the end of May. He certainly met Gouju on 17 June and inspected the depot he had created at le Plessis Grohan to the south-east of Évreux with material collected from a special June drop to the team at Bois-Jérôme-Saint-Ouen. He also probably inspected the main depot in a derelict house in the forêt de Thelle as it was only a smaller depot elsewhere in the forest that had been taken earlier in the month by the communists. The material from the drop in mid-June at Haillancourt had been taken east to the town of Meru. A very unreliable French source mentions my father visiting a depot of material at Sotteville-les-Rouens received on behalf of the nascent Salesman circuit of Philippe Liewer.[13] This is not mentioned in reports of the activities of the Salesman circuit nor is there any mention of receiving arms from Prosper. The first drop to the Salesman circuit was not until September 1943.

My father was back in Paris by 19 June where he had an early morning appointment with a jeweller, Maurice Braun (also a lieutenant in Marcel Fox's Publican circuit), to make new ID cards, including almost certainly those for Pickersgill, Macalister and Raynaud. The Germans had changed the specifications and photos now had to be in profile and attached to the cards with rivets rather than staples.[14]

Sometime that day he moved his lodgings from rue Hautefeuille, 6éme to 18 rue Mazagran, 10éme, and found time to write to his wife and a report for London. He had already written home once after his return to France – a short homesick note:

It seems ages since I left you. I keep on thinking of all the things I should have said to you – I hope my next visit won't be the same rush. I have just spent two days in a house with two children the same age as Anthony and John – the elder had exactly the same voice as Anthony and it made me feel very homesick. Anyway I now have the photographs and they make me feel much better. My journey was comfortable and my leg gave me no trouble at all – I may even have done it good. Goodbye my darling. All my love, Francis.

On 19 June he starts more chattily:

Another opportunity of sending you a few lines. So far I have received no letter from you since my visit and am very hungry for news. Send me a lot of chatty news. I shall know what you are talking about without names etc. Have you heard from my sister? And of course as much about the children as possible. Use air mail paper and write on both sides. I have earmarked a few very good art books here which I shall buy when the time comes. I shall also get some postcard reproductions from the local National Gallery. They used to print some remarkable ones before the war.

But his yearning to be home is again revealed when he writes about the house that they had built together, Little Halden:

Today at lunch I found myself drawing a complete plan of Little H – on the table cloth. I would give a lot to know how the lonicera and the ramblers are faring. They should be in full maturity. Also the orchard. I have been trying for days to remember the name of the cherry tree. I wonder if the D – s have built a retaining wall for the rear garden.

But there are still practical problems like tax:

> I do hope the trouble with the Tax people about my pay is settled once and for all. I am convinced now that my pay during these months will be a yearly recurring point of difference between me and H. M. Board of Commissioners even if I live to be 90!! Goodbye darling. Do look after yourself. All my love, Francis.

The contrast between the letters and his report written the same day is stark (see p. 199); the letter home appears relaxed whilst the report makes it clear that he is the opposite and that he is in fact totally exhausted.

His threat is unlikely to have been implemented as the report did not reach London until the day my father was arrested.

The next day, Sunday 20 June, there was a big lunch party in Paris to which the Director of the National Agricultural College at Grignon-Thiverval, Professor Vandervynckt, came with the Balachowskys and Noor Inayat Khan. Afterwards my father walked with Mme Balachowsky to the station and told her of his concerns about London. That night a Lysander operation organised by Déricourt failed because he did not appear, nor had he collected the two passengers who were booked to return to London, Richard Heslop and an evading RAF officer. There is no official explanation of Déricourt's failure to collect him on 20 June but Weil was told by one of his colleagues that Déricourt had been arrested for 'a short time before Prosper's arrest'.[15] It is also possible that he may have been warned by the Germans about something that was planned that night not far from the landing ground he was proposing to use at Pocé-sur-Cisse, near Amboise.

On the night of 20/21 June the Germans from Blois encircled the region of Bracieux, Neuvy and Dhuizon with a cordon from the police, the military and the Luftwaffe. The owner of a château near Bracieux, that was taken over at 2 a.m. as the headquarters of the operation, was told, 'Do not worry, we have not come to disturb you but there is in this area a centre of English espionage.'[16] When the *maire* of Dhuizon asked why his house was being searched, he was told that they were not searching for material but for someone. Whatever the reason, there had been British aircraft flying around the Sologne on six of the ten nights since the explosions at Neuvy, dropping not just containers but also three agents and one of these agent receptions may have been seen by a German nightfighter. The reason that the area between Bracieux and Dhuizon was chosen appears to have been because of the incident of the exploding containers, in which case it took the Germans ten days to react and there had been no more drops in this particular area since that incident. The group that had been at Neuvy did receive another drop on 17/18 June but this was to a new DZ much further south and chosen because it was considered that the Neuvy DZ should not be used again.

On the night of the encirclement itself, there were four more successful drops, again all outside the encircled area but that to the Villeny group was close. This was the first drop for the Villeny group and Roger Couffrant brought a team from Romorantin to help and train them. After the reception, the Villeny team went home, leaving the Romorantin team with the parachuted material in an abandoned farm on the road to Dhuizon. Very early in the morning André Habert arrived with a lorry to pick them up and take them to unload the material at le Cercle where Culioli had his headquarters. At around 6 a.m. they drove straight into the roadblocks and were promptly arrested.

REPORT PROSPER 19TH JUNE, 1943.

1. Letter Boxes.

(a) Madeleine was apparently given the Monet letter box in spite of the fact that it is cancelled since February (cancellation confirmed personally by me in May visit). Please take disciplinary action. Had Madeleine gone there yesterday afternoon she would have coincided with one of the Gestapo's periodical visits at that flat!

(b) I understand Delphin is with you. Please take disciplinary action against him. While still over here he gave the Monet address to his No. 2 without my consent. His No. 2 was contacted there by Monique who gave him the Rose letter box and told him never again to visit Monet. In spite of that a few days later a message from this No. 2 (which message I enclose) was brought to the Monet letter box and, this time, by a third person - a woman. Heaven knows how many people now know this letter box via Delphin!

I ask for disciplinary action as this makes the position quite clear. Please follow closely.

Either (1) You take disciplinary action in which case all well and good.

Or (2) Delphin manages to convince you that although he realised that it was most undesirable, it was, nevertheless, unavoidable in the circumstances that he should give the address to his No.2, in spite of the fact that he was still in France himself.

In this case, it at once becomes superabundantly clear that similar circumstances can arise at any time and that therefore the whole system of giving to any agent a letter box of another circuit is an obvious invitation to disaster for that circuit. (I hope I have made myself clear. I state, in parenthesis, that it is now 0100 hours 19th June and that I have slept 7 hours since 0500 hours 15th June). The answer is quite obvious. If you give a letter box to an agent it must be given on the understanding that it is to be divulged to NOONE whatever the circumstances, without the consent of the organiser of the circuit to which the letter box belongs. Please make this a standing order, at least in so far as my letter boxes are concerned, with the sanction that any infraction of this order involves immediate and permanent recall.

(c) All my letter boxes and passwords now in force will be cancelled as from midday 19th June and will remain cancelled till I receive your W/T message, "The village postman has recovered", which will mean:-

(i) That as regards these letter boxes my suggested standing order has been accepted and adopted and also made known to agents already over here.

(ii) That the Monet letter box is quite quite quite cancelled and all concerned warned.

N.B. If you are not prepared to accept my suggestion I will, of course on your instruction, immediately reinstate the letter boxes unconditionally. In such case please file this report carefully for production on the inevitable eventual "post mortem" of the "feu" Prosper organisation.

My father's report of 19 June 1943. (HS9/911/1)

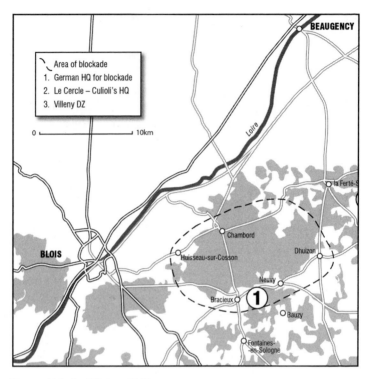

The road block of 21 June 1943.

Around the same time, Culioli and Rudellat were preparing to set off with Pickersgill and Macalister for Beaugency from where they all intended to catch the train for Paris to meet my father, hand over Pickersgill and Macalister to Guerne and collect the new papers for Pierre Raynaud. Raynaud had decided to travel on his own to Paris the day before and made an arrangement to meet Culioli to collect his new papers after Culioli had delivered Pickersgill and Macalister to my father. They did set off, but without waiting for Roger Couffrant and his team to arrive, nor did they see Habert's lorry on the road, which should have been a warning to Culioli that something had gone wrong. Culioli admitted later that, 'I made the error of setting out that morning despite none of my reception chiefs having reported on their operations.'[17] The result was that they also met the roadblocks. Their car was allowed through the first control but stopped at the second on the edge of Dhuizon. The two Canadians were ordered out of the car and told to walk to the *mairie*; there were soldiers stationed every 10m along the road. Another soldier got into the car and ordered Culioli to drive to the *mairie* where they joined a queue to have their papers examined. Culioli took advantage of the wait to place his briefcase behind a chair standing against the wall. He told Ben Bossard after the war that, contrary to all of the rules of security, he never travelled without his briefcase, which was stuffed full with compromising documents.[18] When his papers were examined, he was asked about the surprisingly heavy small package he was carrying addressed to a prisoner-of-war, but his interrogator was satisfied when he replied that it contained charcuterie and he and Rudellat were allowed to leave. However, his briefcase was found and when it was revealed to contain important documents, including his reports on his organisation, a soldier was sent out to bring him back.[19]

As they waited in the car, Culioli left the engine running and, when the soldier ran out of the *mairie* to call them back, he put his foot down and set off, unfortunately on the road to Neuvy and Bracieux. According to an eyewitness, another reason for their recall was the considerable quantity of money that the Canadians were found to be carrying in their belts.[20] Culioli was pursued by much more powerful cars and as he approached the road blocks at Bracieux, a bullet made his windscreen opaque, another hit him in the leg and Rudellat, hit by a bullet in the head, slumped against him, apparently dead. He lost control on a bend, crashed into the wall of a house and ended up in a ditch. (After the war, he claimed that he had deliberately tried to kill himself.) He was dragged from the car but fought back despite the wound in his leg. He was taken back to the *mairie* in Dhuizon where the package was opened, revealing the two small radio receivers, the new crystals and messages labelled 'For Archambaud' and the packages marked 'For Prosper' and 'For Marie-Louise', de Baissac's courier. He was sent to the Luftwaffe field hospital in Blois where he received some basic treatment for his wound. When asked his address he gave that of an apartment in Orléans that he had recently rented as he did not want to implicate his in-laws in Mer or let the Germans know where his headquarters were. He was able to convince the Germans of this address because one of the many documents in his briefcase, retrieved from behind a chair, was a rental agreement for the apartment.

This was not the only significant arrest that day. At Caluire near Lyons the Germans raided a meeting of the Armée Secrète and arrested Jean Moulin and the entire Conseil National de la Résistance (CNR). Moulin had been sent back to France at the end of March 1943 by General de Gaulle to set up the CNR. The large military groups already in existence in the south were ready to accept a central military direction but those in the north needed persuading. Despite disagreements, the north and south coordinating committees were finally fused into the CNR at the end of May but then the entire CNR was caught on 21 June.

Meanwhile, in Paris, Déricourt finally turned up to collect his passengers and took them by train to Amboise. (They did not actually leave France until 23/24 June as the previous night it was the RAF who failed to appear when the generator on the aircraft failed.) My father waited at the agreed time and place for Culioli and his party but was not disturbed when they failed to arrive as it was standard practice that, if a first rendezvous was missed, then it was assumed to be re-arranged for the same time and place on the next day and on the third day after if necessary. That night he was on the DZ at le Roncey for the reception, where a parachuted agent could not be found and nor initially could two radios for Inayat Khan. He left the others to continue the search as he had to meet Jean-Michel Cauchy in Paris and go with him to Antelme's apartment, where Cauchy was given 100,000 francs to enable him to buy a lorry with which to collect the material parachuted at Ancinnes and l'Hermitière and take it Falaise for storage until it could be further distributed to other groups. Cauchy collected half of the material from Ancinnes on 25 June and planned to collect the rest on 2 July as a further drop was expected there on 9 July.

At midday on 21 June my father met Renée Guepin, Darling's fiancée, who came to tell him that at the last operation that Georges Darling had attended, he had taken fright and the operation had failed.[21] He agreed to go to Trie-Château in a couple of days, when the operation was due to be repeated, so as to encourage Darling and uphold his reputation amongst his men. In the evening he met up with the others who had been at le Roncey and asked France Antelme to arrange for the wireless transmitters to be taken to the Sarthe ready for Inayat Khan's use.

By this time Culioli had been transferred from the Luftwaffe hospital to a cell in Blois. The Canadians were also taken to Blois and interrogated but do not appear to have given anything of interest. It was only when the local Gestapo chief Ludwig Bauer got round to interrogating Culioli on 23 June that he realised how important were the documents that he was carrying in his briefcase as they included detailed information about the activities of other parts of the organisation, not

Renée Guepin. (Libre Résistance)

just those in the Sologne. A police report of 6 July noted that the Germans considered the arrests of 21 June were the most important find of arms and espionage to have been made in France since the occupation.[22] According to Culioli,[23] he had decided that, as he was carrying packets to be delivered to Prosper and Archambaud, he would have to admit that he had worked with them but had now lost contact with them as it was no longer possible to meet them because the third of three agreed rendezvous had been missed. However, according to Mona Reimeringer, who worked with Bauer and was his mistress but gave contradictory statements, Culioli immediately offered to give Bauer two names and addresses, which would enable him to break all of the English resistance groups.[24] This ties in with

an admission that Culioli made after the war that he had several addresses in his briefcase, including those of Norman and Borrel, but not that of my father, which he did not know. Whether given by Culioli or found in his briefcase, this information seems to have been the spark that

Ludwig Bauer. (P. Guillaume)

Mona Reimeringer. (P. Guillaume)

made Bauer realise that he would
have to act quickly if he were to
make use of the information.
Culioli was driven to Gestapo HQ
in the Avenue Foch in Paris that
same night.

He arrived shortly before
midnight on 23 June and soon
afterwards an arrest team arrived at the apartment of
Nicolas and Maude Laurent where Norman lodged and
where Borrel also happened to be staying that night. Culioli
initially claimed that he was not taken to Paris until after
the arrest of my father but later admitted at his trial that it
was 23 June. When the Laurents arrived home from visiting
friends, they found Norman and Borrel making false cards.
Nicolas recalled that:

At midnight the bell rang at the Boulevard Lannes entrance
and, as Nicolas was already in bed, Maude answered it. A
man in civilian clothes asked if he could speak to M. Gilbert.
Maude went to fetch her husband who came out of the
house and across the garden to speak to the man. He thinks
that the man said he came on behalf of Gaspard but of
this he is not certain. He remembers thinking it odd that
someone should call for Archambaud at that late hour and
he went to fetch Archambaud. They came back together and
Archambaud opened the garden gate to the man. He was a
young man aged about 24 or 25 speaking French very well.
The young man slipped through the door and behind Nicolas

Nicolas Laurent. (Guy Laurent)

and Archambaud and, when Nicolas turned round, he found a revolver pointed at him. Immediately about ten men in civilian clothes came through the gate saying – Gestapo. They were handcuffed, Archambaud taken to a room up the stairs and Nicolas put into the kitchen on the ground floor. The Germans began to search the house.[25]

Maude gives a more dramatic account, saying that the doorbell rang at a quarter past midnight:

Gilbert and Denise were working in the office and the table was strewn with compromising documents and the seals of all of the Kommandaturs in France, which were being used to stamp the false papers. Nico and I had undressed and intended to go and say goodnight to Gilbert and Denise before going to bed, but the sound of the bell changed all that. Gilbert shouted to Nico to go and answer it. He was our leader. Reluctantly, my husband did as he asked, thinking, like me, that Gilbert must be expecting someone and we didn't know about it, though this was surprising because it was after the curfew. Nico went down the stairs that led to the kitchen and out that way into the garden. He opened up and I heard him call to me, surprised and concerned, Maude! get dressed! That was his greatest concern – as a husband he didn't want twelve men seeing his wife in a see-through slip, which happened

Maud Laurent. (Guy Laurent)

anyway! Well, twelve Gestapo agents burst in on me, with their revolvers raised, and backed up by machine guns, shouting 'hands up'. I did nothing and was filled with anger at this violation of my home. They had already seized Gilbert and were going down to apprehend Nico. Denise tried to escape, but was stopped by the threat of the revolver. Gilbert, Denise and Nico were taken away immediately.[26]

Armel Guerne later met the Gestapo agent who had been responsible:

It appeared that just before midnight, i.e. shortly after Archambaud and Monique had left Guerne, a Gestapo agent came to Archambaud's house. He passed himself off as a recent arrival from London and produced the crystals which Archambaud was expecting. Archambaud was then arrested by two other Germans who entered. Monique was also arrested and prevented from swallowing the organisation code. This code was in any case already known to the Germans. The same Germans spent the rest of the night waiting at Prosper's house and arrested him the following morning on his return from Normandy.[27]

That evening my father had gone to Trie-Château as arranged but the operation, which had failed some nights earlier when

Darling took fright, was not flown again. Before leaving Trie-Château after a wasted night, my father met Marcel Charbonnier, his personal liaison officer, who had been trying to find out why Culioli had failed to make the three rendezvous. He had no news, reporting that Culioli had not sent any message. This must now have become a serious concern. Renée Guepin, who went with my father to the station in Gisors, said that he appeared very worried. 'It's not my health. It's much worse. I have not the right to tell you the trouble which weighs on my mind.'[28] However, the problems with London were an even greater concern and this was confirmed by Charbonnier who stated, 'Well before his arrest Prosper was uneasy concerning the security of his network; I definitely remember him saying "There are hard blows in prospect and it is from London that it is coming."'[29]

As soon as he reached Paris, my father met Marc O'Neill who led an OCM group based in Paris that was affiliated to Claude de Baissac's Scientist circuit. As de Baissac was based in Bordeaux, it had been agreed that O'Neill's group should transfer to Prosper and this was the initial meeting where it was agreed that they should meet again in the afternoon for a formal hand-over.[30] The plan was for O'Neill to organise drops in the eastern Oise and northern Loiret as Physician operations. After the collapse of the Prosper organisation, O'Neill returned to work with de Baissac who sent him Marcel Defence as wireless operator and they organised drops in these areas in August as Scientist operations instead.

My father then returned to his lodgings on the second floor of 18 rue Mazagran. There was no sign of the concierge, Mme Fevre; she was being held by one of the arrest team, which had arrived in the early hours only to find that my father was away. By the time he opened the door of his room it was too late. There were German agents in the room as well as on the stairs above and below him. Despite this it seems he put up quite a fight as the concierge reported that, when he was taken away, 'some two hours later he appeared to me all disfigured, having the appearance of having been beaten and being totally miserable'. She added, 'When I got my room back the following Sunday, I realized that the Germans had destroyed everything. The marble slab of the fireplace had been torn off and broken. The mirror in my wardrobe was shattered. Chairs and armchairs damaged and all over the place.'[31] She was the only French person who records seeing him after his arrest. He was taken straight to the Avenue Foch and there are conflicting reports as to who dealt with him and what happened during the next few days.

The Germans also had a local success in the Oise on the same day, arresting René Davesne, the leader of the Meru group, and one of his men, Gabriel Lhomme. Davesne survived and recorded that he had met a man who gave him the necessary password and told him that he was replacing Jacques (Agazarian) who had left for London, 'We talked about our work. We took an aperitif in a café in Meru and then four Gestapo agents arrested me.'[32] I have not yet managed to piece together the full story of this arrest but Davesne is recorded as being friendly with two women, Mlles Dennery and Leitz, as was a member of the group at La Houssoye, Sylvain Allais. Allais is recorded as having chatted with the women in a café and told them about the parachute operations. He was arrested three days later together with fourteen other members of Darling's groups. It seems that the women were perhaps agents of, or working with, the local police.[33]

The Germans had not planned the arrest of Culioli; he fell into their hands almost by chance but his arrest resulted in the arrests in Paris. Indeed the Gestapo were caught out because they suddenly found themselves with two wireless operators with new crystals, which they could therefore play back, but no one available to do so as their expert, Dr Goetz, had gone to Germany on leave on 19 June to be with his wife who was expecting a baby. He was hurriedly recalled but did not return until 29 June. The Paris Gestapo were also already occupied with the interrogation of the people arrested with Jean Moulin but they put these to one side and gave priority to the Prosper people as, unlike the CNR's administrative role, they had considerable quantities of arms and sabotage material.

Some time over the next two days someone talked. German reports are inconsistent. Kieffer, the most senior officer to comment, stated that:

> Prosper did not want to make any statement but Gilbert (Norman), who had not the integrity of Prosper, made a very full statement. Through Norman and through the documentary material available, we received our first insight into the French Section, and also through Denise.

Mme Balachowsky stated after the war that Borrel was arrested with her briefcase 'in which she was carrying names and

addresses which made possible the arrest of so many persons'.[34] Ernst Vogt, an interpreter for the Paris Gestapo, made a deposition in 1949 in which he states that when my father and Norman were brought to the Gestapo HQ in the Avenue Foch, Kieffer showed

Josef Goetz

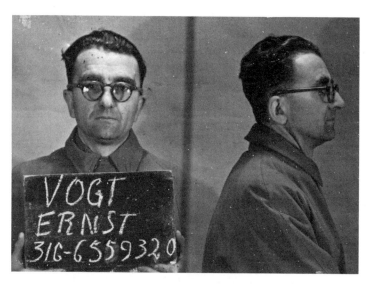

Ernst Vogt

them copies of documents that had been intercepted on their way to London via Déricourt's aircraft. Although he thought most of these were not very important as SOE was not an intelligence gathering organisation and most communication with London was by wireless, there was one important document that gave all of the DZs in the Seine-et-Oise and the Eure – about forty – together with the names and addresses of the local group leaders and their helpers as well as the address of the Paris letter box where documents were left for Déricourt to send to London. Vogt said that my father and Norman were shattered when they saw these documents. Kieffer did not tell them where these documents came from, letting them believe that he had an important agent in the HQ of the French Section in London and, realising that everything was lost, my father and Norman agreed to an accord.

Josef Placke

Kieffer asked Suttill and Norman to detail all of their activities for the French Section in England and in France, to name all of their collaborators in France, to give the location of all of their depots of arms and material, the names and addresses of the people who had created these depots or were now looking after them. They must also both agree to order their collaborators to whom they were presented to adopt the same conduct as themselves. In exchange, Kieffer would agree, when they gave their word of honour, that both, together with all of their collaborators, would be perfectly treated and that they would not be brought before a tribunal, but purely and simply sent to a concentration camp in Germany until the end of the

war. Suttill and Norman accepted on condition that the only people to be arrested would be those that they had indicated as having taken part in their clandestine activities and not those who only knew about these activities, such as the families. Kieffer agreed.[35]

Hans Kieffer.

In a letter to the author J.O. Fuller in 1958 Vogt gives a somewhat different version of these events:

Prosper and Archambaud refused to make any statement for forty-eight hours after their arrest, this to leave time for the other members of their group to change domicile … During the forty-eight hours after their arrest Prosper and Archambaud maintained a complete silence, refusing to make any statement, even to give us their real names and nationalities. During these forty-eight hours, Scherer, von Kapri, Goetz and I took it in relays to be with Prosper and Archambaud night and day separately (they were held separately in separate offices) and we had formal orders from Kieffer not to touch them, not to press them to make a statement and above all Kieffer ordered us not to subject them to any ill-treatment. To take our meals with them (the properly prepared meals which were brought to us) and

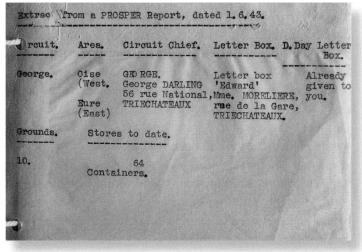

Extrac from a PROSPER Report, dated 1.6.43.

rcuit.	Area.	Circuit Chief.	Letter Box.	D. Day Letter Box.
George.	Oise (West. Eure (East)	GEORGE. George DARLING 56 rue National, TRIECHATEAUX	Letter box 'Edward' Mme. MORELIERE, rue de la Gare, TRIECHATEAUX.	Already given to you.
Grounds.		Stores to date.		
10.		64 Containers.		

My father's report of 1 June 1943.

to give them as many English cigarettes as they wanted. (Archambaud did not smoke at all.) None of us knew anything about Prosper and Archambaud and we had for these forty-eight hours to keep on asking them the same question – What is your real name and activity? It was only at the end of these forty-eight hours that Kieffer intervened personally and showed them the photostatted copies of the reports they had sent to London and told them he knew all about their activity. It was only after this that the famous pact was concluded between Prosper and Kieffer.

He also told her that when the pact was made 'no one else was present; only Prosper, Kieffer and himself as intermediary', adding that my father had asked him, 'Can I trust your chief?' When he replied 'Yes', the pact was obtained from Berlin, stamped with the seal of the RSHA and given to my father.[36]

However this is contradicted by an earlier statement that he made where he says that he only learnt that Prosper had made an arrangement from Norman.[37] It looks as though, when he spoke to Fuller and knew who had survived and who had died, he decided to give himself a more important role.

There are also problems with the statements of Josef Placke, a member of the Paris Gestapo involved in several arrests. In a deposition he states that my father was interrogated for forty-eight hours non-stop by one of his colleagues Karl Langer, Dr Goetz and himself. As we know, Goetz did not return to Paris until 29 June and there is no mention of Kieffer. He goes on to say that Prosper gave the address of Darling and wrote him a note asking him to give arms to the persons presenting this note but he admits that he only heard this from Langer; indeed he emphasises that he himself was not present. He later says that after giving up Darling, Prosper gave all the other arms depots and the names of the men holding them but he again says that he was not present at the interrogations at which this was supposed to have been said.[38] Vogt claimed that only he, Scherer, von Kapri and Goetz were involved in the first forty-eight hours, whilst Placke claims it was he, Langer and Goetz. The only name in both of these statements is Goetz and he did not arrive back in Paris until five days after the arrests and never made any claim to have interrogated my father.

Goetz made a statement in 1946:

I was recalled from this leave by Kieffer at the end of June in order to take up the transmission of Archambaud. Before this time, the organisation of the French Section was unknown but following the details supplied by Archambaud, we obtained a precise insight into the whole organisation. Archambaud helped me to carry on transmissions after he had noticed that London had failed to observe the security checks.[39]

Kieffer and Boemelburg sitting in a Paris café.

In a later statement he says that:

> As I was absent at the time of the arrests, I can only tell you about the information that was collected whilst I was on leave and when I read these, I think that I remember that in the file there was a long deposition by Culioli telling of his work for the French Section. He probably gave the names and addresses of members of the French Section. I have the impression that Culioli was very explicit and that he sought to save himself by making unreserved admissions.

He also said, 'I deduced that the massive arrests in the Buckmaster circuits were due in part to the information provided by Culioli and Valentin (Macalister).'[40]

Notes

1. D. L'heureux, *La Résistance 'Action-Buckmaster' Sylvestre-Farmer avec le Capitaine 'Michel'*, Geai Bleu, 2001.
2. PP BA 1748 and PP BS 11 carton 25, Archives de la Prefecture de Police de Paris.
3. Rapport Final Allemand, origin unclear but French translation published in Les Nouvelles de Falaise, 21 September 1961.
4. Rapport 28.04.1945, HS 9/379/8, TNA.
5. Culioli continued with this claim after the war and decided to call his organisation Adolphe. This caused confusion for those trying to wind up the affairs of the various circuits for not only did he include most Monkeypuzzle operations and those at Étrépagny in the Eure but there already existed a real SOE circuit called Adolphe in Finistère known to SOE as Racketeer. Although his groups are now generally known by the name Adolphe, this is not correct; the groups that he and Yvonne Rudellat organised in the Sologne were simply one of the several sub-circuits of Prosper/Physician without any official unique name.
6. General Report July 1943, HS 9/42, TNA.
7. Interview 08-09.05.1945, HS 6/440, TNA.
8. J.O. Fuller, *The German Penetration of SOE*, William Kimber, 1975.
9. C. Wighton, *Pin-Stripe Saboteur*, Odhams, 1959.
10. Z 6 NL 17339, Archives Nationales.
11. Draft Briefing 05.08.1943, HS 9/21/4, TNA.

12. HS 9/520/8, TNA.

13. R. Ruffin, *Résistance Normande et Jour J*, Presses de la Cité, 1994.

14. *Le Réseau Publican*, Les Cahiers de la Résistance Seine-et-Marne, No. 4, undated.

15. See 7 above.

16. P. Guillaume, *La Sologne au Temps de l'Héröisme et de la Trahaison.*

17. See 4 above.

18. See 16 above.

19. 1375 W 70, Archives départementales, Blois. de Loir-et-Cher.

20. 1221 W 11, Archives départmentales, Orléans.

21. 1375 W70, Archives départmentales, Blois.

22. See 21 above.

23. See 4 above.

24. See 16 above.

25. Interrogation 04.05.1945, HS 6/440, TNA.

26. Document given to author by Nicolas Laurent.

27. First Interrogation Report 14-20.05.1944, HS 9/631/5, TNA.

28. See 8 above.

29. J.O. Fuller, *Double Agent?*, Pan 1961.

30. Interview 27.08.1943, HS 9/75, TNA.

31. Proces-Verbal 08.10.1947, Trial papers of Pierre Culioli, DCAJM.

32. 16 P 160161, SHD.

33. Archives départementales, Beauvais.

34. See 8 above.

35. See 29 above.

36. See 29 above.

37. See 16 above.

38. 1221 W11, Archives départmentales, Orleans.

39. Voluntary Statement 20.11.1946, HS 9/836/5, TNA.

40. 1221 W11, Archives départmentales, Orleans.

A WAVE OF ARRESTS

The first action of the Germans after the Paris arrests was to send a lorry on 26 June to Trie-Château to collect arms using, according to Placke's hearsay evidence, one of the promissory notes signed by my father. Members of the local team arrived at the bois d'Etoile to help load the lorry, assuming it was another visit from the communist group from Paris. It was only when Georges Darling arrived on his motorbike that they realised that it was not the same people. Darling shouted a warning – '*Nous sommes foutous!*' (We've had it!) – but it was too late.[1] Darling took off towards Chambors on his motorbike but was hit and found later with a bullet in his liver. He died the next day in Gisors hospital. All but one of the other members of the group who were there managed to escape with Pierre Perret who, as forest guard, knew the wood intimately but the local baker's boy from the Bussy bakery in Trie-Château, Joseph Fournier, was caught. The Germans later went to the bakery and arrested Fernande Bussy and one of the workers, Adolphe Redelsperger; the baker Bussy escaped. Yvonne, the wife of the forest guard, Pierre Perret, was also arrested and deported but survived.

I have already commented on the unreliability of Placke's testimony as his story of the promissory note is by his own admission only hearsay. If one was used, it is not known whether it was specifically written for the Germans or whether it was a sample found on my father when he was arrested, which he had been planning to show or give to those he was due to meet in the next few days. I have also found three other possible explanations for this German raid. As has already been noted, the Germans had started to infiltrate Darling's organisation and had arrested two of the Meru group two days earlier. I have also seen a police report that states that it was a Henri Amand who gave them the location of the Trie-Château depot.[2] Finally, an English relative of Darling who was also in France during the war was sure that he had been betrayed by an ex-lover, Michelle Carré, and that this might lead to his arrest as well, as had already happened to Georges Darling's 72-year-old father.

I think the most likely explanation is in the deposition of Ernst Vogt where he says he was shown a document giving the name and address of the group leader in the Seine-et-Oise and Eure.[3] I was puzzled by this remark until I discovered that Georges Darling had a personal file[4] and in it I found a copy of part of the report by my father dated 1 June 1943 (see p.154). There are no similar extracts on the files of other group leaders so this may have been the first with reports on the other groups still being prepared, such as perhaps that referred to by Vogt as having been being prepared by Culioli. So there was no need for the Germans to ask for Darling's address or how many DZs he had or how much material he had received. They already had this information, which could only have come to them from Déricourt allowing the mail to be copied. Placke's version therefore seems to be an attempt to hide their sources.

After the arrests in Trie-Château, there was a pause for three days and then the arrests in the rest of the circuit started in earnest and continued over the next few weeks. On 29 June the Germans returned to Darling's area and arrested fifteen people, destroying the groups in Neaufles-Saint-Martin,

La Landelle, Meru, Bois-Jérôme-Saint-Ouen and the group that had received the drop near Jouy-la-Grange. They also arrested Marcel Gouju at Évreux.

At Neaufles-Saint-Martin an eyewitness described seeing the local leader, the retired gendarme Alexandre Laurent, brought out of a house 'in an appalling state, bloody all over, his clothes torn, his eyes and ears swollen, bruises all over his body'.[5] When the Germans arrived at the Sénécaux yard, they had a plan showing the steps to a loft and knew the number of sacks of arms that should have been there. The Sénécaux family, hearing of the death of Georges Darling, had moved the arms from the loft and buried them in surrounding woods and fields but they were soon found. Sylvain and Pauline Sénécaux were arrested together with their son but their 13-year-old daughter was left to fend for herself. They were taken to the Avenue Foch and confronted with Gilbert Norman but he denied knowing them. Pauline and her son were released a month later but Sylvain was deported together with Alexandre Laurent and his wife, Antonine, as well as Jules and Olga Villegas; only the last two returned.

In the forêt de Thelle the chief forest guard, Maxime Aubry was arrested together with one of the team from the east of the forest at La Landelle, Camille Bigot and his partner Ginette Boulanger; they all died in Germany. According to another member of the group who survived, Aubry:

> had given away everything he knew about other members of the group to save himself and his wife. Apparently he had had some quarrel with Darling, as he wanted to form an independent group under his own leadership rather than take orders from Darling. When he was arrested, a photograph of the Darling group was found in his room and he immediately gave all particulars to the Germans.[6]

Author being shown where the arms were hidden in the Sénécaux yard. (F Dury)

On the other side of the forest the man who had talked to Mlles Leitz and Dennery about the parachute receptions three days earlier, Sylvain Allais, was arrested as were two other members of that team, Marcel Schwartz and Roland Boyeldieu; all three died in the camps.

Two more of the Meru team were picked up: Victor Lucas, who worked in the *mairie*, and Marcel Ponléve, the butcher who had taken other members of the group to the DZ at Haillancourt in his van. Both were deported but only Ponléve returned. The Germans also called at the home of the gamekeeper at Étrépagny, Gustave Tiercelin, who had helped at the very first drop to the circuit in November 1942 and lodged my father, but they only found his wife at home and arrested her. She was released soon afterwards together with her son Gaston who was caught the next day but his brother Gilbert, who had been one of the look-outs when the sucrerie was sabotaged, did not return until 1945.

The final arrests that day in the groups of Georges Darling involved dramatic scenes in Bois-Jérôme-Saint-Ouen. When the Germans arrived, some of the Perret family were in the family café in the middle of the village where my father had stayed. Ernst Vogt was involved and described the raid:

In this village the name 'Perret' belonged to multiple families. The team charged with making the arrests apprehended all the men with the name Perret, about twenty odd of them, and locked them in a room in the town hall. Kieffer was informed about this state of affairs and went immediately to the village, asking me to go with him. In arriving in the village he had all of the arrested men put into a truck and driven near to a wood a few hundred metres away. There he had me get into the truck and make sure that the prisoners understood what he said. He was going to take them, one after another, into the woods on the pretext of shooting them until one of them told the truth. A few moments after the first man had been led into the woods, we heard a gunshot coming from that direction. Straight away a young man among the prisoners asked particularly to speak to me. I acquiesced. He stated that it was the man we had just shot who was responsible for the parachute drop and storage operations. I told Kieffer immediately. With the informer, we searched for the stores in a wood about a kilometre from the village. They were concealed among piles of wood. The arms and sabotage supplies were put back into their containers. According to the intelligence from Paris, what we had found there was about half of what had been dropped. The young man assured us that these were the only stores that he knew about. Before we left the village, Kieffer had everyone released except for the young man and the man we had

pretended to shoot. Some weeks later I was told that the
young man, who was being brought from the prison at
Fresnes to be interrogated had asked to speak to me. When
he was brought to my office, he stated that he knew where
the other containers were. When asked why he hadn't told
the truth straight away, he told me that he had acted thus
so that he would be able to make a trip back home after his
arrest. Almost immediately we went to the scene. Kieffer
led the expedition himself. In fact, we found the rest of the
containers hidden in the same area as the others. No arrest
was made on this second expedition. The young Perret
was allowed to go home and collect some other personal
belongings. We had dinner in the café where he lived while
he was left to pack his suitcase as he wished.[7]

When I met Alfred Perret in 2008, he told me that he was
'the young man' that Vogt referred to but he remembered
the incident differently. Early in the morning of 29 June he
had set off on his motorbike as usual to make charcoal. As he
passed the home of his brother Marcel he remembered that
the men from Évreux were due to arrive to collect some of
the parachuted material so when he saw a lorry parked there,
he thought it was them arriving early. By the time he realised
it was a German lorry, it was too late and he was arrested by
the police under a German officer. The police gathered some
thirty to forty men and women from the village and held
them in the *mairie* for nine hours. But they knew who they
were really looking for and he and a few close members of his
family were driven to a quarry. Marcel was asked to reveal
the location of the depot of arms and when he refused, he was
taken into the quarry and they heard a shot. Then the same
happened with his father, Lucien. Thinking that his father
and brother were dead, he decided to tell the Germans about

one of the depots so that other members of his family who
were not involved did not suffer the same fate. His father and
brother were then brought out of the quarry and the three of
them together with their brother-in-law, André Delfosse, were
taken to the Avenue Foch and confronted with the man who
had given them away, Gilbert Norman, who ordered them
to reveal the location of the main arms depot, which was in
an old tile kiln. The three Perrets survived deportation but
Delfosse did not.

The last arrests that day were in Évreux. The group leader,
Marcel Gouju, was arrested with his wife and the wife of
another local man, Madeleine Lainey, as well as a worker
at the distillery who had driven the lorry carrying the arms,
Georges Bernard, and the director of the distillery, Georges
Piedplus, which explains why Gouju and his men were not
in Bois-Jérôme-Saint-Ouen. They were arrested early in the
morning by a team led by Josef Placke: 'Taken to the SD
police station in town, they were interrogated by Mabiot,

Author with Alfred Perret. (Author)

Robert Perret show-
ing author where
the arms were
hidden in an old tile
kiln. (F. Dury)

and in the course of the interrogation were knocked about,
punched by two German soldiers from l'Avenue Foch.'
Gouju stated:

> They interrogated me all morning, passing me from one
> to another to be beaten. They had found out about our
> network from our radio a contact, an Englishman, who
> transmitted for the English, and from whom they had been
> taking the messages for some time without being able to
> decipher them. That is how they had got my name. From
> him they knew that there was a store of explosives at Plessi
> Grohan that I transported from Bois-Jérôme using a vehicle
> belonging to the Évreux distilleries.[8]

Gouju recorded that this was another attempt by Placke to minimise his involvement as it was actually Placke himself and not Mabiot who had interrogated him and allowed him to be beaten.[9] He also stated that, 'I do not think I have known a more painful moment in my life than when, on 4 July 1943, Gilbert Norman came towards me and said with the most beautiful poise – You can tell them everything. They are stronger than we are.'[10] The news of Gouju's arrest spread very quickly and all of the other members of the group managed to avoid arrest. The wives of Gouju and Lainey were later released as was Piedplus but both Gouju and Bernard survived deportation.

The Germans returned to finish clearing Darling's people on 9 August. At 6 a.m. the Heuillard house in Neuf-Marché was surrounded but Georges had fled to hide in Paris, so his wife and 18-year-old son were arrested. When they were pushed into a lorry they found that they were not the first. Already in the lorry were Jean Argence, a forest guard with a depot of arms in the forêt de Lyons, and the gravedigger from Neuf-Marché, François Dupressoir. For some reason the Germans thought that some of the material was buried in the cemetery in Neuf-Marché but in fact this was in Martagny. All were taken to the tannery in Trie-Château, where the owner, Léon Henaff, had been tied to a chair. Later a Spanish boy was brought in who had been arrested in a village to the south of Trie-Château. José Iglesias had strangulation marks around his neck and was in a pitiable state. It is still not known whether he was involved with Darling or why he was arrested. Also brought in was Alexandre Barbier from the farm at Champ Mauger near Sérifontaine where the police had disrupted a proposed drop in February, but he had also been involved in the movement of arms to the communists earlier in the month. They were interrogated throughout the rest of the day before being taken to the Avenue Foch. The Heuillards were released soon afterwards but Georges was caught later and deported; having left France weighing 117kg, he returned weighing only 47kg. The five from the tannery were all deported and only Argence returned.

As well as the finding of arms depots at Évreux and Meru, Placke mentioned another found at the same time at Creil. This is in the eastern Oise, near to two of the DZs used by the French groups under Marcel Sailly, but it appears to have been found because of Sailly's links with the Prosper organisation and this is also the reason that he gives for his own arrest in November.[11]

As explained in the last chapter, the organisation in the Montargis area of the Loiret to the east of Orléans is the one that I know least about. However, from French documents I have managed to find the sequence of arrests there from which it appears that the Germans were not initially as well informed about this group as they had been about Georges Darling's organisation. They started on 28 June by arresting Micheline Conter, who was the liaison officer between Montargis and Paris, and two of her nephews, Jean and Pierre Cassier, who had been part of the reception team. Two days later they arrested four more men, three of whom had also been involved in the June drop and one of these, Roger Narcy, cooperated after his wife talked.

In the middle of the night of 8 July, the Carmignac family in the village of Chuelles were woken by shots. Lucien Carmignac rushed downstairs with his revolver, two of his sons close behind him, but despite killing two of their attackers, they were outnumbered. Lucien and his son Norbert were killed and although the other son Roger was wounded, he managed to get away, only to be caught later in the hospital in Montargis. At 4.30 a.m. reinforcements

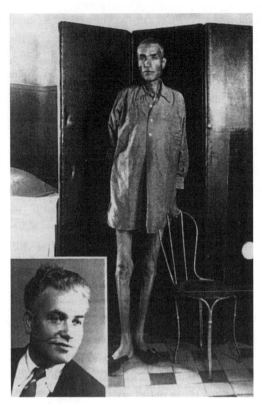

Georges Heuillard on his return from deportation. (Libre Résistance)

arrived and a search was made for the arms the family held. When they found nothing, Narcy was brought in from the car where he was being held and he showed them where the cache had been but it was now empty. When they had heard of the arrests in Montargis, the Carmignacs had moved their arms to the farm where Kleber Gauthier already had a cache. The next night the other depot was found at the garage of Albert Guellemin in the village of Chantecoq to the north of Chuelles and he was arrested. The Germans next went to the farm of Gauthier but Kleber was not there as he was out burying his arms in a wood to which he had

Micheline Conter.
(Libre Résistance)

moved them after the shootings at the Carmignacs. His wife was held so that she could not warn him and he was arrested as soon as he returned. Next it was the turn of the Lehmann family who were neighbours of the Carmignacs and held some of the arms. They were arrested but nothing was found. The family had found time to collect the arms from their cellar and throw them into a pond near the courtyard where they are still believed to lie. While these raids took place, more arrests were made in Montargis. Altogether some twenty-three people were arrested and deported; only twelve returned, one of whom was Narcy, but he never came back to Montargis. The chief of the group, Jean Vessière, escaped but his son Jacques was caught and was one of those who died in the camps. Jean had an appointment with my father in Paris on 28 June but he did not find him or anyone to warn him about the arrests in Paris.[12]

The arrests in Meung-sur-Loire on the other side of Orléans started on 1 July. The Germans had no problem in knowing where to go here and went straight to the house of Maurice Lequeux where they arrested both him and his wife, and then went to Petit-Aunay where they arrested the chicken farmers, Edouard and Marguerite Flamencourt and their secretary, Jacqueline Durand. Both of the circuits' wireless operators had lodged with them as had Culioli. Lequeux and Flamencourt were taken to Paris and confronted with

Lucien CARMIGNAC
Chef du réseau « PROSPER » du Gâtinais
(assassiné par les Allemands le 8 juillet 1944).

Madame CARMIGNAC
à son retour de déportation.

Roger CARMIGNAC
à son retour de déportation.

Luce CARMIGNAC
Combattant F. F. I.
(Croix de guerre).

Norbert CARMIGNAC
Assassiné par les Allemands
le 8 juillet 1944.

La famille CARMIGNAC, de Chuelles
(Réseau « Prosper »).

The Carmignacs. (P. Guillaume)

Norman who told them that he had made an accord with the Germans and asked them to abide by it. The Germans returned to Petit-Aunay on 5 July with Lequeux and retrieved the wireless transmitter hidden in a chimney. Hearing of his arrest, the abbé Pasty moved his cache from his cellar to an abandoned well outside the presbytery. They then arrested Louis Rivière but he denied having any arms so he was confronted with Leqeux and, realising that he could no longer deny having a cache, he revealed the location but there was hardly anything in it. He had also moved most of his arms to a barn but the next day he was persuaded to reveal this as well. When the Germans arrived at the Bordier farm at Langlochère, they saw Robert Boqueho about to cycle away; he had come to the farm to warn the Bordiers. He was stopped and his papers found to be in order and he was about to continue on his way when Leqeux emerged from one of the vehicles and identified him as one of the team. Jean Bordier also initially denied having any arms but like Rivière realised that he had no option when Lequeux insisted that there was a depot at the farm. The same scenario was repeated at the home of André Raimbault and he was also persuaded to reveal the new hiding place of the arms held by the abbé Pasty, which he had helped the abbé to move, so the abbé was arrested later.

The four men were taken to the prison in Orléans where they met Lequeux again. He wanted to make sure that that they had given up all of the material that had been parachuted but he warned them to say nothing about their sabotage activities as this was a more serious offence than holding arms caches. When they discovered he was going to betray even more people, they threatened to harm his son. He did not give away the extra people he had mentioned to them but he did shortly afterwards give the Germans full details of the sabotage attacks and the names of those who had taken part. He also gave away the family of Paul Philbée and Georges Vappereau from Orléans, who had organised food and other equipment for the possible landings of troops and who had organised considerable funding for the circuit, as well as Alain and Marie de Robien, who had agreed to lodge English officers in their château nearby at Huisseau-sur-Mauves.[13] The abbé Pasty died soon afterwards in prison whilst his governess, Marie-Thérèse Billard, was deported together with Maurice Lequeux and his wife, Jean Bordier, André Raimbault, Louis Rivière, Edouard Flamencourt with his wife Marguerite and brother Jean, Robert Boqueho, Georges Vappereau and Paul Philbée with one of his sons Jean. Of the fifteen deported, six died.

In Falaise in Calvados the Germans also arrived on 1 July and again went straight to the house of the leader of the group. Jean-Michel Cauchy and his wife were arrested and the property searched. A German report claims, 'The description of the courtyard, the garage as well as all of the buildings were indicated exactly by Prosper.'[14] However, all they found were some English cigarettes and tobacco and a small box of sabotage material, which Cauchy claimed had been given to him by someone whose name he did not know in a café in Paris. Failing to find Pierre Bar, who was the liaison officer for the group with the leaders in Paris, they arrested his wife but she was released when they caught him later in the day. Realising that the cache had been moved and that Cauchy was not going to tell them where it was, despite some serious interrogation, the three arrested were taken to Paris for a confrontation with Norman. As a result the arms were found the next day and the rest of the group were rounded up, although the de la Rochefoucaulds had been arrested earlier and Pierre Bar saw Bernard when he was taken to Paris. An author claimed that the confrontation was with my father and that he gave away other members of the group[15] but Pierre Bar said he only saw Norman and was not aware at the time that my father had been arrested.[16]

From the amount of material found, the Germans realised that it was more than could have come from the single drop near Falaise in May. They record finding fifteen of one type of inner cylinder, which tallies with the drop near Falaise of five C-type containers each containing three cells. The contents included more than 20 machine guns, 100 hand grenades, 15 revolvers and 7,000 rounds of ammunition, 10kg of explosives, 10kg of plastic explosives and the same of fuses and primers. But they also found 19 cells of a different type dropped elsewhere and brought to Falaise in Cauchy's recently acquired lorry. Kieffer ordered the search to be extended throughout the Sarthe and in the area of Angers.

On 9 July they arrived in the village of Ancinnes just to the south-east of Alençon and went straight to the garage of Paul Lottin; he had unwisely taken some of the empty cylinders back to his workshop. André Malo heard the Germans pulling up outside the house where he lodged and quickly left by the back door, only to see two members of the Gestapo with Paul Lottin just the other side of a fence. One of the policemen, pointing a revolver at him, shouted at him to give himself up but he ran away across the fields under fire and escaped. When the Germans knocked at the door of Paul Drecq, his wife refused to let them in for long enough for him to escape and hide in the bell tower of the church with the help of the abbé Luçon.[17] They did, however, find the arms cache in the tunnel in the wood. (The thirty-one found here, including the three taken by Lottin, totalled thirty-one, which, with the nineteen found at Falaise, makes a total of fifty cells, which tallies with the

Pierre Bar. (Nicole Trupin)

drop of ten H-type containers, each holding five cells.)

Arthur de Montalembert was not there that day but when he returned and heard that the Germans had arrived with 'a civilian', he not unnaturally thought that it must have been Jean-Michel Cauchy from Falaise. He reported this to France Antelme who reported it when he returned to London. Through a local historian, I was put into contact with some of the descendants of the Falaise group, including the son and daughter of Cauchy and the daughter of Pierre Bar. They invited me to a reunion, which put me in a difficult position as at that time, I had only seen the report made by Antelme and did not know how to deal with people whose father I thought had betrayed the Ancinnes group. The reunion was put off for a year and in the interim another local historian sent me testimonies from the two men who had escaped the Germans at Ancinnes. They both said that the betrayer was a local garage owner, René Rolet, who was jealous of the more successful business of Paul Lottin and had earlier caused his arrest for distributing anti-German tracts. At the end of the war, Rolet was almost lynched by the villagers; he was tied to a post where he was sworn at and hit by every passer-by and would have been summarily killed if the abbé Luçon had not intervened. He was later tried and although the second betrayal was not proved, the villagers still believe it was him.

Happy that the situation had been resolved, I attended a reunion in 2008 at which a plaque was unveiled to commemorate the activities of the Falaise group. This was the first time that a local memorial in France had included the name of my father, which I found very moving. Of the Falaise group only three of the nine returned from Germany. Paul Lottin was deported and killed in a gas chamber. Arthur de Montalembert was arrested later and died in Mauthausen after being dowsed in cold water and left outside on a freezing night.[18]

On 11 July it was the turn of the Celier family at the château d'Eporce. Pierre had been contacted the day before by the Montalembert family who had heard about the raid on Ancinnes and wanted him to go there to warn Arthur, but he could not find him. A local gendarme in Eporce, Julien Collet, heard about the Germans arriving at the château and warned his chief, Moreau, who he knew was involved. Moreau asked him to visit Jacques Morand, the gamekeeper, and when he was told that the Germans were looking for arms, he warned a colleague, Leclercq, who had some of the arms hidden in a rabbit hutch, and he moved them. Collet then met an abbé who had tried to contact the Celiers to give him false papers for Drecq from Ancinnes who was due to collect them at 8 a.m. the next morning. This was the abbé Luçon from Ancinnes and together they managed to intercept Drecq and give him the papers the next morning before he reached the château. Collet was arrested a few days later but released as it was his chief, Moreau, who was being sought. Moreau was warned in time and escaped. The female members of the Celier family were arrested but soon released. Jean was not so lucky. According to his nephew, he was treated brutally, having his eyes gouged and his fingernails pulled out. He was about to be deported when he fell into a coma. He was

kept in various hospitals for the rest of the war but died in
September 1944.

When the du Mascureaus were warned about the events
at Eporce:

> With the help of my mother and sisters, I immediately got
> rid of the compromising objects left over from the parachute
> operations which had been brought into the château and hid
> that night in the forest of Charnie where I had a rendezvous
> the next day with my cousin Pierre de Montalembert
> (from Hauterive in the Mayenne) to study the possibility
> of parachute operations in the Torce en Charnie – St Denis
> d'Orques area. I was hidden for four months in a hut in the
> forest with the help of a guard, Meslier, then I succeeded
> in obtaining a new identity and under the name of Michel
> Martineau, I went to the Loire inférieure. Not finding me
> when they raided la Renaudiére, the Gestapo imprisoned my
> mother and my sisters, at first for several days in the prison
> in Le Mans, then in the Pre–Pigeon in Angers from where
> they were released after a month.[19]

Morand and three farmers were arrested and deported. The
cache of arms at la Renaudiére was found in the cellar of a
sheep shed, which the current owner, Antoine de Mascureau,
showed me; he thought that the location must have been a
local betrayal. He also told me that he has a recording in which
all the members of the family involved give their memories of
the events. He was hoping to persuade his son to transcribe
it. Another cache was found after a four-day search at a farm
called Feulon.

On 13 July the Germans arrived at l'Hermitière looking for
Guillaume and Aymard de Courson and one of their workers,
Jean Reiss. The brothers had heard about the arrest of their

cousins, the Celiers, and had left. Reiss was badly beaten but took an opportunity to jump out of a second floor window and escape into the woods despite being handcuffed. He was later killed whilst fighting with the maquis in the Nièvre. In the absence of Guillaume and Aymard, their mother, the Comtesse, was arrested and died in Bergen-Belsen. Maurice Duthilleul, who worked with France Antelme, was sent to collect the material from the June drop, which had been destined for Falaise and so was still only covered in branches where it fell.[20]

Octave Simon escaped the raids and reached England where he was trained as an SOE agent. Emile Garry also escaped but was considered experienced enough to be tasked, without further training, with establishing his own circuit called Phono with the help of de Montalembert and Duthilleul and with Noor Inayat Khan as their wireless operator. It was planned to install wireless transmitters for her in the tower of the de Montalembert property in Ancinnes known as Vaubezon and in the château de l'Hermitière. Duthilleul was arrested at the end of September and almost immediately took the Germans to l'Hermitière and showed them where the material from the first drop in May was hidden.[21]

Another raid on 1 July was on the farm le Roncey in the commune of Bazémont where the drops had taken place for the group at the National Agricultural College at Grignon. The police had Gilbert Norman with them and the arms were found, including forty boxes of dynamite, 14 tonnes of weapons, a radio and twenty parachutes. The farmer, Guillaume Abgrall, and his labourer, Jean Toulis, were arrested as well as the owner, M. Parent, but the latter was released in October. At 4.30 p.m. some sixty German-led police arrived at the college, which was closed down and surrounded whilst a search was made of all of the buildings

The sheep pen at château de Renaudiére where arms were hidden. (Author)

and the grounds, but nothing was found. The Director, Eugene Vandervynckt, described what happened next: 'These police told me that they were enquiring about arms parachuted at the College or nearby and hidden at the college and about some English people who were hidden at the College.'[22] Following this interrogation, at around 9 p.m., he was called into the courtyard where all the College workers had been assembled and, when he again denied knowing anything, the six oldest pupils and the ten labourers were taken by bus to a nearby wooded area and a simulated shooting took place, as had happened at Bois-Jérôme-Saint-Ouen. When they had all been put through this mock execution without anyone revealing anything of interest to the Germans, they announced that the enquiry was over.

At 3 a.m. the next morning, Professor Balachowsky was arrested at his home in Versailles and taken straight to the Avenue Foch. He denied everything until he was surprised to be confronted with Gilbert Norman, who had a beard and was generally unkempt but bore no marks of blows or torture:

> The chief asked me if I knew Gilbert. I replied that I had never seen him and that this was the first time. When Gilbert was asked the same question, he replied – Yes – and addressing me, he said – Serge, it is necessary to tell everything, they know everything in the most minute detail, it is useless to deny, this will only aggravate your case and even more that of others and will mean involving all of the little people of no importance who mostly remain at liberty.

In the ensuing interrogation, he realised that his interrogator really did know everything and that there was nothing that he could add.[23]

Two days later, the gardener at the college, Marius Maillard, and the son-in-law of the Director, Robert Douillet, were arrested. Maillard was brought back on 10 July and the radio that had been buried in the vegetable garden next to the greenhouse was unearthed but they could not find the eight parachutes that he had hidden in a barn. Vandervynckt was forced to admit that he had moved them; they were recovered and he was arrested. Vandervynckt, Douillet, Maillard and Abgrall all died in the camps; only Balachowsky survived.

Pierre Culioli, having been taken to the Avenue Foch late on 23 June, was only briefly interrogated about his identity before being sent to the prison of Fresnes in the same car as Maude Laurent, from whom he heard about the arrests of Norman and Borrel. His real interrogation did not begin until around 1 July when Karl Langer told him:

> We know everything. We have someone in your HQ in London. For several months now we have known

everything the organisation has been doing, through the wireless transmissions and the messages sent to London by Lysander.[24]

Langer made it clear that he already knew many details such as the address of the Bouton letterbox and the A and B messages warning of D-Day, and he had a Michelin map marked with the location of sixteen of his DZs. He said to Culioli:

Give us the arms and explosives and we will forget the rest. Those arrested as a result will be interned until the end of the war. This is an arrangement that we have made with Prosper. The depots at Gisors and Montargis are already collected. If this does not happen the villages around where we think the depots are will be burnt and the inhabitants killed.

Richard de Courson points to the window at the château de l'Hermitière from which Jean Reiss jumped. (Author)

When Culioli said he would first like to have a meeting with Prosper, Langer replied, 'We do not have time to lose. I will get Archambaud, to confirm this.' Langer returned a few minutes later with Archambaud who was in chains but appeared to be at ease. He said, 'It's true. They have known about everything for a long time, but they are being very nice and will not shoot anybody if they retrieve the material. Prosper has agreed that the depots be given.'

Langer left Culioli with pencil and paper and said he would return the next day. Culioli decided to reveal some of his depots. He did not feel obliged to follow Norman's order but he decided it was for the best. In the morning he gave Langer a report indicating the address of Couffrant of Romorantin who had about thirty containers; that of Gatignon at Noyers-sur-Cher who had some twenty; that of Cordellet at Vallières-les-Grandes who had some twenty-five; and that of Lemeur at Chambord who had fourteen, all of which represented about half of the total that he had actually received. He had written a letter to each of them in these terms:

> It is with great regret that I am obliged to involve you. We have underestimated our adversary, they have seen through most of our secrets, but they seem benevolent and have agreed not to condemn anyone to death if the material is given up to them. I would ask you therefore to show the Gestapo where your depots are with as few people as possible being put at risk. If your stocks are mined, take steps to ensure that no harm comes to the German troops.[25]

Before these letters were delivered, some precautions had been taken by those left at liberty in the Sologne. When André Brasseur heard of the arrests, he was worried because he had lent a bicycle with his name on it to one of those arrested with Roger Couffrant so he decided to leave the area. The daughter of the family who owned the château d'Herbault, which the Germans had taken over as their HQ on the night of 20/21 June, managed to warn the de Bernards at Nanteuil and they in turn got word to Marcel Buhler who was expecting a drop on the night of 22/23 June at a new DZ near Huisseau-en-Beauce to the north-west of Blois. The de Bernards also asked Georges Duchet to clear anything incriminating from Culioli's HQ at le Cercle as they remembered that they had lent Yvonne Rudellat a book with their name in it.

Albert Lemeur in Chambord decided that it would be wise to hide but after a few days he decided it was safe to return home, only to find the Germans arriving in force on 2 July. They presented him with the letter from Culioli but he refused to believe it was true and made a run for it. He was brought down by a bullet, which went through his neck and lodged in his mouth. The news spread fast and in neighbouring Bracieux, François Cortambert also decided to hide but, when the Germans arrived at his house in the afternoon, he returned and tried to play innocent. He and his wife were arrested together with Lemeur's family. Lemeur decided to reveal his depots to save the lives of his family and the Cortamberts. From the drops at Neuvy, he had some material buried but most was hidden in a nearby farm, des Haies, and the material from the drop at Chassenais was hidden under brushwood at the entrance to a nearby wood. However, most had subsequently been moved so little was found, but when the Germans agreed to release his family and the Cortamberts, he asked Cortambert to replace all the material that had been moved and the Germans later retrieved it all. Lemeur had also founded a group in Montdoubleau to the north-west of Blois under Auguste Cordelet and this group had moved arms from one of the drops at Chaumont-

Auguste Cordelet. (Blois museum)

sur-Loire to their own commune on 24 June, and this was also found on 2 July and Cordelet arrested.

On the same day the Germans appeared in Contres. Raymonde Nadau cycled to Noyers-sur-Cher to warn the Gatignons but arrived at the same time as another force of Germans led by Karl Langer. Langer knew exactly where the arms were hidden, which surprised André Gatignon as he thought he was the only one to know, but he felt he had no option but to cooperate. He did, however, manage to warn other members of his team and only he was arrested on this occasion. Meanwhile on the same day in Romorantin, the Germans arriving at Roger Couffrant's house found that he was being held in Blois following his arrest on 21 June. He was brought home and shown photos of the chiefs of the réseau and a map showing the location of all of the terrains de parachutage and depots of arms. When he still refused to cooperate, he was given Culioli's letter and threatened with a raid on Romorantin, which would have resulted in many more arrests. Only then did he agree to take them to his depots and he wrote to each of their guardians saying, 'Our activities have been divulged from above. The Germans know of all our depots in the region. I ask you to give up the material. This will pain you but it is the price for the lives of all of the Frenchmen who have been arrested.'[26] He also went with the Germans to ensure there were no problems. At the farm de la Guilloterie of Paul Sausset they found twelve machine guns and sixty hand grenades and more arms were found at a house in Veillens. At Châtres-sur-Cher 200kg were found in the electrical works and Prosper Legourd was arrested, and another 100kg were found in an electrical transformer station at Selles-sur-Cher but their keeper Pierre Chassagne managed to escape.

The Germans released Cordelet, Gatignon and Cortambert almost immediately but then re-arrested them two weeks later. In the meantime they also arrested René Bouton but did not search his home, so they did not find the 40kg of plastic explosive he was hiding or discover his involvement in some of the drops. They appeared to be only interested in his house being the letter box for messages from the chiefs in Paris and known only to them. Norman not only gave the Germans this address but also the password necessary to contact Bouton. His colleague from the drop on 20/21 June, Georges Duchet, managed to escape. At the end of the month the team that had been recruited for the new DZ at the farm Chassenais were rounded up – first the blacksmith, Maxime Bigot, and then the farmer, Armand Goleau – whilst Henri Caillard from the *mairie* in Neuvy and two others from that village were also picked up. On 29 July Culioli's brothers-in-law, Jean and Guy Dutems, who had helped at the Monkeypuzzle receptions on their father's land, were arrested; another betrayal by Norman according to Vogt. Neither the group at Boisgenceau outside Romorantin under Pierre Constant nor the team at Villeny were ever investigated.

In the middle of July Culioli thought that if he could persuade the Germans to take him to the Sologne, he might find a chance to escape. He told Langer that he had forgotten a depot of five containers near Chaumont-sur-Tharonne and drew a plan that was not correct. When the depot was not found, he was taken there to show them where the containers were hidden in a thicket. He was not, however, able to get away; indeed his leg was still so bad that he had to be carried to the hiding place. On the return journey, Langer became mellow after a good meal and revealed to Culioli some of what he already knew, such as:

- the addresses of Odile (Lise de Baisac) in Poitiers and Antoine (France Antelme) at Auteuil;
- the fact that Honore (Ben Cowburn) and his wireless operator, whom Culioli had received in April, were now operating around Troyes;
- the presence of Cinema (Henri Garry) in the Le Mans area;
- the existence of other F section agents such as David (Claude de Baissac), Ernest (Marcel Fox), Olive (Francis Basin) and Peter Churchill;
- the involvement of some of the people in other Prosper groups such as Guerne, Gouju, Balachowsky, Darling and Forcinal;
- the names of those responsible for Culioli's groups in Contres and Pontlevoy;
- the location of the safe house of Jean Charmaison where Pickersgill, Macalister and Raynaud had been lodged; and
- the sabotage operations Culiloi had carried out.[27]

In the middle of August, Marcel Buhler was arrested, followed on 9 September by the de Bernards. They were interrogated about the failed parachute operation in February north of Blois which Norman and Guerne attended but not Culioli as this was before he was involved with this group. The de Bernards' interrogator even knew what they had given Norman to eat – a meal of tripe. They were never asked about their later involvement with Culioli. Also in August the Germans arrived in Montrichard but the daughter of Georges Fermé saw them and her father managed to escape. The Germans took his wife, Henriette, instead and she survived deportation.

Occasional apparently random arrests continued for the rest of the year and well into 1944 so it is difficult to work out how many people from this group were arrested as a direct consequence of the collapse of the circuit, but it is certain that fifteen of those who were so arrested, and were deported, did not return. One of these was Yvonne Rudellat. Plans were made to rescue her from the hospital in Blois but the continuous arrests made this impossible. Some four months later she was transferred to Paris, and despite having been trepanned and told that she still had two bullets in her head, she was declared fit and sent to Fresnes prison. Her cellmates found that she was suffering from amnesia and could not even remember her own name, although she had vague memories of the chase in the car and a large town where she had lived and had a daughter. She struggled to find words but one day she used the English word 'window' and found she was able to express herself more clearly in English.[28] She was deported to Ravensbrück in August 1944 and then to Belsen in the closing weeks of the war. She was still alive when the camp was liberated but very ill and living under another name that was not on the SOE search list. She died a few days later.[29]

Notes

1. G. Harny testimony, 2012, e-mail.
2. 998 W 47190, Archives départementales, Beauvais.
3. 16P 364747, SHD.
4. HS 9/395/3, TNA.
5. C. Menard, *Les Cahiers de la Societe Historique et Geographique du Bassin d'Epte*, No 25, 1990.

6. Interview with Jean Argence 31.05.1945, HS 6/440, TNA.

7. See 3 above.

8. *La deportation dans le department de l'Eure*, Lynda Ligier, Université de Caen, 1996–1997.

9. P. Guillaume, *La Sologne au Temps de l'Héröisme et de la Trahaison*.

10. J.O. Fuller, *Déricourt: The Chequered Spy*, Michael Russel, 1989.

11. 16 P 530436, SHD archives, Paris.

12. P. Guillaume, *Au Temps de l'Héröisme et de la Trahaison*.

13. P. Guillaume, *L'abbé Emile Pasty*, Orléans, 1946.

14. Rapport Final Allemand, origin unclear but French translation published in *Les Nouvelles de Falaise*, 21 September 1961.

15. R. Ruffin, *La Résistance Normande Face à la Gestapo*, Press de la Cité, 1977.

16. Testimony sent to me by his daughter.

17. Souvenirs de M. André Malo, Malo family papers, 1994, Archives départmentales, Le Mans.

18. Testimony of fellow prisoner sent to me by de Montalembert's sister-in-law.

19. ADS/18 J 740, Archives Départementales, Le Mans.

20. *L'Hermitiere*, Cahiers Percherons, No. 75, 1983.

21. André Pioger, Les Circuits Satirist, Physician & Bricklayer dans la Sarthe, Gens de la Lune, Nos 180–183, 15.04.1978 & 15.07. 1978.

22. Letter 04.07.1943, Archives departmentales, Yvelines.

23. 72 AJ 39I, Archives Nationales.

24. Rapport 28.04.1945, HS 9/379/8, TNA.

25. HS 9/379/8, TNA.

26. 1375 W 70, Archives Départementales, Blois.

27. See 9 above.

28. N. Hany-Lefebvre, *Six Mois à Fresnes*, Edition Flammarion, 1946.

29. S. King, *Jacqueline*, Arms and Armour, 1989.

CONSEQUENCES

Back in Paris, the disappearance of my father, Norman and Borrel on 24 June was noticed almost immediately. When my father met Marc O'Neill at 9 a.m. that morning, they had agreed to meet again at 2.30 p.m. where they were to introduce their chief lieutenants to each other to formalise the affiliation of O'Neill's group into the Physician circuit. Even before that, Claude de Baissac had waited at a rendezvous at 10.30 a.m. that he thought he had arranged by leaving a note requesting it at Borrel's apartment the day before. As she decided to go with Norman to his apartment that night, she would not have seen that note. When my father did not appear at 10.30 a.m., de Baissac was concerned as my father had always previously been punctual, so he went again to Borrel's apartment at 11.30 a.m. where the concierge told him that she had not returned the previous day but that two policeman had just taken away all of her possessions; they had a key and knew exactly where her rooms were. De Baissac spent the rest of the day making sure he was not being followed and at 8 p.m. he again ran into O'Neill and, after hearing of his failed afternoon rendezvous, concluded that all three had been arrested. O'Neill told him that my father had mentioned, as they parted in the morning, that he was due to meet up with Norman and Borrel at the Gare Saint-Lazare. Norman had two other appointments that day: at the café Garnier near the Gare Saint-Lazare at 2 p.m. with Ben Bossard to receive a loan of 150,000 francs and with Jacques Weil and

Gaston Cohen at 3 p.m., after which he had arranged to go to Grignon for a couple of days to help Noor Inayat Khan with her transmissions.

The Gestapo missed the opportunity to do even more damage to the French Section since not only did they not know of my father's appointments on 24 June but also that he had arranged another for the next day with Michael Trotobas at 11.30 a.m. nor of his frequent meetings with Antelme who had gone to Poitiers early on 24 June. The latter only heard of the disappearances when he returned on the evening of 25 June and found Henri Garry and Noor Inayat Khan waiting at his rooms to tell him. Inayat Khan had been waiting for Norman at Grignon as arranged when Serge Balachowsky told her that he had just been informed that my father, Borrel and fifteen others had been arrested but that Norman had escaped. They buried her wireless set in the vegetable garden and she returned to Paris to warn Garry. Antelme decided to move in with his friends Raymond Andrès and Germaine Aigran, and Inayat Khan moved into a separate flat that Andrès maintained in the same building in Square Malesherbes, 16éme. He also went to Borrel's apartment and was told the same as de Baissac; Jacques Weil claimed that he sent someone there too. Antelme then went to the apartment where Norman had lodged and broke in. Norman's room was tidy with only a tie left in the wardrobe, but his bicycle was there, indicating that he had returned the previous night after he and Borrel had dined with Armel Guerne; Antelme knew from Guerne that Norman had left on his bicycle and Borrel by the metro. The Laurents' room was, however, in great disorder, suggesting to Antelme that they had made a hurried departure.

On 27 June Antelme met Peregrine, Guerne's wife, by chance at Chez Tutulle. This was a black market restaurant run by the Tourets and used as a meeting place by all members of the circuit and their associates. She had come to warn the Tourets and to ask them to warn one of the other regular customers, Charles Grover-Williams. In the afternoon he also met Guerne himself there, who told him that he and his wife had also moved and were now staying with the Bussoz family in the Square Clignancourt. Antelme was disturbed to be told that Peregrine kept returning to their apartment to hear news from the concierge and his foreboding was confirmed on the morning of 1 July when, despite having already removed all potentially incriminating documents, she decided to go into their flat and found it occupied by the police. She was tied up whilst they searched her bag and found Antelme's ration card. Alain Bussoz had kept watch outside and after a time he thought it would be safe to go up to the flat and opened the door. He immediately turned and ran back down the stairs hotly pursued, only to be stopped by a French policeman a few streets away. However, this gave Peregrine time to cut herself loose, tear out and eat one page of Antelme's ration book and escape before her capturers returned with Bussoz. She went again to Chez Tutulle to warn Jean Worms who was another regular there and to get a message to Antelme that the Germans had his old address from the food card found in her bag. She found Worms with two of his men and soon afterwards her husband joined them. They were all arrested as they left, just as Jacques Weil was walking down the street to join them, and he escaped. Antelme, who had left earlier, and Weil were lucky; the continued use of this venue after the arrests of 24 June broke the most basic rules of security. As a result of this carelessness, two days later Worms' group in Thibié were arrested and between 8 and 20 July those in the area of Vitry-le-François and Chatelraould were rounded up.

Soon afterwards Antelme heard that the Germans had visited his apartment so he and Inayat Khan moved again at the beginning of July. They went to stay with Maurice Benoîst on his family estate near Rambouillet to the south-west of Paris. This was the base for Charles Grover-Williams' Chestnut sabotage circuit and the material from his parachute drops between April and June had been stored there. Antelme realised that it was time to leave France again and he and his friend William Savy, who was also being pursued as his address was one of those found in Borrel's papers, were picked up by a Déricourt operation on the night of 19/20 July. Inayat Khan moved back to the apartment in the Square Malesherbes. Her wireless set had been sent to Le Mans in readiness for Garry to take over the Prosper groups in the Sarthe and the Orne, so she borrowed one from Dowlen, the Chestnut radio operator.

At the last minute and with no prior warning, Déricourt joined Antelme on the flight to England, returned two nights later and received Nicolas Bodington and Jack Agazarian the following night. Bodington, with Agazarian as his wireless operator, had been sent in 'To investigate the position of the Physician circuit following the arrest of its leaders' – Operation Gamekeeper.[1] This had been arranged through Norman's radio as London thought at this time that he was still free but in hiding. On 15 July he was asked for 'a completely safe contact as we hoped to send a London representative already known to him whose arrival would be announced by a BBC message'.[2] Norman replied the same day, giving a contact address and saying that he supposed the London representative would be Agazarian. He also warned that all Prosper post boxes and safe houses should be considered to be blown. This meant that once in France there was only one way they could contact Norman and that was a way dictated by Norman's radio. Déricourt had clearly been told to expect and look after this representative over the radio of either Inayat Khan or Dowlen and he may also have been told that Bodington was coming as well. It seems to me that the reason for his sudden visit to London was his concern about keeping his visitor(s) safe. He would not have wanted everyone in London to know about his contacts with the Gestapo and I suspect that he must have managed to contact Bodington during this visit and make a plan. A special flight had to be hurriedly arranged outside the moon-period to drop Déricourt back into France in time to meet his visitors.

They had been told to contact a Mme Gasiorowski but not before 26 July. Agazarian went there and was given a note, which he recognised was written by Norman, asking for a meeting the next day at the café Garnier near the Gare Saint-Lazare. They thought this was very suspicious as this café was one of the regular meeting places of the Prosper organisation and should therefore be considered to be completely blown. However, the note made provision for an alternative rendezvous at the apartment of a Mme Filipowski, so they phoned her around 6.30 p.m. that evening and Agazarian went there half an hour later as they thought a trap could not be set for them that quickly. They were wrong and Agazarian did not return. After the war, Bodington claimed

that they had tossed a coin to decide who should go to the rendezvous but Jean Besnard, with whom they were staying, stated that he remembered quite clearly that Bodington had ordered Agazarian to go.

Bodington had now lost his wireless operator and, rather

Nicolas Bodington. (SFC)

surprisingly, decided to try to contact Norman through a couple of letterboxes despite the warning he had received but they were no longer operational. However, he was in contact with Inayat Khan and through her he met Garry and Arthur de Montalembert, who were able to give him a good idea of the scale of the arrests. Apart from Garry's new circuit, the only possibility that Bodington could see for further activity was to send Pickersgill and Macalister, whom he thought were still free, to Hirson rather than the Ardennes, which he thought was lost. This was despite the fact, which he does not mention in his report, that he also met Robert Gieules, who had been asked by Antelme to look for contacts in the east-north-east of France, preferably the Ardennes, and to help the agents who had been sent to organise this sector.[3] Gieules had been given the name of M. Desprez, the director of a foundry in Hirson, and he gave Bodington a password to enable contact to be made. London had received the first message from Macalister's set just before Bodington left London. The message said that Macalister had seen Norman and had received a radio from him. Bodington concluded his report on his visit to France: 'It seems to me difficult to believe that Butcher (Norman) is not probably under extreme duress and even under the influence of drugs being used as a tool by the Gestapo.' He recommended that Norman be ordered to return to England via Spain, which would either end any game or give him the chance to explain.

Bodington claims that he also discovered, without saying how, that:

the sinking of the Prosper organisation had been the priority A task of the Paris Gestapo for five weeks preceding Prosper's arrest and there is no doubt that considerable infiltration had been made in various quarters. The arrests in widely different places occurred in the space of about five days and there is every reason to believe that they were the result of action, planned and admirably carried out by the Gestapo.

He then adds:

Without in any way wishing to criticise unduly a man such as Prosper who worked wholeheartedly for our cause, I cannot help placing on record my despair when I realised the lack of security which he showed towards the end in connection with the meetings he had to carry out with members of his organisation. These meetings were often made with five or six people at a time and apparently very little effort made to disguise the nature of the conversation. Prosper himself was far too active and should never have participated in some of the actions necessary for the running of his groups. He also allowed far too great a contact to exist between his different circuits. I am sure that this was due to his anxiety that his organisation should develop as quickly and as profitably as possible, but the result could only be and was – disaster.

He does not support this sweeping statement with any evidence and goes on to make another amazing, and totally erroneous, statement:

Incidentally, Prosper played far too freely with the communist element, laying himself open to another form of double-crossing. After his disappearance, and I consider Prosper is now probably dead, the communists calmly seized all of the arms deposited in the Oise department. No doubt good use will be made of these arms, but it does show that the communists were perfectly aware of where the hiding places were situated – information which they should never have had.[4]

As has already been noted, large quantities of arms had been given to the communists in June; they did not, however, seize any after the arrests as there was little left after the German raids.

Bodington was also contacted by Henri Frager who had heard about Bodington's visit from Hugo Bleicher, the Abwehr agent who had caught Peter Churchill. Frager wrote a note to Bodington on 3 August telling him that he had been approached by this apparently friendly German who told him:

- That the Gestapo and his branch of the Service were at daggers drawn but that, in the course of his duties as an Intelligence Officer, he acquired knowledge of the Gestapo's counter-espionage activities;
- That the Gestapo knew that Major Bodington had recently arrived but that although they could arrest him, they were holding their hand for fear of losing thereby a first class source of information;
- That a number of our transmitters were in the hands of the Gestapo and were working for them;
- That the chief source of the Gestapo's information was the agent in charge of receptions – (Gilbert);
- That the contents of Frager's June courier were known to the Gestapo;
- That Archambaud was a traitor but that the Gestapo had been working to make HQ believe that he was still at liberty and intact.[5]

Frager met Bodington the next day and Bodington dismissed his accusations. After the war Bleicher told MI5 that it was

Kieffer of the Gestapo who had told him of Bodington's visit in the hope that he would find out where he was staying and confirmed that Kieffer told him it was Déricourt who had told him about the visit.[6]

Despite all these accusations, Bodington was still in denial about the role of Déricourt, writing on his return to London, 'I can say here and now that Gilbert's organisation, which consists of three people, has not the slightest possibility of being infiltrated and that the Germans obviously do not know the real identity of Gilbert.' He goes even further on the copying of Frager's report, writing, 'If this story is true, I do not know how it is possible for the Gestapo to have had a copy of the report ... handed directly to Gilbert in the presence of Claire who never let it go until he handed it over at the take-off of the bomber.'

Although he was in contact with Inayat Khan, she was not able to make contact with London so he turned to Dowlen, but he was arrested before he could send any of Bodington's messages. On 31 July German direction finders pinpointed Dowlen's position and caught him at his set.

Grover-Williams was caught two days later as was Robert Benoîst but the latter made a dramatic escape from the vehicle taking him to the Avenue Foch. Bodington then tried to send messages through Dubois in Tours but local police activity thwarted this. These problems seem surprising as, at the same time,

Henri Frager. (SFC)

Déricourt seems to have had no problems in arranging two operations through Inayat Khan's set for the second half of August. The first on 16/17 August picked up Bodington and Claude and Lise de Baissac who were leaving France as a consequence of the collapse of the Prosper organisation. The second on 19/20 August picked up Robert Benoîst and two refugees from the Physician arrests, Octave Simon from the Sarthe and de Ganay from the Grignon group. The latter were both trained as agents and returned to France in 1944.

Roger Landes, de Baissac's wireless operator, was now left in charge of the Bordeaux area and he told me that de Baissac had been wise to leave when he did because Landes, who had met Norman, saw him or his double in Bordeaux in August or September. Norman failed to recognise him and Landes warned all of his friends to beware, and one of them soon afterwards reported having seen Norman in a car with Germans.[7]

London was informed very quickly of the arrests of 24 June. A message was received through Gaston Cohen on 25 June, 'Be worried about Prosper, Gilbert and Denise' ('*Sois inquiet sur Prosper, Gilbert et Denise*').[8] On 2 July a message through Landes stated, 'Prosper, Butcher and Monique had disappeared since 24 June. Suzanne and Adolphe appeared to have fallen into a trap, and had been surrounded or killed.' Later messages were received from Noor Inayat Khan, Dowlen, Barrett and Dubois. Whilst it was soon accepted that my father and Borrel had been arrested, the situation of Norman was unclear. Antelme believed that he had escaped and had probably gone to Meung-sur-Loire where he had a radio. The Germans had clearly not, despite what Bodington claimed he was told, been expecting to make these arrests. If they had known that they were about to capture not one but two wireless operators, they would not have allowed their radio game expert, Goetz, to go home to Germany to visit his wife on 19 June. He was hastily recalled

Hugo Bleicher.

and returned to Paris on 29 June to discover that one of his colleagues had already sent London three messages, which had been found uncoded on Norman when he was arrested. This had given Norman the opportunity to warn London that he was no longer free by coding the messages but leaving out a security check. The Germans did not realise what he had done but it was noted immediately by the coding experts in London as Norman had never been known to make such a mistake. Before his past messages could be re-checked to be sure, Maurice Buckmaster decided to send a message to Norman to inform him that he had forgotten to insert his security check, and accused him of committing 'a serious breach of security which must not, repeat must not be allowed to happen again'.[9] This reply was received in Paris after Goetz had returned and taken control. According to Goetz, Norman felt that as his attempts to warn London had been ignored, he now believed that he was free of all responsibility and he agreed to correct and code messages but not transmit them, which did not worry Goetz as he had a technician who could copy Norman's style of transmitting.[10] London was reassured since the following messages, although showing some initial hesitation, contained the correct security checks.

Goetz was delighted when shortly afterwards a message was received from London that two men were coming to see Norman. A contact address was sent and this was kept under constant surveillance, which was how Agazarian had been arrested. Goetz claimed that it was Agazarian who told them that he had come to France with Bodington and, although Goetz did not know whether they had parachuted or been brought in by Déricourt, he stated, 'In any case, it is quite possible that Déricourt has confirmed the arrival of these two agents.' He also stated that he had been hoping to order parachute drops through Norman's set but that after the arrest of Agazarian, London cut the contact.

Antelme had returned to London on 20 July just before Bodington left for France and it is likely that they met, which would have given Bodington a foretaste of the uncertainty and suspicion he would meet in France. Antelme's first comment about the possibility of Norman transmitting for the Germans was that he was 'sure Norman would rather have shot himself than talk or transmit under duress'.[11] By the beginning of August, after many debriefings with Antelme, London was no longer sure that Norman was transmitting freely, if at all. Antelme could not understand why Norman had made no attempt to contact Déricourt or even mentioned him in his messages. Nor had he mentioned the arrests of Pierre Culiloi and Yvonne Rudellat, simply reporting that he had no trace of them. On 7 August Buckmaster wrote on a memo, 'I am coming to the conclusion that Butcher is a gonner. For working purposes, we must assume Butcher to be in enemy hands and take all consequential steps, such as cancelling messages we know him to have had.'[12]

The group that started as part of the Physician organisation around Nantes and my father's groups in Muno in the Ardennes and Origny-en-Thiérache were not affected by the first wave of arrests. There was, however, a raid on the latter on 6 July. As Geelen had lost contact with the organisation, he sent two of his men to contact Guerne in Paris. Guerne does not seem to have given a cut-out address so the men went straight to his apartment, where they were arrested as it was still under surveillance. The Germans raided their houses in Origny-en-Thiérache but found nothing as two wireless sets and other compromising material had been well hidden. Geelen and Marly were arrested by a patrol but managed to escape.

Armel Guerne was involved with all three of these groups but was not asked about them for some time. At his first interrogation he was immediately confronted with Norman, 'who explained that the Gestapo knew everything about the Prosper organisation since his own and Prosper's arrival in Paris about December 1942 but had allowed it to run on without hindrance'.[13] Norman then told him that he had agreed to a proposal made by the Commandant of the Paris Gestapo that if he and Guerne surrendered all the arms depots, the Germans would spare the lives of all members of the group except its chiefs and would stop their files reaching a military court. Guerne emphasised that the German proposals were put forward by Norman as an agreement already accepted by Norman, who had accepted it in order to save the lives of his subordinates. Guerne said that he was also shown a large volume containing photostat copies of all the messages sent to London by amongst others Prosper and Norman and even a copy of a personal letter from Prosper to his wife. In view of the evidence held by the Germans, Guerne decided to adopt a similar attitude to that already adopted by Norman, although he was not at that time asked to indicate the location of any depots.[14]

He was only asked about the Nantes organisation in the first week of August, just after his brother-in-law, Charles Berruet, was arrested there on 29 July, but Guerne only confirmed what Berruet had already told his interrogators. Guerne claimed at his British interrogation that it was not until September that he was approached about the depot in Origny-en-Thiérache. He said that the Germans knew the depot was somewhere in the mill and asked him to write a note to the director, Elisée Manesse, requesting him to surrender the arms. He said that he did this in accordance with Norman's agreement but he denied revealing the exact location. This timing is contradicted by Pierre Geelen who had made plans to save the material by handing it over to a resistance group from Charleville. Some of their men had visited the mill on 20 August and had only just left when the Germans arrived to arrest Manesse. They demanded a screwdriver and went straight to the hiding place and opened the cases of arms. The miller, Emile Plancoulaine, and his son Claude were also arrested a few days later. All

Armel Guerne. (©Les Amis d'Armel Guerne *asbl*)

three were deported and only Emile returned.

Also on 20 August, Georges Lefèvre at Carignan was approached by two men claiming to have just been released from Fresnes, where they said Armel Guerne had asked them to contact Geelen and Marly and let them know whether the arms dropped in this area were still safely hidden. Lefèvre was suspicious and so denied any knowledge. He was right to do so as he later learnt that the car the men were travelling in showed German papers when it drove into Belgium. On 1 September, two cars arrived at Lefèvre's hotel and one of the men introduced himself as 'Gaspard' and presented Lefèvre with half of a 10 franc note. Lefèvre had never met Guerne but he did possess the other half of this note. However, when he was given it, he had been told that the other half would be presented by 'François' who was expected to come and give them sabotage instruction. Lefèvre therefore again denied all knowledge, despite further pleas from Guerne to cooperate, so he was taken to a nearby wood, suspended from a tree with his hands manacled behind his back and beaten until he lost consciousness. He still refused to talk. Guerne decided that if he could not find the location of the arms from Lefèvre, he would have to try and find Geelen. He therefore took the Germans accompanying him and Lefèvre to Muno, where he knew that the mayor had been in contact with Geelen, but the mayor was warned and disappeared. The Germans arrested his nephew Marcel Godfrin and one of the reception team, Gaston Biazot, and they and Lefèvre were imprisoned for the night. The next morning Lefèvre decided to take the Germans to the DZ where he had helped at the reception in May, as he knew that the arms from that drop had been taken away. What he did not know was that there had been a further drop on 21/22 June and that the material from this drop had not yet been moved from its temporary hiding place in a ditch on the edge of the DZ. The Germans were delighted but knew that this was only part of the material that had been parachuted. The material from the earlier drop had been taken to a local resistance group in Banel, on the French side of the frontier between Carignan and Muno, and the Germans found this soon afterwards. According to Guerne, this was the last of eighty-seven depots on the Germans' list.

The three men all survived deportation and made accusations against Guerne. Gaston Biazot and the other two had met Guerne again in Compiègne at the end of November 1943 and they were astonished when Guerne told them, 'The Germans did not know about the parachute operations in the Ardennes; if I told them about these, it was to demonstrate to the Germans that I acted loyally and in that way saved people's lives.'[15] This contradicts what he told his British interrogator, which was that the Germans asked him to help them find these depots, implying that they already knew about them, and he reaffirmed this in a statement that the Germans knew about these depots 'without my telling them'. Norman would certainly have known about them as he would have requested the drops that supplied them, but Guerne said in another statement that Norman did not tell the Germans of the depots for which he knew Guerne was responsible.[16] Guerne would not have been aware that the

Georges Lefèvre. (Libre Résistance)

Germans would have known the location of all of the depots used in May and June when they were able to decode Norman's back messages.

Having removed the SOE resistance groups in Origny and the Ardennes, the Germans were ready to try and set up a controlled Archdeacon circuit using the identities of Pickersgill and Macalister. They were replaced by Josef Placke and Karl-Horst Holdorf, the latter speaking fluent English with an American accent. Through a German who had copied Macalister's fist and using the coding information he had on him when he was arrested, they established wireless contact with London and were sent the contact arrangements and password to meet M. Desprez in Hirson. However, when they went to Hirson at the end of

August, they made two mistakes; they went to M. Desprez's house rather than his office as had been arranged and they were rather ostentatiously driving a Paris registered car. M. Desprez did not respond to the password. When they reported this failure

Joseph-Marcel Godfrin.
(Libre Résistance)

Gaston Biazot. (Libre
Résistance)

to London, Inayat Khan was
sent a message on 15 September
asking for another meeting to
be arranged with M. Desprez.
Gieules arranged this for 25
September but in Paris in his
presence rather than Hirson. At
this meeting he was told that a
British officer, Jacques, had just arrived and asked if he wanted
to meet him. It so happened that the previous day, Maurice
Duthilleul had asked him if he had any news of a 'traveller'
who was due to arrive, so he thought it would be safe to
meet him. He and Duthilleul went to this further meeting on
29 September but it was a trap and they were arrested. The
Germans had in fact caught a new agent, François Michel, who
had dropped on 21/22 September to be the sabotage instructor
in the Archdeacon circuit and went to a contact address
arranged over the German controlled radio. The Germans
tried to persuade Gieules to help them trap Inayat Khan but
he succeeded instead in warning her of the trap.

The Garrys moved back to Paris from Le Mans at the end
of August. He had found a DZ at the farm Chambrin, north
of Luché-Pringe, and through Inayat Khan he arranged a
drop of fifteen containers, Operation Phono 1, on the night
of 15/16 September, although one drifted away and was
handed in to the police. This drop was received by Arthur de
Montalembert and Maurice Duthilleul with a local team. The
BBC message was '*Une mansarde à Paris, une chaumière en
Touraine*' (An attic in Paris, a cottage in Touraine).

Notes

1. General report undated, HS 9/171/1, TNA.
2. Memo 22.03.1945, HS 6/439, TNA.
3. Rapport undated, HS/9/581/4, TNA.
4. See 1 above.
5. HS 9/531/1, TNA.
6. S. Helm, *A Life in Secrets*, Little Brown, 2005.
7. Interrogation 24.01.1944, HS 6/436, TNA.
8. KV 2/1131, TNA.
9. L. Marks, *Between Silk and Cyanide*, HarperCollins, 1998.
10. Z 6 NL 17339, Archives Nationales.
11. Memo 05.08.1943, HS 9/42, TNA.
12. See 11 above.
13. First Interrogation 14-20.05.1944, HS 9/631/5, TNA.
14. HS/9/631/5, TNA.
15. A. Biazot & P. Lecler, *Face à la Gestapo*, Euromedia, 2011.
16. Z 6 NL 17339, Archives Nationales.

THEORIES AND LIES

Much of the information that I have recorded so far has only recently come to light, in particular the unfortunate series of accidental events and security failures that resulted in the arrests of 24 June 1943. Immediately after the war, the reasons for the collapse of my father's organisation, and the speed with which it occurred, seemed to be an impenetrable mystery and, as so often happens in the absence of the truth, conspiracy theories developed. These revolved around the suggestion that my father's arrest and the collapse of his organisation were part of the deception plans that were developed by the Allies to confuse the Germans as to the real intentions of the Allies in 1943.

This deception plan was code-named Operation Cockade and had three parts:

- Operation Starkey involved heavy bombing of the Boulogne area in early September followed by an amphibious feint towards that coast with the intention of keeping German forces in that area and drawing out and destroying the Luftwaffe;
- Operation Wadham was directed towards the Brest area later in September; and
- Operation Tindall was directed towards Norway.

The plan failed; the Luftwaffe stayed grounded and ten divisions were withdrawn from the threatened areas in France.

The first details of such deception plans became known in 1950 when General Sir Frederick Morgan published *Overture to Overlord*.[1] He referred to a plan for:

> an elaborate scheme of diversionary operations to extend over the whole summer of 1943 for the purpose of pinning down the enemy in the West so that he might not reinforce at will his active fronts against the Russians in the East and against the Forces of the Western Allies in Italy.

He stresses that nothing planned for this operation should be detrimental to plans for the full-scale assault in 1944.

Morgan discusses the problem of what to tell the resistance groups:

> In their own interests they could not be told too much. The tension was by now so great in the Maquis that the smallest of sparks would have sufficed to cause the most violent of explosions. And it is not necessary to expand upon the ghastly effect that would have attended a premature uprising. All we could do was drum into these sorely-tried people the absolutely vital necessity, come hell or high water, of waiting for the word from London. Whatever they saw, whatever they heard, whatever they felt, there was only one word to be obeyed and that word would come from one place.

In the 1950s, Maurice Buckmaster published two books that seem to contradict each other on this issue. In the first, *Specially Employed*,[2] he wrote:

As early as April 1943 the rumour ran like wildfire that the Allies were about to land in France. The patriotic upsurge of enthusiasm was dangerous. It had to be quelled ... We decided that we must bring Prosper back to London ... The fires of enthusiasm would have to be damped down. Only a first class man like Prosper could convey that message successfully.

In *They Fought Alone*,[3] he wrote, 'In the middle of 1943 we had a top secret message telling us that D-Day might be closer than we thought ... and we of course acted upon it without question.'

The idea of a betrayal was first suggested in a book by Barry Wynne. The story is set in Holland where the Germans had successfully taken over SOE's activities between mid-1942 and mid-1943. Against this background of uncertainty in the Dutch resistance in 1944, two agents are brought to London and deliberately briefed with false information, i.e. that the invasion would be through Holland. The team briefing them included a German agent who did not realise that she was being used and so passed on the details of the agents to Germany. When they were returned to Holland they were soon arrested and the details of the invasion plan extracted from them. Although the author claimed that it was based on a true story, it should be noted that the German control of the Dutch resistance had effectively ceased by the end of 1943.[4]

In 1958 J.O. Fuller reported a conversation with Déricourt in which he suggested that London knew the Prosper organisation had been compromised and penetrated right from the start. A decision was therefore taken, at a level above Colonel Buckmaster, to let it continue for as long as it could to keep the German counter-espionage teams occupied and thus distracted from another British organisation in France, 'which had been launched upon a different and more serious basis'. No evidence is given for this assertion but I assume this refers to the intelligence gathering networks and that those purportedly taking these decisions were therefore in the Secret Intelligence Service.[5]

The following year, Charles Wighton published the (somewhat exaggerated) story of Jacques Weil, who became the locally recruited second-in-command in the Juggler circuit led by Jean Worms, which started as a sub-circuit of Physician. The book claims that, as mid-summer 1943 approached, those in France, including Weil and my father, 'became quite certain – from hints literally "dropped" from London – that the Second Front was but a few weeks distant' but this is not explained. Later in the book, the author suggests that the Prosper organisation was betrayed by a triple agent as part of an Allied deception plan. Déricourt is not named but is clearly meant. Again no explanation or evidence is provided either as to the betrayal or how the betrayal was orchestrated.[6]

The only suggestion that I have found for an attempt at deliberate betrayal was that the explosion of the containers on 10/11 June was a unique event and so must have been designed to alert the Germans. It was not a unique event; there were at least six occasions in various parts of France when containers exploded.[7] As it happened, these explosions did contribute to the chain of events that resulted in the arrest of Culioli, which ultimately led to the arrest of my father, but that chain of events would have been impossible to predict.

Morgan's book is referred to by Wighton but he ends by saying, 'What is certain is that any sacrifice made by the Resistance as a result of London deliberately feeding false information to the Germans in Paris in the middle of 1943, almost certainly saved many thousands of British and American lives.' Such an idea is clearly contrary to what

Morgan wrote as the loss of such a large part of the resistance was clearly detrimental to the plans for 1944.

Wighton's suggestions were elaborated upon by Gilles Perrault. He met Weil who suggested to him that captured agents were presented with so much information about SOE by the Germans that this information must have come from London. Weil would not have been aware how much information about the structure and training methods of SOE had been obtained through the German control of SOE in Holland. Perrault on the other hand talks about the book by Barry Wynne and yet fails to make the connection to this source of much of the German knowledge. How much the Germans knew about SOE at the time of the arrest of my father is dealt with in a later chapter.[8]

In 1966, the official history appeared – *SOE in France* by M.R.D. Foot, a professor of History at Manchester University. Foot discusses various stories surrounding the collapse of the Prosper organisation, including its deliberate betrayal by the British. He poses one question that is key to understanding whether any such strategy is plausible or not – 'What object useful to British strategy could have been served by it?' The only such purpose suggested at that time was that it was part of a deception plan to draw German attention away from the invasion of Sicily. Foot dismisses any SOE contribution to such a strategy as being totally out of character and too open to chance compared with all other parts of the deception plan.[9]

Foot also deals with the question of whether my father was sent back to France in May 1943 still believing that the invasion was imminent or having been told that it had been put off to 1944. He quotes from Buckmaster's second book that suggests that the invasion was imminent, although his first book is not so clear. He also quotes from an interrogation of the Juggler circuit's radio operator, Gaston Cohen, on 11 October 1943, which says that my father was sent back to Paris 'with an alert signal, warning the whole circuit to stand by'. Although Foot then suggests that this may have arisen from a misunderstanding, he ends by saying, 'Suttill returned to clandestine duty in the belief that an invasion was probably imminent.'

In 1966, E.H. Cookridge suggested that the arrest of Prosper resulted from information discovered by the Germans in May 1943 when the two German agents from Holland contacted members of the Prosper organisation in error, but he gives no evidence to justify this claim and I have not found any.[10]

The COSSAC file 'COCKADE': Cover Plan, was opened to the public in 1973 at the Public Record Office (now The National Archives).[11] These papers confirm what Morgan had written, making it quite clear that any increased activity by resistance groups or the loss of such groups would be counter-productive to the deception strategy. This is spelt out in the Joint Planning Staff Report to the War Cabinet dated 16 June 1943 and elaborated in a PWE/SOE report dated 8 July and approved by the Chiefs of Staffs Committee on 22 July 1943. It was only after this date (a month after the arrest of my father) that Buckmaster, and the other SOE country chiefs, were told that the invasion had been put off to 1944.

Up to this year, writers had relied on the fact that the relevant documents had not been released. Now that they were available, it might be expected that the conspiracy theorists would retreat but they did not; they either distorted what was in these documents or ignored them and in some cases went on claiming that no documents had been released.

Following the release of the COSSAC papers in the USA, Anthony Cave Brown claimed that, as part of the Cockade deception plan, certain agents, including Prosper, were deliberately not told that the September action was only a rehearsal so that they would act as though it were a real invasion. He says that the deception planners thought that this would add to the 'full flavour of authenticity'. He states that Cockade also involved the resistance in France being stirred into activity and says that it was this, together with their lack of security, that led to the arrests. I can find nothing in the Cockade papers to support any of these statements. These papers make no mention of any role for SOE agents and they specifically rule out any undue activity by resistance groups.[12]

In 1977 John Vader published a book based around the activities of the French poet, Armel Guerne, who worked with my father. This book considers three ideas. First, the Western Allies deliberately disrupted French resistance to convince the Russians that a full invasion had to be postponed to 1944. The problem with this theory is that this postponement had already been agreed at Casablanca by Churchill, Roosevelt and Stalin in January 1943. So the Russians were well aware of the real reasons for the postponement and the sacrifice of part of the resistance for this purpose would therefore have been of no benefit. Second, the destruction of SOE networks and de Gaulle's political movement would have strengthened the communists and the Western Allies would have made slower progress in any invasion allowing the Russians to move further in from the east. Such an action would have been a year too early. Third, he suggests that by 1943, resistance circuits were so badly penetrated and insecure that they were allowed to disintegrate to keep the Germans occupied while other more secure circuits were developed, but he presents no evidence for this.[13]

Then in 1983 the conspiracy theorists were presented with a gift, and from an unexpected quarter; Colonel Buckmaster announced in a BBC interview that when he wrote in 1953 that, 'We had decided Prosper must be brought back to London', it was a decision of Winston Churchill who wanted to meet him. Buckmaster claimed that my father was closeted with Churchill and the Cabinet Office for a long time as Churchill explained that Stalin was bullying him into making more trouble in France. He claimed that Churchill then asked, 'Are you prepared to risk your life in these circumstances? I want you to make as much disruption as possible. Ignore the security rules, stir things up.' And that my father replied, 'Yes, sir.'

This suggestion of an agent meeting Churchill was picked up immediately by a novelist, Larry Collins who takes the deliberate sacrifice theory one stage further by suggesting that MI6, thinking that the Prosper organisation was penetrated, betrayed them to the Germans to ensure that false information about the invasion was revealed to the Germans under interrogation. He wove a meeting between my father and Churchill into this theory.[14]

This suggestion was taken even further when the BBC aired a Timewatch programme – *All the King's Men* – on 1 May 1986. The programme's producer, Robert Marshall, followed this with a book of the same title, which included information that he had not been able to fit in the television programme. The cover described the contents as, 'The astonishing wartime story of how MI6 treachery led to the loss of over 400 British and French agents' and under the first page title 'The Truth Behind SOE's Greatest Wartime Disaster'.[15]

The basic thesis of this book was yet again that the largest F Section network in northern France in the middle of 1943, my father's Prosper circuit, had been deliberately betrayed to the Germans as part of a deception plan designed to convince the Germans that a large-scale Allied invasion was imminent. But Marshall went further and claimed that my father had been recalled to London in May 1943 to be briefed by Churchill himself to expect the invasion to take place in September 1943. He also repeated the claim he had made in the television programme that, although the betrayal of the Prosper network was dressed up as part of a deception plan, the real reason was simply vindictiveness on the part of the Vice Chief of MI6, Claude Dansey.

I saw the Timewatch programme some 15 years before I started my own research. It affected me deeply as it was very convincing, despite Michael Foot describing it as 'imaginative fiction; an ingenious story, but not a true one'.[16] The book at first reading seemed to be even more convincing but when I read it again and looked more closely at what appeared to be a comprehensive list of footnotes, I noticed that evidence for the most crucial links was missing. For example, most of his story relies on his claim that Déricourt, Bodington and the Gestapo chief Boemelburg knew each other before the war, but his evidence for this is 'Private information' which is of no evidential value. I did write to Marshall to ask him to clarify a couple of factual points but received no answer despite the BBC assuring me that he had seen my letter. I wondered why he was not keen to communicate with me and this deepened my suspicions that there were fundamental flaws in his arguments.

Another novelist, Ted Allbeury, mixed Vader's and Marshall's suggestions but went further, suggesting that an order to increase resistance activity as though an invasion was imminent was given by Churchill face to face with Suttill, with the primary purpose of bluffing Stalin that the invasion would be in 1943, a reason dismissed earlier in this chapter.[17]

Also in 1990 appeared the official history of the British use of deception in the Second World War. No mention is made of any use of SOE or its agents in Operation COCKADE.

The book makes it clear that by 1942, three things had been realised:

1. deception plans, to be useful, must be based around real action;
2. plans for real action must therefore be prepared first; and
3. deception plans must be continuously acted upon to maintain the value of double agents and to keep the enemy guessing.

At the end of 1942, a cross-channel invasion was still part of the overall strategy and therefore deception planning was built around this action. When the overall strategy was changed at the Casablanca Conference in January 1943 to a cross-channel invasion in 1944, it was also decided that the possibility of an invasion in 1943 should be maintained by deception. However, this change of overall strategy was not formulated into an action plan until April 1943, so the existing deception strategy had to be continued to protect the value of double agents passing false information and to keep the Germans constantly confused. As stated earlier, details of the real strategy were not passed to SOE's country chiefs until the second half of 1943.[18]

In 1992, even an ex-agent, Bob Maloubier, fell under the spell of the conspiracy theories and suggested that Antelme was with my father when he met Churchill and that they were fed an invasion date of September 1943 in accordance with a plan prepared by Dansey to deceive both the Germans and the Russians.[19]

Also, in 1992 there appeared a book by Jacques Bureau, a radio expert on the fringe of the circuit who agreed to work for the Germans after his arrest. There may be elements of truth in this book but he has rewritten so many events and invented others in a very obvious attempt to justify his betrayal theories that it is of no value as evidence, especially as there are no sources given. As an example, he takes the Churchill meeting to an extreme, claiming that Churchill told my father the truth about the invasion being put off but asked him to get himself arrested, reveal a September date for the invasion under torture and make a pact with the Germans to salvage as many lives as possible. And not to tell Buckmaster or anyone else! He even suggests that the address my father moved to on 19 June was agreed in London in May and passed by Dansey to the Germans.[20] Although he claims in this book to have known my father well, Antelme noted in a report that although Bureau was a friend of Armel Guerne, he 'is not known to Prosper'.[21] I also noted that he did not register as a member of the circuit after the war.

There are many other accounts that use the same elements, sometimes in different combinations, but do not add anything new. Richard Seiler was a television journalist and, although he only relied on secondary sources, his book has been successful with the result that these myths have unfortunately been carried into several student theses.[22] This is one of the books that still claims that the relevant papers have not yet been released, despite the release of the COSSAC papers in 1973, and this claim was repeated in a France3 television programme in 2010 by Charles Lebrun, who had translated Vader's book. I did write to Lebrun on several occasions but had no reply. I wrote to him again in 2018 when he elaborated his theories in a book still without giving any evidence. This time I asked him for his sources for some of his key statements on the understanding that, if he did not answer yet again, I would take it to mean he was unable to provide any evidence. He did not reply.

There was, however, one author who not only challenged the tide of conspiracy theory but also suggested an alternative, which in my view was nearer the truth. This was Rita Kramer, writing about four of the F Section couriers including Andrée Borrel:

> It is conceivable that those responsible for planning and implementing strategy, appraising the consequences of the mistakes that had been made in France, decided to profit from the situation, to use it as a contribution to the military victory that was their aim and the purpose of everything they did. No one knew how things would turn out or what would eventually have proved decisive in determining the war's outcome.[23]

The evidence that I have found shows that the arrest of my father was the consequence of a series of unfortunate events, not the result of any betrayal as part of a deception plan. The arrest of Culioli, Rudellat, Pickersgill and Macalister was the result of a local initiative by the Blois Gestapo and Luftwaffe. The priority of the Paris Gestapo that day, 21 June, was the arrest of Jean Moulin at Caliures near Lyons. Indeed it has been claimed that Bauer, the Gestapo chief in Blois, was probably in Lyons that day and may not have returned to Blois until 23 June. Some writers claim incorrectly that the containers exploding at Neuvy on the night of 10/11 June was a unique event and was a deliberate plan to alert the Germans. It is clear that this incident was one of the main reasons for the deployment of troops on 21 June that caught Culioli and ultimately resulted in the Paris arrests. It would have been impossible for these particular containers to have been sabotaged and, even if this had been possible, the results

would have been impossible to predict as suggested by Paul
Raynaud after the war.

   If Culioli had not set out until he was sure that the reception
teams operating the previous night had returned home
safely, as he admitted he should have done, he would have
realised that something had happened to Couffrant's team
from Romorantin and he would not have set out to catch the
train to Paris. Whether Culioli then volunteered information
to his interrogators in Blois or was persuaded to do so, the
address of Archambaud/Norman would in any event have
been found in his briefcase and this was one of the names
clearly written on the packages that he was carrying. This led
the Germans to the apartment of Nicolas and Maud Laurent
where Norman was staying and where Borrel also happened
to be staying on the night of 23/24 June. There is no definitive
information on what then led the Germans to go a couple
of hours later to my father's address, which Culioli did not
know or have in his briefcase. Maud Laurent stated that the
table in the apartment was covered in false documents of one
sort or another. Amongst them the Germans found an identity
card photo of my father and asked Nicolas to confirm that it
was 'François'. The regulations for identity cards had been
changed in June and the need for Pickersgill, Macalister and
Raynaud to have the new style cards was the reason that their
transfer to Paris had been delayed. My father would also have
needed a new identity card and addresses had to be shown
on these cards. It seems to me to be likely that the Germans
found enough evidence of the address of my father amongst
the papers in the apartment of the Laurents to justify sending
an arrest team there.

   Many of the writers mentioned, and even some of those
involved, claim that my father's organisation had been

penetrated by the Germans and that this led to the arrests. Some of the German interrogators also told those arrested that they had known all about the circuit ever since it was established and Déricourt suggested that the circuit had been compromised from an early date as it was built on contaminated contacts from previously penetrated circuits. Although it is now clear that the arrests were not the result of German penetration, there had been some major opportunities for such a penetration.

The first such opportunity was the loss by a Carte courier of the names and addresses of 200 Carte members that he was taking to Paris by train in November 1942. This included the address of Germaine Tambour, who had been Carte's secretary but then joined my father's circuit, having been one of his first contacts in France. This was an Abwehr coup but they do not seem to have acted on it for some months as Tambour was not arrested until the second half of April 1943 and even then she was only asked about her Carte contacts. She was not asked about her work with my father until after his arrest.[24] This was a missed opportunity for the Abwehr, which had previously been successful in penetrating and breaking the circuits of Pierre de Vomecourt and Peter Churchill and by mid-1943 had penetrated Frager's Donkeyman circuit so successfully that Frager was not aware of it when he met Bodington. Bodington should have been suspicious as my father was certainly aware that there was something wrong and had warned London in April in no uncertain terms, 'Please, please, please avoid all contact between me and (Frager). I have had reliable reports which induce me to distrust him or at least his methods. I can, if necessary, give you chapter and verse for this.'[25] And he probably did when he went to London shortly afterwards, although there is no record of this.

Another opportunity for penetration was during the visit of the false Dutch agents who came to Paris to contact Déricourt in May. This was an Abwehr operation but it seems that the Paris Gestapo became involved (see next chapter), which would tie in with Bodington's assertion that the arrests had been their priority 'A' task for the five weeks preceding his visit, but as already noted, their priority task was in fact the arrest of Moulin. Furthermore it is clear that the Gestapo were not expecting to arrest one, let alone two, wireless operators as they allowed their radio expert, Josef Goetz, to go home on leave on 19 June, five days before the arrests. So although the Gestapo may have started to take an active interest in the activities of the Prosper organisation in May, there is no evidence they did anything about it apart from securing Déricourt as a double agent.

A further, less specific, suggestion of penetration used by some authors appears to be due to a misunderstanding of comments made by my father in the days before his arrest. After Mme Balachowsky and the others from Grignon came to Paris to meet my father for lunch on 20 June, he told her that there was something wrong in London and that he needed to protect those he had involved in his work. When he left Renée Guepin at Gisors station on the morning of 23 June, she later said that she had the feeling that this was the last time she would see him for, having said goodbye, he came back and said goodbye twice more. His personal liaison officer, Marcel Charbonnier, records my father telling him around this time that, 'There are some hard knocks coming and they are coming from London'.[26] These comments have been interpreted by some to mean that my father suspected that there was a traitor in London but no explanation is given for this interpretation. It seems clear to me that the explanation for these comments is contained in his furious report of 19 June in which he makes it clear that London is seriously compromising his security by giving details not only of a contact address to an F Section agent after he had cancelled it, but also to an agent from another Section who, despite being specifically ordered by my father not to, continued to use it and even passed on the address to others. He had already complained about his letter boxes being given to other agents without his knowledge in his report of 18 April.

There was of course one part of the organisation that had just started to be penetrated, leading to the arrest of one of the group leaders, René Davesne, also on 24 June and it seems that they also knew the location of one of Georges Darling's arms depots, which they raided on 26 June. Whether that penetration could have been contained is now only an academic question but I think it would have been difficult because of the unrelated arrests soon afterwards of the two communists from whom the Germans were able to extract the exact location of the much larger depot in the forêt de Thelle.

There are differing views in these books as to whether, on his return to France in May, my father was expecting an imminent invasion, had been given a date or had been told it had been deferred to 1944, with some writers even suggesting that he had been told about the deferral but had been ordered to carry on as though the invasion was imminent. The most far-fetched of these suggestions invent a meeting between my father and Winston Churchill, which is simply untrue. Churchill left Scotland on board the *Queen Mary* on 5 May for the Trident Conference in Washington and did not return until early June.[27] My father was in London between 15 and 20 May.[28]

Once this became known, some writers, instead of accepting that this whole story was a fiction, simply said that my father must have met someone representing Churchill but they present no evidence for such a meeting. As far as I am aware, the only person from outside SOE that my father met in London was someone called Colquhoun, whom Maurice Buckmaster recorded in his diary had dined with him and my father on 17 May. I have not yet managed to identify Colquhoun but he may have been from Air Intelligence, which organised reports from the field on the results of parachute operations.

When my father first went to France, all those involved expected there to be a cross-channel invasion in 1943 and this was official policy. At the highest strategic level this was changed to 1944 at the Casablanca Conference in January 1943, by which time it had become clear that were only enough resources available in 1943 to enable a smaller scale invasion into Sicily. Although this change of policy was not made public, it had to filter down through the various levels of command as was considered necessary. The pertinent question here is when were the SOE Country Chiefs such as Buckmaster told and when were agents going to, or already in France, made aware.

My father went back to France with France Antelme on the night of 20/21 May. Antelme returned to London in late July and the reports that he made then concerning the feeding and financing of an invading force make it clear that his instructions in May had been that plans for adequate food and money had to be in place immediately. For example, in his report 'Feeding Invading Troops', he records that such a scheme would be in place all along the coast between the Belgian and Spanish frontiers by the end of July but he warns:

> These arrangements, of course, while they have been fully organised as far as the food situation is concerned, cannot

be relied upon for an indefinite period. It must be borne in mind that it has meant considerable work and risk and that, while every organiser will be able to guarantee the feeding of troops, subject to an invasion in the near future, it would be impossible for them to guarantee that the same conditions would prevail if it became a matter of several months.[29]

That Buckmaster was also not given the new date until well after the Paris arrests is confirmed in his report 'Future Programme', dated 29 July 1943. Having mentioned the main tasks allotted to SOE at the time of an invasion of France, he continues, '… it is most probable that we shall be asked on very short notice, and in the very near future, if we are capable of carrying out a certain number of jobs that have not to date been specifically enjoined on us'. But he adds later in the report, 'It is of course quite possible that the Chiefs of Staff will decide to do nothing on a very large scale this year.' He also warned, 'It is also undoubted that failure to invade this autumn will involve considerable losses among our own personnel and to morale among sympathisers.' (I was interested to note that this report includes proposals for an extra 200 personnel in the field by the end of the year, including another five organisers and ten wireless operators for the Physician circuit!) The official Directive finally informing the French Country Section that 'an invasion of France is no longer possible this year' is not dated; an accompanying note states only that it was 'prepared at the end of 1943'.[30]

As for the 'alert' signal warning the whole circuit to stand by, which Gaston Cohen reported, he only claims to have heard it discussed but not to have known the precise orders.[31] He could not have been referring to the official messages warning that the invasion was due, as no such plan existed.

The 'alert' that he heard almost certainly related to the target messages for the Le Mans area which Antelme reports were given to my father during his visit to London in May.

The question of whether the deception planners had any responsibility for the collapse of the circuit is not so black and white. The evidence of how the arrests happened makes it clear that it was not due to any deliberate betrayal as part of such a plan but perhaps it might have been an unintended consequence. The exponential increase in drops to the circuit in June was set to continue in July. Some visible increase in resistance activity in the northern half of France was compatible with what the deception planners wanted and so the fact that an increase was already happening meant that there was no need for them to become involved with SOE to arrange such an increase.

The man in charge of deception planning was Colonel John Bevan who led a small team of specialist officers named the London Controlling Section. Just before Bevan died, Sir Michael Howard, the official historian of deception planning, asked him about the collapse of the Prosper organisation. Sir Michael told me that Bevan had admitted that he still had feelings of guilt about this as he considered that this collapse had resulted from the pressure on the circuit to increase their activities for what they thought would be an imminent invasion. He felt in hindsight that the pressure put on that organisation would have been an acceptable risk if there really had been a landing in France planned for 1943. As this was not the plan, the Prosper activities could actually have been reduced somewhat without damaging the deception strategy. The problem was how this could have been done without letting SOE know the truth.

Bevan also confirmed that the collapse of such a major circuit had been counter-productive to both Starkey and, more importantly, the overall strategy. However, this was not to the extent that Hitler:

> Believed, or at any rate hoped, that the break-up of the Prosper circuit – of which he too exaggerated the importance – represented a serious setback for Anglo-American plans to liberate France. Interrogations of captured SD officers made it clear that he took a good deal of personal interest in F Section's repression; as usually happens when high commanders start interfering in detail, he got his perspectives wrong. In fact of course Prosper's troubles had no impact whatsoever on the decision about when the invasion would take place, which was made on other and weightier grounds.[32]

I think that Bevan's hindsight is correct. The reason for the deployment of German troops that caught Culioli was clearly related to the explosion of some containers during a drop ten days earlier. My father was asked to halt the drops in the Sologne for a while as a result of this incident, but instead ordered it to continue because he thought the invasion was imminent. If he had halted operations for a while, then the Germans would not have caught Culioli with two newly arrived agents because they would not have arrived and he would not have been driving them to the station to go to Paris. Even if this had happened, the organisation is unlikely to have lasted much longer as the penetration in the Trie-Château groups would almost certainly have become toxic for the wider organisation.

One of the most outrageous suggestions made about the collapse of the circuit was that Claude Dansey, the deputy head of MI6, had so detested SOE that he had personally taken steps to sabotage it.[33] It is now clear that this could not have happened but it certainly appears to have been something that Dansey might have liked to happen. Patrick Reilly, who was personal assistant to the Chief of MI6, Sir Stewart Menzies, records:

> My own most vivid memory of Dansey is of seeing him come into my room opposite Menzies', rubbing his hands with glee. 'Great news', he said, 'great news'! I expected to hear news of some splendid intelligence coup. The cause of his glee was the destruction of a major SOE network in France – probably the Prosper organisation whose terrible fate is recounted in M.R.D. Foot's *SOE in France*. Misery, torture and death for many brave men and women, British and French: and Dansey gloated. I remember feeling physically sick.

Reilly considered Dansey to be one of the very few people he had met who seemed to him to have been truly wicked. 'He seemed to be consumed by hate, of everything and everybody.'[34] If the Dansey my father met in 1942 was the same man then this celebration might well suggest that he harboured a grudge for whatever they had disagreed about when they met.

Notes

1. F. Morgan, *Overture to Overlord*, Hodder & Stoughton, 1950.
2. M. Buckmaster, *Specially Employed*, Batchworth, 1952.
3. M .Buckmaster, *They Fought Alone*, Odhams, 1958.
4. B. Wynne, *Count Five and Die*, Souvenir Press, 1958.
5. J.O. Fuller, *Double Webs*, Putnam, 1958.
6. C. Wighton, *Pin-Stripe Saboteur*, Odhams, 1959.
7. HS 7/135, TNA.
8. G. Perrault, *Le Secret du Jour J*, Fayard, 1964.
9. The first 1966 edition published by HMSO is not now used as it was officially amended and republished in 1968. A revised and updated

edition was published by Frank Cass in 2004 and a French translation of this edition was published in 2008 by Tallandier under the title *Des Anglais dans la Résistance*.
10. E.H. Cookridge, *Inside SOE*, Arthur Baker, 1966.
11. WO 106/4223, TNA.
12. Anthony Cave Brown, *Bodyguard of Lies*, W H Allen, 1976.
13. J. Vader, *The Prosper Double-Cross*, Sunrise Press, 1977. French translation by C Lebrun, *Nous n'avons pas joue*, Le Capucin, 2002.
14. L. Collins, *Fall from Grace*, Granada, 1985.
15. R. Marshall, *All the King's Men*, Collins, 1988.
16. Letter to the *Observer*, 11 May 1986.
17. T. Allbeury, *A Time Without Shadows*, Hodder, 1990.
18. M. Howard, *British Intelligence in the Second World War*, Volume Five – Strategic Deception, HMSO,1990.
19. J. Larteguy & B. Maloubier, *Triple Jeu*, Laffont, Paris, 1992.
20. J. Bureau, *Un Soldat Menteur*, Robert Laffont, 1992.
21. Memo 05.08.1943, HS 9/42-44, TNA.
22. R. Seiler, *La Tragédie du Réseau Prosper*, Pygmalion, 2003.
23. R .Kramer, *Flames in the Field*, Michael Joseph, 1995.
24. Interview with Mme Flamencourt 26.04.1945, HS 9/517/8, TNA.
25. Prosper report 18.04.1943, HS 9/11/1, TNA.
26. 1221 W 11, Archives départmentales, Orléans.
27. www.ww2troopships.com.
28. In *SOE in France* (see 9 above), Michael Foot incorrectly stated that my father returned to France on 12 June. This may explain why some writers say that there could have been such a meeting as Churchill returned to England a week or so before 12 June. The date of my father's return has been corrected in the 2004 edition of the book.
29. 28.07.1943, HS 9/42, TNA.
30. In the OSS/SOE War Diary for 1944, it is recorded that SOE were 'not made fully cognizant of plan 'Overlord' until August 1943. American National Archives, reference unknown.
31. Interrogation 11.10.1943, HS 6/568, TNA.
32. See 9 above.
33. R. Marshall, *All the King's Men*.
34. Ms Eng c 6918 (fols 200-50), Special collections, Bodleian Library.

THE ROLE OF DÉRICOURT

There have been many suggestions that Henri Déricourt was responsible for the collapse of the Prosper organisation and even for the arrest of my father. Although the evidence shows that he was not responsible for my father's arrest, there is plenty of evidence that at some stage, in exchange for the safe passage of his aircraft, he started to let the Gestapo have or make copies of the mail that agents were sending to London on these aircraft. There is also evidence that he told them of the location of some of his operations, which enabled the Gestapo to send people to follow and arrest agents, and there are many events in his story which are difficult to explain.

Most SOE agents were trained to find suitable grounds for parachute operations. Finding fields where specialist aircraft such as Lysanders and Hudsons could land to drop off and pick up agents and other passengers was a more specialist job. This required experienced pilots who were trained as Air Movement Officers. Such a person was needed in northern France in 1942 and when Déricourt arrived in England in September, he appeared to have all of the right qualifications as he had been a commercial pilot before the war employed by Air Bleu and had toured France giving air shows.

He joined the French Section of SOE at the end of November 1942 and was given the operational name of Farrier. In the field he was to be known as Gilbert. Two attempts were made to parachute him into France on 23/24 and 29/30 December but the weather was too bad and he spent Christmas at Tempsford where he met another agent waiting to go to France, Pierre Natzler. He was finally dropped, with Jean Worms, organiser of the Juggler circuit, between Pithiviers and Montargis (Loiret) on the night of 22/23 January 1943.

As soon as he arrived in Paris, he contacted an old friend, Julienne Aisner. He told her about his mission and asked her to help him. She became the circuit's courier. He next went to Marseilles to collect his wife and to recruit an old colleague, Remy Clement, who had been a Flying Officer in the French Air Force. He became Déricourt's second in command. After returning to Paris with his wife, he started looking for suitable landing fields. He was supposed to work through Lise de Baissac in Poitiers but, once he had based himself in Paris, he came more and more into contact with members of the Prosper organisation, especially as he had to rely on their radios for communication with London.

He organised his first operation on 17/18 March when four agents arrived and four departed. His next was on 14/15 April, bringing in another four and taking Marcel Clech out. This operation was not without incident as it took some time for the aircraft to take off again after flying through a tree before landing; Déricourt had not provided enough bicycles for the number of passengers; and the incoming passengers had to make a run for it next morning when the school where they were staying was visited by Germans, although they turned out to be a commission inspecting school books. The next night Pierre Natzler finally arrived and was left with a bicycle that he could not ride. He was supposed to cross the demarcation line and go to Lyons but he went instead to Paris where he stayed for over a month, causing my father problems. By this aircraft, Déricourt sent his courier, Julienne Aisner, to London to be properly trained.

As a result of the incident with the tree, Déricourt was recalled to London where he stayed for 12 days over Easter, returning on 5/6 May. Many suggestions have been made about the people whom he might have met on this visit, including Bodington and Dansey of SIS, but no evidence has been produced to justify these claims.

When he returned to Paris he found that his security was becoming more and more endangered. He often used to meet other agents in the same restaurants and bars, and when one of these agents, Natzler, with whom he had spent the previous Christmas at Tempsford, asked him publicly whether he had had a good time in London over Easter, he decided that he had better take steps to protect his operations. He retired to Marseilles to see someone about an exfiltration but ran into more trouble; some of his pre-war colleagues who were now flying commercial flights for the Germans wanted him to join them. He had received a similar approach earlier in the year but had not then been alarmed. This time he took it more seriously and in a report on 11 May he comments that he had, 'serious bother at Marseilles where the Luftwaffe is looking for personnel. I have been solicited. I will have difficulty getting out of it but expect I will be able to do so on medical grounds with the help of a doctor.'[1]

This was the day that some claimed that he met up with my father at Amboise, although the operation did not take place until the night of 14/15 May. It was a double Lysander operation bringing back Julienne Aisner, now a fully-trained courier, and three agents who were to form the Inventor circuit. The only passenger to London was my father. I found the form (A.T.F 13 – Operation Instructions for Despatch of Personnel and Stores) giving the dates during which the reception team should be on stand-by to receive this operation. This showed the stand-by period starting on 12 May so, if they did arrive in Amboise on 11 May, there would have to have been another reason for them to have left Paris early. [2]

A possible reason is the expected arrival of Adrien and Arnaud, claiming to be SOE agents from Holland; they were in fact Abwehr agents. The Abwehr in Holland had managed to take over SOE's operation there completely, arresting all of its agents and successfully playing back their radios so that SOE in London was not aware that anything was wrong. The mastermind behind this was Abwehr Colonel Giskes and he had been so successful that he had convinced London that there was a viable Secret Army established in Holland. However, a problem arose for him when the Chiefs of Staff in London decided that this organisation was so important that its chief, Kale, should come to London to report. A team of three agents was dropped in to exfiltrate him but they were immediately captured. When instructions for this team from London were received on one of the captured radios that Kale should be taken to Paris for exfiltration by air, Giskes replied that Kale was too busy (he was of course a prisoner) but that he would send his trusted second in command. This part was to be played by an Abwehr NCO called Karl Bodens and he was to be escorted by another agent, Richard Christmann.

Giskes' plan was that they should contact and make the necessary arrangements with the agent in Paris responsible for exfiltrations by air and, at the last minute, the local Abwehr would arrest Bodens publicly so that it would be witnessed by the relevant SOE agents, who would report it to London, making the Dutch Section of SOE believe that there had been a genuine attempt to send to London the man they had asked for.

In response to Giskes' message that Kale would not be able to go himself, London sent him instructions that Kale's second-in-command should go to an address in Paris, the café Monthalon in the square Clignancourt, by 10 May or as soon as possible thereafter, using the name Adrien. There he was to use the password '*Je suis un ami de Roger Dumont*' (I am a friend of Roger Dumont) and, when he received the reply '*Il y a plus d'un mois que je n'ai l'ai vu*' (I have not seen him for over a month), he was to ask for 'Gilbert'. He was then to stay somewhere quietly until called for by Gilbert with the same password. When Christmann went to the cafe and asked for Gilbert, the proprietor told him that Gilbert was in a flat nearby playing poker. Christmann went straight there, only to discover that he had found the wrong Gilbert. He had found Gilbert Norman, not Déricourt. Agazarian, who was also at the game, took it on himself to make the necessary arrangements and to arrange another rendezvous, as he was sending and receiving wireless messages for Déricourt who was out of town.

On 17 May, Agazarian met with Christmann, this time with Bodens, at a safe house and told them that having spoken to Déricourt, no flights were possible for the rest of the May moon period. He arranged to meet them again at the Royal Capucines on 9 June and let them return to Brussels. When Agazarian returned to London later in June, he reported:

I first met Adrien on 17 May. He therefore missed the May operation and as Gilbert, not having received further instructions from you, refused to allow us to do another operation unless we could find another passenger in time (which was impossible). I decided to allow Adrien to return to Brussels until the first June operation. I did not try to prevent them doing this as, whilst in Paris, I discovered he

had slept with a woman at his hotel and, as he speaks not
a word of French, I thought this bad security.[3]

When they did meet as arranged, Bodens was arrested
but Christmann and Agazarian were able to leave the café
separately. Agazarian met up with Borrel at another café
and then reported the arrest to Déricourt and to London so
that this part of Giskes' plan was successful. But it was not
the Abwehr who made the arrest; it was the Gestapo, which
suggests that they had been made aware of the plan and taken
over the arrest, perhaps to warn the Abwehr not to trespass
on their territory. But how had the Gestapo found out? The
only person in France who could have known anything about
the plan in advance, apart from the Abwehr, was Déricourt.
He must have been very surprised to be asked to arrange
a pick-up for a Dutch agent as this meant that his contact
details were being given to agents in Holland. This seems
likely to be the moment when he decided that his security
was now so compromised that he must take urgent steps
to protect his activities if they were to continue safely. The
message with contact instructions from London to Giskes
was sent on 28 April. This means that the arrangements
to exfiltrate Kale were being made whilst Déricourt was in
London from 23 April to 5 May. If he was informed of these
plans then, as seems likely, he would have had the opportunity
to discuss their implications for the security of his operation
with someone in London. Maurice Buckmaster does not
mention meeting Déricourt during his visit, so it could have
been Nicolas Bodington because the person that Déricourt
appears to have ended up seeing on his return to Paris was
the head of the Paris Gestapo, Karl Boemelburg, whom some
claim that Bodington knew before the war. Goetz stated after
the war that he knew exactly how Déricourt was recruited by

Boemelburg. Sometime before the June arrests, attempts were made to recruit Déricourt into flying with them by Luftwaffe officers that he had known before the war. To avoid this, he asked them to introduce him to Boemelburg.[4]

Déricourt would certainly have been aware that the fake Dutch agents had orders to arrive in Paris on or soon after 10 May. The fact that he may have removed both himself and my father himself from Paris on 11 May, a day earlier than was required to wait for the pick-up, did ensure that neither he nor my father became involved with the Dutch problem until he returned to Paris after this operation, by which time it was too late to put Bodens on that flight. It looks to me as though Déricourt's first contact with the Gestapo was between his return to France on 6 May and leaving for Amboise on 11 May, in which case he might have been ordered by them to leave Paris as early as possible to give the Gestapo time to take over the public 'arrest' of Bodens from the Abwehr.

He would have wanted to give something to the Gestapo as a show of goodwill and he was able to do this. He knew that one of his incoming passengers on his 14/15 May operation was a wireless operator who would have with him all of his codes and schedules and the Gestapo were at this time very keen to get hold of such information in order to play a radio back to London. On arrival, Clech's suitcase was left in the care of Déricourt's team and the vital documents were stolen and given to the Gestapo. Ironically, the evidence for this was provided by

Karl Boemelburg.

Hugo Bleicher of the Abwehr, who felt cheated because he had also planned that one of his agents should steal these documents for him. He records that Déricourt, 'had handed over to Kieffer the transmitter timetable of (Clech) the wireless operator which was meant to reach me'.[5]

It is known that at some stage Déricourt started to allow the Gestapo to have or to make copies of reports and letters that had been given to him to pass on to London via his aircraft and involved Aisner in this. Bardet who worked with Frager records, 'One day, Frager asked Leigh if she was happy with her lodgings and whether she had everything she needed. Leigh answered that she shared a bedroom with Aisner who often stayed up very late copying out documents for Gilbert.'[6] Besnard stated after the war that Bodington told him that he knew Déricourt worked for the Germans and encouraged him to continue but that Aisner was not aware of this although she knew that he met Germans. Besnard was not concerned as he understood from Bodington that it was on the advice of London.

The earliest evidence that I have found is that some of the June mail was copied. Some of those arrested were shown a dossier of reports and letters and Armel Guerne records that one was from Prosper to his wife. There are two such letters that he wrote after his return to France, one dated 19 June, the same date as his last report, and the other undated but clearly written soon after his return (see p. 195–96).

If the letter in the Gestapo's dossier was the first letter, then they would have known the names of his two sons and that he had a photo of us. They would no doubt have made good use of this information in an attempt to demoralise my father. I did wonder whether the second letter and the report of the same date might have been carried by Agazarian rather than given to Déricourt but Agazarian records that he last saw my father on 12 June. If mail was copied in May, it would not have been likely to include Prosper mail as my father would not have given it to Déricourt when he could carry it himself.

Very few of my father's reports have survived so it is not known how many he made between his return on 21 May and his arrest. The only full report is his angry one of 19 June, already discussed. After his return to London, Agazarian refers to a letter from my father giving his reasons for sending Agazarian and his wife back, which must have been written in this period but the only part of it that has come to light is the part relating to the Agazarians. In another file there are notes of addresses that should be considered as 'blown', which are noted as coming from a Prosper report dated 1 June.

Another part of this report included details of Georges Darling's sub-circuit, giving his address, the name and address of his local letter box, the number of DZs in his area and the number of containers dropped to each.[7] When I first found this extract I assumed it was part of a comprehensive report covering all parts of the organisation and that the extracts relating to the other parts of the organisation had been lost from the files of the leaders of the other sub-circuits and groups. However, it seems that this was the only part of the organisation for which such a report had been made, as Ernst Vogt stated that, when he was charged with the interrogation of Norman, he was given some copies of intercepted documents, the most important of which was a report 'listing all of the parachute grounds in the departments of Seine-et-Oise et Eure' with the names and addresses of the local leaders and their principal helpers. He said it was this document that enabled the Germans to make the first arrests in these areas.

If the Germans had a copy of such detailed information, it is surprising that they did not act sooner, which suggests that they only saw it just before the Paris arrests. If it had been in the mail given to Déricourt for his operation on 23 June, it might only have been copied a day or so before the flight and by the time they were ready to react, my father had fallen into their hands for other reasons, but it does explain why Georges Darling's area was the first to be raided and implicates Déricourt in his death.

The next troubling incident involving Déricourt is what happened at the time of his second June operation at the end of the month. A Lysander carrying two agents arrived over his ground at Pocé-sur-Cisse just to the north of Amboise on the night of 20/21 June but saw no reception. The operation was tried again on 22/23 June but this time it was abandoned due to a problem with the engine of the aircraft. The next night the operation was successful. There were two people to be picked up. Richard Heslop was leaving his activities with the Privet circuit in Angers following the arrest of Wilkinson on 6 June. The other was a meteorologist with the RAF who had been in an aircraft that had crash-landed in the Orne and needed to be returned to England urgently. He was put into contact with the Prosper group in Falaise in Normandy and taken to Paris on 20 June. This was the day he and Heslop were to be handed over to Déricourt to be taken to Amboise in time for the pick-up that night, but the handover did not take place. It was that night that the Germans were deploying their troops in the Sologne and it is tempting to think that Déricourt might have been warned but his ground was not near the deployment and it is more probable that Taylor did not reach Paris in time.

This was, however, an operation that Déricourt had told the Gestapo about and they sent some of their men to wait at Amboise station to follow the new arrivals. Robert Lyon was followed for a time and then allowed to go on his way but Colonel Bonoteaux was arrested. He was later shot at Dachau.[8]

I think it is unlikely that Déricourt told the Gestapo about his next two operations. On 19/20, July France Antelme and William Savy were returned to London. Verity does not record Déricourt travelling on this operation but Foot writes that he 'seized the opportunity of a flying visit to London'. He stayed the night in the flat of André Simon, a French Section HQ officer, and was taken back to France on 22 June in time to receive Nicolas Bodington and Jack Agazarian that night. Simon met Déricourt at Tangmere so London must have known that he was coming. There is no record of the reason for this visit but it seems to me to be likely to have been in connection with the impending visit of Bodington. Déricourt was in contact with the Gestapo by this time and his sudden visit suggests to me that the French Section may not have been aware of this. If they had been aware of his contacts, it would have been madness to send such a senior officer to France without being assured by Déricourt that he would be safe. The fact that Bodington did go to France, but only after Déricourt's visit to London, suggests to me that this was the moment when Déricourt felt that he had to reveal the extent of his contacts. He did keep Bodington safe but not Agazarian. At the time of Bodington's visit, Déricourt knew that Norman had been arrested (which is why Déricourt was having to use other wireless operators) and that his transmissions were therefore controlled by the Germans, so he would have known that the messages from Norman's radio making a rendezvous were a trap into which he could not let Bodington fall. Norman and Déricourt must share responsibility for Agazarian's arrest and subsequent death in Germany but whether Bodington was party to this is not clear.

The last incident concerning Déricourt that affected part of the Prosper organisation was the arrest of Inayat Khan. As already mentioned, the Gestapo were in contact with her through Macalister's wireless and as a result she had already met the two Gestapo agents playing the parts of the arrested Canadians. London became increasingly concerned. 'Knowing the risks she was taking, Buckmaster ordered her to return to London but she refused to leave until she was satisfied that he'd found a replacement for her. He assured her that he had, and she finally agreed to be picked up by Lysander in mid-October.'[9] She told friends in Paris that she was to be picked up on 14 October.[10] As she was the wireless link for all of the messages arranging such operations, she would have received a message to tell Déricourt that he should be on stand-by at the ground for this pick-up between 11 and 21 October. In fact, Déricourt's next operation did not take place until the night of 16/17 October. The orders for this operation were to take two agents to France and to bring back two or three. The agents coming in were not only Déricourt's deputy, Remy Clement, but a wireless operator for his exclusive use, Arthur Watt. As soon as Déricourt heard from Inayat Khan the date of Watt's arrival, Déricourt no longer needed her. Only two agents were picked up in France leaving the intriguing question as to whether the possible third might have been Inayat Khan who had been arrested on either 10 or 11 October.

It seems to me to be a remarkable coincidence that just at this moment the Gestapo claim that she was betrayed by Garry's sister, Renée. I have not found any mention of the date she is said to have first approached the Gestapo, except for Vogt saying it was the end of October or early November, when she was arrested on 13 October. It was Vogt who was sent to meet Renée Garry and to prove her sincerity she took him to the flat where Inayat Khan was staying and showed him both where a key was hidden and a wireless set. Vogt noted that it was a Mark II. A few days later she called him to say that Inayat Khan was due to return and an agent was sent to wait for her. I cannot understand why the Gestapo had to wait for this denunciation as they could contact her at any time through her wireless, as they had already done on more than one occasion. They had tried to trap her at the end of September after she had unwittingly enabled them to arrest Gieules and Duthilleul but Gieules managed to warn her. Perhaps this made her suspicious of further contact with those claiming to be Pickersgill and Macalister. It should be remembered that Renée Garry was tried for this alleged betrayal after the war and acquitted, with the help of evidence from Gieules.[11]

Notes

1. KV 2/1131, TNA.
2. AIR 20/8493.
3. General Report 23.06.1943, HS 9/11/1, TNA.
4. Proces Verbal, 29.11.1945, dossier Z6 NL 17339, Archives nationales.
5. H. Bleicher, *Colonel Henri's Story*, William Kimber, 1954.
6. Interrogatoire 20.01.1945, P 303057, SHD.
7. HS 9/395/3, TNA.
8. Three of the arrivals on Déricourt's operation of 15/16 November were similarly followed and arrested. These were all French Section agents, André Maugenet, Jean Menesson and Paul Pardi, and they also were killed in German camps. Ernst Vogt claims that this happened because one of the men was thought to be France Antelme whom they were looking for.
9. L. Marks, *Between Silk and Cyanide*, HarperCollins, 1998.
10. S. Basu, *Spy Princess*, Sutton Publishing, 2006.
11. There is a telegram on Inayat Khan's file in which Sonia Olschanezsky reports on 1 October 1943 that 'Ernest, Maurice and Madeleine' had been arrested and that Madeleine is a wireless operator. Ernest/Marcel Fox was arrested on 7 September and Maurice Braun on 20 September together with another member of their circuit, Madeleine Clayssen. Olschanezky seems to have thought, wrongly, that Madeleine was Inayat Khan.

COOPERATION

As has already been noted, the statements of the various Germans involved are unclear and contradictory on the subject of how much those arrested might have talked. Hans Kieffer, the most senior, commented that my father did not want to make any statement but that Norman had not the same integrity and made a very full statement whilst some information was obtained from Borrel.[1]

Josef Goetz, on his return to Paris five days after the arrests, was charged with trying to play back the wireless of Norman. He claimed that he was supplied with information already obtained from Norman, Culioli and Macalister.[2] In another document he commented that my father had talked but with much more reticence.[3]

Ernst Vogt stated that he interrogated Norman whilst my father was interrogated by Scherer.[4] Vogt also interrogated Borrel, who he said had agreed to talk on Norman's orders. Vogt commented that Norman had a less than average intelligence but an incredible memory. I had earlier noticed that one of his training instructors had commented that, 'He talks too much.'[5] As revealed by the extract in the file of Georges Darling, the Gestapo had information about this group from a Prosper report to London, which Déricourt had given to them. When confronted with this report, Vogt stated that my father and Norman were told that the Gestapo had an agent in London, but he also commented that the mail from Déricourt was not of great consequence as the agents were not spies and carried out most of their communication with London by radio.[6]

Josef Placke not only claimed that my father had told them about the group of Georges Darling but that, when he was told about what had happened at Trie-Château on 26 June, my father realised that he had made a mistake and in further interrogations, gave all of the other depots and the names of those holding them. However, he repeatedly states that he was not involved in any of the interrogations of my father and is only passing on what he heard from others and that the depots revealed were only those of the Darling group. He does also state that my father gave the arms depot at Hirson, but this was in September by which time my father was in Sachsenhausen.

Hugo Bleicher told Frager that Norman was working for the Gestapo but made no mention of my father.[7]

There are two German claims that my father gave specific information: the contact for Georges Darling and the plan showing the location of the Falaise depot. What actually led them to Trie-Château remains unclear. There is the version mentioned by Placke, which he admits is hearsay, and his reference to a note written by my father may simply be an attempt to hide the fact that they possessed the extract from my father's report that Déricourt had given the Gestapo giving Darling's name and address. Or he may have had a copy on him when arrested. There are also two reports, one claiming that the Trie-Château depot had been betrayed by Henri Amand and the other that the Germans had already started to make arrests in Darling's Meru group two days earlier on 24 June. The only survivor to mention any involvement of his chiefs in his arrest was Marcel Gouju of Évreux, who stated that it was Norman, who had given the Gestapo his name and revealed the fact that he had an arms depot at Le Plessis-Grohan.

At Falaise, the plan showing the exact location of the depot, which it is claimed was drawn by my father, was found not to be correct. Unfortunately this did not help keep it hidden as the leader of the group and his liaison officer, Pierre Bar, were taken to Paris on 1 July where they were confronted with Norman after which the correct location was revealed. In recording this incident, Bar noted that he was not aware at this date that my father had been arrested.

Another accusation made against my father is that he accompanied the Germans when they went to clear the arms depots, his presence helping to convince the keepers that it was all over and that they should not resist. Harry Peuleve records Vogt telling him this when he was arrested in 1944 as part of an attempt to persuade him to cooperate. Not a single one of those who survived the arrests claims to have seen my father after his arrest. Bearing in mind that my father had apparently been disfigured when he was arrested, I can imagine that the Germans would not have wished others to see him as they would either not have believed that he had agreed anything or that he had done so only under extreme duress, which would have reduced their willingness to cooperate. However, several refer to being visited by or confronted with Norman. The first time this happened was on the morning of 1 July when the arms were found that had been dropped for the Grignon group; the farmer's wife recognised Norman accompanying the Germans. The same day Culioli was being interrogated in Fresnes and asked to see my father, but he was only allowed to see Norman who asked him to give up his depots.[8] The next day it was Balachowsky who was confronted in Fresnes by Norman and told to reveal everything.[9]

On 4 July it was not only Marcel Gouju who was confronted with Norman at Fresnes but also Edouard Flamencourt of the Lequeux group, who was told to reveal everything. He also stated that it was Norman who had given him away. Germaine Tambour told Flamencourt's wife, Marguerite, that:

> She had been very much surprised and shocked to find (Norman) present at her interrogation and more so to find that each time she forgot a detail or feigned ignorance, he prompted her with – Come on Germaine you must remember – or some such phrase. He stood in front of a map and pointed out to the Germans where the arms were hidden. He seemed on excellent terms with them and they spoke to him with friendly familiarity, sending him to make tea, etc.

She was another who was shown documents that she was told had been copied in London.[10]

On the evening of 19 July Norman arrived with three Germans at the house where Robert Arend, Andrée Borrel's brother-in-law, was staying with his parents to avoid being taken to Germany to work. Norman had come to collect a wireless set that he had left there. Robert was out and his father could only find four of the five parts, so they had to wait until Robert came back to give him the fifth part. Unfortunately his father let slip that Robert was a *réfractaire* and the Germans arrested him; he survived deportation.[11]

Norman participated at the arrest of Dr Helmer, who was the personal letter box for my father and had housed agents. He helped to search her apartment and confronted her again in the Avenue Foch.[12] Also in the second half of July Norman and Borrel were seen together in Orléans by Georges Brault of the Romorantin group. As he was being taken for interrogation he passed them. 'Whereas I was escorted by a policeman with a revolver, they were unguarded, talking to each other, at ease.'[13]

The next month Roger Landes saw Norman in Bordeaux. The Germans were still looking for de Baissac in August and asked Culioli about him as he had told them about my father's meeting with de Baissac; he offered to take them to the places that he knew de Baissac frequented in Bordeaux but his offer was not taken up. Landes and Norman had parachuted into France together in November 1942 and had met again in Paris soon afterwards. Landes commented that if it was not Norman, it was his double, but Norman failed to recognise him. He warned his team and one of them later reported that he had seen Norman in a car with Germans.[14] It was at this time that Norman gave the Germans the address of one of Landes' safe houses according to Friedrich Dhose, the Gestapo officer who was pursuing de Baissac.

Another SOE agent who was confronted with Norman was the wireless operator for the Butler circuit, Marcel Rousset, who was arrested on 7 September 1943 with his organiser, Jean Bouguennec, and the organiser of the Publican circuit, Marcel Fox. Norman told him that the Gestapo had full information about the SOE organisation and that, in view of this knowledge, he and Prosper had decided to admit everything in order to save their lives and he advised Rousset to do likewise. He was told

Author with Roger Landes in 2004.
(D. Harrison)

the same by Bouguennec. When Rousset was sent to Germany in April 1944, Norman was on the same train in a lamentable condition. He was limping terribly, having tried to escape and been shot.[15] Alain Antelme, a nephew of the SOE agent France Antelme, told me that he was told the same story when he met Rousset in Paris 30 years later but Rousset had added that Norman had implored the forgiveness of his fellow deportees for what he had done.

There have been many suggestions that there was some sort of formal agreement, accord or arrangement between my father and/or Norman on the one hand and the Gestapo on the other, by the terms of which lives would be protected if arms depots were given up. Nothing on these lines is mentioned in the official statements made immediately after the war by either Kieffer or Goetz but Vogt later remembered that:

Kieffer asked Suttill and Norman to give him precise details of all of their activities for the French Section in England and in France, to point out all of their helpers in France, to give the location of all of the depots of arms and material, the names and addresses of the people who created these depots or were guarding them. They must also both undertake that they would order their helpers with whom they were confronted, to behave in the same way as themselves. In exchange, Kieffer would undertake, on their giving their word of honour, that they would both, together with their helpers, be treated fairly and not be placed before a tribunal but purely and simply sent to a concentration camp in Germany until the end of the war. Suttill and Norman accepted on condition that the only people to be arrested would be those who had taken an active part in their clandestine activities and not those who were simply aware of their activities, for example, their families. Kieffer agreed. To my knowledge the conditions were adhered to strictly by both sides.[16]

However in a different document, Vogt said that he heard all of this from Norman when he interrogated him.[17]

Placke stated that he was told by Langer that my father had waited several days before giving the depots because he believed that the contacts would have been cut and this was in accordance with London's instructions to give up depots to save himself. 'Moreover I believe that the commandant Kieffer had given his word that none of his helpers would be shot. Contrary to the hopes of Prosper, the contacts were not cut and numerous arrests followed.'[18]

Guerne, when asked by British interrogators in 1944 what he knew of the arrangement, said much the same but claimed that the lives of the chiefs of the organisation would be exempted from the arrangement and this is the version that appears in the official history. It looks as though the Vogt version was not available to Foot. For some reason, Guerne placed himself in this exempted category but he was treated by the Germans like all of the other helpers.[19] It was only Culioli who was treated as an equal of the officers and he was sent to Germany with a group of them on 8 August 1944.

Most writers now refer to this arrangement as a 'pact of honour' but this is not how it was described originally. Culioli was told by Norman that an 'accord' had been made and the Germans who told Lequeux about it used the same word. Guerne told his British interrogators that Norman had told him that it was he who had agreed a 'proposal'. As far as I can find, the writer J.O. Fuller was the first to publicise the word 'pact', saying that she had heard mutterings of a pact from some of the survivors that she spoke to in the 1950s and this was the word she said that Vogt used when she met him in 1950. In the official history, which first appeared in 1966, several words are used – 'bargain', 'arrangement' and also 'the pact that is supposed to have been made'. In the same year E.H. Cookridge introduced the phrase 'Pact of Honour' and this was made popular in France when it appeared in Henri Nogueres' history of the resistance as *'pacte d'honneur'*.

None of these references suggest a formal written arrangement but a few years later Vogt changed his story dramatically. Whereas he had stated in one of his depositions that he had heard about the pact from Norman, who had been party to it, he wrote to J.O. Fuller in 1958 stating that the pact had been made by my father and Kieffer only, 'No one else was present: only Prosper, Kieffer and myself as intermediary,' He then added, 'The pact was obtained from Berlin, stamped with the seal of the RHSA and given to Prosper.' Elsewhere in the letter he refers to 'the famous pact' and he seems to me to have exaggerated both his role in it and the formality of it. It should be noted that a formal but unwritten agreement had been made by Pierre de Vomecourt in the previous year but this was with the Abwehr, not the Gestapo, and was adhered to.

Pierre de Vomecourt was told by Bleicher that he and Roger (Cottin) would be part of the next 500 hostages to be shot. On the next day, Bleicher came to him and said that he was authorised to make him an offer; if he would tell the Germans all about his organisation, he and all his comrades would be treated as PoWs. He asked for time to think it over, which was granted. When they came back for his answer, he said that he must first of all talk the matter over with Roger as the latter had already refused to save his own life and that, although he felt inclined to accept Bleicher's offer himself, he could not answer for Roger. He was allowed to see Roger but the Germans stayed in the room. He therefore told them that he would not speak to Roger while they were present and they were left alone. He was thus able to explain to Roger his plan and to brief him on what he had to say. When the Germans returned, he said that he and Roger had decided to accept the offer but on two conditions: firstly that the offer should be made to them officially by an officer of the Wehrmacht in uniform and secondly, that his wife should be allowed to see him and should be told of the offer. These conditions were accepted by the Germans. On 1 May 1942, the offer was made to him and Roger officially by a Hauptmann in uniform, who made the promise *on the word of a German officer*, and his wife was allowed to be present. After this, he and Roger were left alone for two hours to compile a list of names of people involved. [20]

If there had been a written document, it is incomprehensible that no one else ever saw it, especially those who questioned whether there was any such agreement, such as Culioli or Peuleve. I cannot imagine what my father was supposed to do with such a document. I think that my father would in any event have not taken any such document seriously, especially in view of the fact that he was a lawyer. As Foot wrote, 'They had fought the Germans long enough to know their enemies' word was worthless.'

The available evidence shows that it was only some of the Germans and Norman who claimed that my father agreed to a pact. The only other evidence that I have found suggests the opposite. This is a deposition by Maurice Braun who was a member of Marcel Fox's Publican circuit. He records that in September 1943 he was for a short while placed in a cell in Fresnes with Fox, Jean Worms and two lieutenants of Prosper whose names he did not know. Fox and Worms told him that it was Norman who had sold them out and that there was no point in hiding anything as Norman had told them everything. This was confirmed by the two lieutenants of Prosper, who added that Norman had given the Prosper circuit and, 'that he had assisted at the interrogation of Prosper which lasted without interruption for several days and several nights and that little by little Norman completed or made Prosper give up the details that the latter wished to hide'.[21] This is not a description of a man who has agreed to tell the Gestapo everything; quite the contrary.

This picture fits with a comment about my father given by one of the German secretaries in Avenue Foch, 'They did not take to Prosper much, who had been very English and haughty under interrogation, and that he had just sat in a chair and smoked cigarettes.'[22] It appears that my father did not tell the Gestapo anything willingly and that the few details that he may have been asked to give because they were not known to Norman, were given under considerable pressure if they were given at all. Even then, although he appears to have given some details, he did still, for example, try to protect his depot at Falaise by giving an incorrect location.[23]

There is a letter written by Renee Guepin of the Darling organisation claiming that my father was interrogated without a break for seventy-two hours during which he had to remain standing without anything to eat or drink but did not say a word despite being savagely beaten, including having one of his arms broken, and this is quoted in the official history. Although her reference to seventy-two hours ties in with Braun's statement of several days, there were serious inaccuracies in other parts of this letter, and I felt I could not give it credence without further corroborating evidence. Since first publication, I have found this evidence in a statement by a woman who worked in Avenue Foch as a cleaner, Rose-Marie Holwedts, née Cordonnier. She said that my father was interrogated for seventy-two hours and tortured, and that he must have given something away. She added that as a rule they didn't torture the English.[24]

I can only speculate on why Norman behaved as he did. Yvonne Rudellat told Anne-Marie de Bernard that Norman had said 'If I am taken, I will do whatever it takes to get away without concerning myself about the fate of others. They will have to cope as best they can.' From the dates of the arrests in the groups it is clear that his interrogation and that of my father, at which Norman assisted, was basically complete before Goetz returned to Paris on 29 June. It was only after that date that London reminded him not to forget his security checks, so this was not the reason for his degree of cooperation as many have claimed. When he and Borrel were arrested the Germans must have realised that they were lovers and threats to her may have been a powerful incentive. There is a record that she wrote in a note to her sister from Fresnes that Norman was protecting her. Another factor may have been the amount of information that Culioli was caught with in Blois. Whatever he said or gave Bauer on 23 June was important enough for Bauer to take him straight to Paris that same day. Culioli knew not only the details of most of the drops and sabotage activities of his own and Lequeux's groups but also many of the groups in Darling's area, which were the first to be raided by the Germans. Faced with such a fait accompli and the threat of reprisals unless all of the organisation's material was given up 'to the last pistol' as Langer had requested, he may have felt that all was lost and decided to cooperate despite my father clearly taking an opposite view.

Michael Foot left the question of my father's role in the collapse of the circuit open when he wrote his history, but he revised that soon afterwards and sent his conclusion to Colonel Buckmaster who passed them on to our family. (See opposite page)

By the time I met Michael Foot many years later, he could not initially remember the new information that led him to

UNIVERSITY OF MANCHESTER
MANCHESTER 13

TELEPHONE:
061-273 3333

Department of History

from Professor M.R.D. Foot

29 July 1969.

My dear Colonel

In the course of revising my 'SOE in France' for a second edition, I have
had to go over again carefully the whole sad and complicated story of the
downfall of Francis Suttbill's 'Prosper' circuit. I have now been able to see
several people, previously inaccessible to me, who knew and worked with him;
and to consult various private as well as official papers. As I know you knew
him well and valued him highly, you may like to have advance notice of my
conclusion about him.

It is, that I now have no shred of doubt left that his personal integrity,
his loyalty to his friends, and his patriotism all remained absolutely intact,
to the end.

I am quite sure that he was no party to making or sanctioning or implementing
any sort of bargain with the Germans. And everyone I met, whether among the
senior survivors of the circuit, or elsewhere in F section who had known him
well, spoke most warmly in praise of his character and his courage.

How much of this I shall be able to get into public print, I cannot yet tell:
the copyright is not mine, nor is the decision whether to publish at all. But I
would like you to know what, as the official historian, I have in the end decided
about this; and would of course have no sort of objection if you passed my
conclusions on to his family. They need trouble no longer about unfounded
allegations in old newspapers, or in books whose authors had too few data to
work on.

Yours most sincerely

Michael Foot

Colonel M.J. Buckmaster OBE

Michael Foot's letter. (Author)

this revised opinion but, when I showed him the deposition
of Maurice Braun, he immediately said that this was the vital
document. He also told me that Norman's father, who had
initially fought the accusations against his son, had by the
time the official history was published accepted what his son
had done. He telephoned Michael Foot soon after publication

just to say that he wished the book could have been delayed until after his death.

There were several controversies after the war on the subject of who else might have cooperated and to what extent, and some members of the organisation even ended up going to court. This is water under the bridge as far as I am concerned but it is interesting that some appear to have cooperated willingly whilst others did so because they were told to by Norman himself or by someone down the line whom he had ordered to do the same. Of the two main lieutenants, Darling did not have a chance to be confronted as he was killed. When Culioli was confronted by Norman he pretended to cooperate completely by revealing what he claimed were half of his stores, hoping that the Germans would think he had declared all of them. In fact the four of his team leaders whom he asked to give up their depots held 129 of the 166 containers dropped to Culioli, which is just over three-quarters of his total not the half he claimed after the war. He later showed the Germans where the five-container drop at Chaumont-sur-Tharonne was hidden but not the other drop of twelve. He then discovered that Norman had denounced his brothers-in-law and given the locations of his headquarters and details of his sabotage operations and after this, he decided to declare everything. It should be noted that this is what Culioli claimed after the war whereas he appears to have cooperated as soon as he was arrested either willingly or because he had no option but to do so if he was carrying a report detailing all of his activities.

Maurice Lequeux agreed to reveal all he knew in accordance with the terms of the agreement and was only prevented from revealing every last detail by some of his team, who persuaded him that this was not necessary. The depot at Falaise was finally found but whether this was a result of the confrontation of Cauchy with Norman or the treatment Cauchy received in prison will never be known. In Montargis, I have only found a little information but enough to be clear that Roger Narcy did talk. I do not know whether he did so willingly or after some maltreatment but he did not return to the area after the war. Maurice Duthilleul was another who went somewhere else after the war, after apparently willingly giving up not only the depot at l'Hermitière in the Orne but also Garry's depot from his September drop.

Armel Guerne decided to act in the same way as Norman after a confrontation between them in July. When the Germans asked him about a depot at Origny-en-Thiérache organised by a group for which he acted as liaison with Paris, he wrote a note to the owner of the mill who was holding them and he appears to have told them the exact location as, when the Germans arrived at the mill to arrest the owner, they asked for a screwdriver and went straight to where the arms were hidden. Guerne did not know where the arms of the other group in this area were hidden; nor the people involved as he had never been there and he said later that the Germans did not even know about this group. In fact the Germans would have known about these drops after they decoded Norman's messages for May and June.

As has already been mentioned, the German explanation for much of the information that they showed to those they caught was that they had an agent in London. The SOE agent Marcus Bloom, whose wireless was the first that Goetz tried to play back, had on him when arrested a photograph of his organiser, Maurice Pertschuk, in British uniform. This should have been taken from him by the security staff who searched him before he left for France. Other captured agents shown this photograph could easily believe that it had come from a German agent in London and the Germans played on this.

In reality their extensive knowledge of the structure of SOE and its training schools came from the many agents captured in Holland. Their interrogations included, for example, twenty questions about each of the training schools they had attended; including its exact location and the names of the instructors and other trainees, and full details of what they were taught.[25] Some of their information about the Prosper organisation came from the mail sent to London via Déricourt. They had information on Frager's organisation from the same source, as he had to make detailed written reports rather than report by wireless after Clech's codes and schedules were stolen in May. These were backed up by Bardet giving copies of these reports to Bleicher of the Abwehr before he passed them to Déricourt. The Abwehr had an earlier success in 1942 when one of Frager's men, André Marsac, fell asleep in a train from Marseilles to Paris and his briefcase containing the names and addresses of 200 members of Carte was stolen. Germaine Tambour told Marguerite Flamencourt that her arrest in April was a result of her Carte connections, almost certainly revealed by Marsac's list, but that she had only been interrogated about her Prosper contacts after Norman's arrest and in his presence.

Another source of information came from the packages of instructions and letters addressed 'For Prosper' and 'For Archambaud' which had been brought to France by Pickersgill and Raynaud and found in Culioli's car. Balachowsky records what he thought was just a story of my father, 'being left for forty-eight hours with the complete German dossier on his own case and, at the end of his reading, congratulating the Germans on having some documents addressed to him before he himself had received them'.[26]

As well as finding Norman's address in Culioli's briefcase, Goetz claimed that information had been obtained from a deposition made by Culioli before he returned to Paris on 29 June, whilst Vogt claimed that Borrel had talked after being ordered to do so by Norman, and Mme Balachowsky claimed that when Borrel was arrested, she had her briefcase with her containing names and addresses, 'which made possible the arrests of so many persons'.[27] Gustave Tiercelin records that he was confronted with Norman after his arrest at Étrépagny on 2 August 1943. Norman told him that the Germans had found out about Tiercelin after they had been able to decrypt a message Norman had sent on his behalf.[28]

Marcel Gouju reported that the Gestapo had copies of Norman's messages but had not been able to decipher them until after his arrest. In one of Guillaume's books he mentions that these messages covered May and June, which were of course the busiest months for the circuit, and deciphering these messages would have enabled the Germans to identify the locations of the DZs approved in those months as their coordinates would have been given and would also have revealed the existence of others previously approved but used again in this period.[29]

Michael Foot records that whilst Pickersgill and Macalister were waiting for Culioli to obtain new papers for them, Pickersgill wrote out his operational instructions and Macalister noted down his security checks. These were found on them and enabled the Germans to set up their own bogus Archdeacon circuit.[30]

Being shown this vast collection of information must have undermined the resistance of captured agents and it appears that the Germans varied what they told captured agents to produce the maximum effect on whoever was being interrogated. Maurice Braun, for example, was told about statements made by Jacques Weil without realising that Weil had not even been arrested. Nicolas Laurent was told that the radio crystals with his address on them had been found in a crashed aircraft when in fact the crystals were found in Culioli's car and his address in Culioli's briefcase. Harry Peuleve was told that my father had taken the Germans around to convince people to co-operate when this was only done by Norman. In a letter that Michael Foot wrote to me he said:

Do remember that all the Germans that you quote were professional liars and good at their job. The evidential value of anything that they said while interrogating prisoners is not high. Apart possibly from Goetz and Kieffer, the rest were simply out to get anything they could out of any captive, and no holds were barred.

It was the comprehensive information that the Germans already possessed together with that obtained from some of those interrogated in the first few days that enabled them to round up most of the people in the groups within two weeks of the arrests of the chiefs on 24 June. It must also have required considerable reorganisation. The Gestapo had arrested Jean Moulin and his group only three days before but decided to transfer their attentions to the Prosper organisation as the quantity of arms and sabotage material it had received posed a more immediate threat. Misselwitz, another of the Germans in the Avenue Foch, who had been involved in the initial interrogation of some of the Moulin group, reported that Kieffer lost all interest in the remainder of this group after the arrest of my father and many were released a few months later.[31]

The Gestapo in Lyons had of course failed to capitalise on the arrest of Moulin when they beat him so badly that he was put into a coma without ever admitting that he was Moulin. He was brought to Paris and lodged in Boemelburg's own villa before being put on a train to Berlin, where he died at Metz station on 8 July.

Vogt mentions that my father was sent to Berlin some two weeks after his arrest at the request of an important officer in Gestapo headquarters and Kieffer confirmed this to Vera Atkins, adding that the important officer was Kaltenbrunner, his chief in Berlin. Two weeks from 24 June is 8 July. It is possible therefore that my father was on the same train as the dying Moulin or was sent immediately after, and because of, his death. Records from Sachsenhausen show my father arriving there on 3 September 1943.

Notes

1. Deposition 19.01.1947, HS 6/426, TNA.
2. Voluntary Statement 20.11.1946, HS 9/836/5, TNA.
3. Deposition 13.03.1947, Z6 NL 17339, Archives Nationales.
4. Scherer was later killed by Dubois so there is no post-war deposition.
5. HS 9/1110/5, TNA.
6. Deposition 29.03.1949, 16 P 364747, SHD.
7. Interrogation 25-26.10.1943, HS 9/536/1, TNA.
8. Report 28.04.1945, HS 9/379/8, TNA.
9. 2nd Interrogation 27.04.1945, HS 6/440, TNA.
10. Interview 26.04.1945, HS 9/517/8, TNA.
11. Interrogation 15.05.1945, HS 6/440, TNA.
12. P. Guillaume, *La Solonge au Temps de l'Héröisme et de la Trahaison.*
13. J.O. Fuller, *Déricourt: The Chequered Spy*, Michael Russell, 1989.
14. Interrogation 24.01.1944, HS 6/436, TNA.
15. Interrogation 11.09.1944, HS 9/1286/13, TNA.
16. See 6 above.
17. See 12 above.
18. See 3 above.
19. First Interrogation 14-20.05.1944, HS 9/631/5, TNA.

20. HS 9/1539/6, Interrogation 21.04.1945, TNA.
21. Deposition 11.10.1950, 72 AJ/39/I/piece 10b, Archives Nationales. Norman also helped the Germans in their interrogation of François Reeve from the Farmer circuit who was arrested at the end of November.
22. Interrogation 13.06.1945, HS 9/1395/3, TNA.
23. Letter from Renee Guepin 17.03.1948, HS 6/426, TNA. Interrogation of Rose-Marie Holwedts 10.04.1945, HS 9/1406/8, TNA.
24. Declaration, cote 55 J 4, Archives departementales du Loir-et-Cher.
25. M.R.D. Foot, *SOE in the Low Countries*, St Ermins, 2001.
26. See 9 above.
27. J.O. Fuller, *The German Penetration of SOE*, William Kimber, 1975.
28. Cote III/144, Dossier judiciaire – Pierre Culioli, TMP Metz, jgt n° 183/4526, 17/031949.
29. See 12 above.
30. M.R.D. Foot, *SOE: An Outline History*, BBC, 1984.
31. Deposition of Misselwitz quoted in Le Monde 25 July 1997.

THE CONCENTRATION CAMPS

When Heinrich Himmler was appointed head of the Gestapo in 1936, he ordered a new prison to be built in Oranienburg. Work started immediately whilst, some 35km to the south, Hitler was attempting to show the world the glories of Nazi policies by staging the Olympic Games in Berlin. Sachsenhausen concentration camp was finished in 1941. It contained 50 huts each designed to hold 140 prisoners but by the end of the year it already held more than 200 per hut. Over 200,000 people were sent to this camp. They would all have had to pass through the main entrance with its gates displaying the infamous slogan – *Arbeit macht Frei/* (Work makes you free). In 1938 the administrative centre for all concentration camps was established outside the camp entrance and, before reaching the gates, the prisoners would have to pass this building and an enormous SS barracks where concentration camp staff were trained.

Sachsenhausen was originally intended as a work camp but the addition of a gas chamber and additional ovens in 1943 enabled large numbers of prisoners to be disposed of. The killing area was outside the walls of the camp in an area called the Industriehof, which the SS cynically called Station Z to reflect the end of the journey from the guard tower A on top of the main entrance. These additional facilities were built by Anton Kaindl who became commandant of the camp in 1942.

1. Main gate A
2. Prison/Zellenbau
3. Killing and cremation area

Aerial view of Sachsenhausen concentration camp.

The camp had its own prison or Zellenbau. This was a T-shaped block of eighty cells where prisoners were mostly kept in solitary confinement. Normal prisoners had light and rations; more serious prisoners had light but reduced rations; and the most serious were held in darkened cells. Most of those in the first category were known as *Prominenten* and were potential hostages. These included Paul Reynaud, the Prime Minister of France in 1940, together with some of his cabinet ministers. The most serious prisoners did not usually stay long.

For each incoming prisoner, Kaindl would decide the type of cell and food and whether any privileges were allowed, such as smoking or reading. The chief warder of the prison was Kurt Eccarius. He remembered that my father, Grover-Williams and four other SOE prisoners were to receive standard prisoner food, not the SS rations that some others were allowed, and had no privileges. There were four other men in the Zellenbau from SOE. This was the Locksmith team – Lieutenant Commander Cumberlege and Sergeants Steele, Davies and Handley who had been captured in uniform in Greece after laying charges to block the Corinth canal. Kaindl would make twice weekly visits and on one of these sometime in the summer of 1944, my father asked Kaindl if he and Grover-Williams could share a cell but Kaindl turned this down.[1]

The conditions in which they were held were confirmed by Paul Schroeter, one of the prison orderlies. These were people who had been imprisoned for belonging to banned Bible study groups and took round food to the cells:

The health of these men can be well imagined on a diet of wurzels cooked in water. They never received Red Cross parcels. We orderlies managed however to converse with Allied officer POWs in transit in the Zellenbau (they were usually there for about ten weeks before being passed on) to tell them of the plight of the six and from them we smuggled items from their Red Cross parcels. ... We orderlies too, when it was possible, gave them extra swill if there was any left over which we smuggled into them at night. Despite this the six were very emaciated. They never required the attendance of the MO though they suffered, however, from skin complaints from time to time, or teeth ailments. All six were held in solitary confinement in their cells. Every morning only they were allowed out for 15 minutes exercise in the yard, but it was always avoided that they came together. ... The cells were fairly dark as the small windows were glazed with frosted glass covered on the outside with fine wire mesh.

He added that, 'Captain Williams received the most brutal treatment of all of the men.'[2]

At the beginning of 1945 the Germans realised that they needed to try and empty the concentration camps before the arrival of Allied troops revealed what had taken place in them. At this time Sachsenhausen held the second highest number of prisoners, only Buchenwald held more. Camp records show that there were 47,665 male and 13,214 women prisoners.[3] As a first step, according to Rudolf Hoess who worked in the Headquarters building outside the camp, all camps were asked at the end of January to submit lists of prisoners likely to be dangerous in the event of an evacuation to be approved for immediate execution. The list from Sachsenhausen was sent the next day and he was told about a week later that all had been executed.[4] At the evening roll call on 1 February the names of some 400 to 500 prisoners were called out for 'transport', a euphemism that invariably meant execution, and this included the names of the seven members of a Naval Commando unit held in the camp. Five of that team from Operation Checkmate in Norway came forward; one was in hospital and the seventh decided not to come forward.[5] The transport's departure from the camp was delayed due to a major air raid and when the march out of the camp did begin at 4 a.m., there was an uprising. The leader of the

The main Gate 'A' of Sachsenhausen.

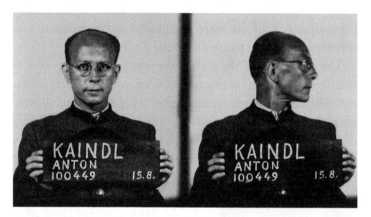

Anton Kaindl.

Commandos, John Godwin, is said to have seized the rifle of one of the guards and killed him whilst another group of prisoners took over a factory building, but all were ultimately gunned down with gunfire continuing until daybreak.[6]

There is no record of anyone from the Zellenbau being included in this 'transport', but soon afterwards, those who were not to be killed started to be moved out and some of these were contacted after the war to see if they had any

information on the fate of the six. Some were members of
SOE such as Hugh Falconer, a trained wireless operator
caught in North Africa, and five Danish officers. Four others
were part of the seventy-seven who had tunnelled out of
Stalag Luft III in March 1944, 'The Great Escape'. The four
were brought to Sachsenhausen and held in special housing
just outside the main wall of the concentration camp as the
Germans thought they had potential as hostages. Here they
met Jack Churchill, a Commando officer captured in Italy
but not killed immediately in accordance with Hitler's order
because he was thought to be related to Winston Churchill.
An irrepressible bunch, they tunnelled out at the end of
September but all five were recaptured within a month and
this time they were thrown into the Zellenbau.

The first to leave the Zellenbau was John Dodge, one of
the tunnellers, who was sent to Berlin on 2 February 1945.
A fortnight later, his three colleagues and Jack Churchill were
sent back to the special housing (where the guards had been
doubled) before being moved to Flossenburg on 3 April. One of
them, 'Wings' Day, stated that my father was moved sometime
between late January and mid-February whilst another, Sydney

Dowse, said he was moved on
12 February but neither knew what
had happened to the SOE prisoners.
However, Hugh Falconer said that
they were still there when he left on
23 February and one of the Danes,
Max Mikkelsen, said that he spoke
to my father on 28 February, the

Kurt Eccarius.

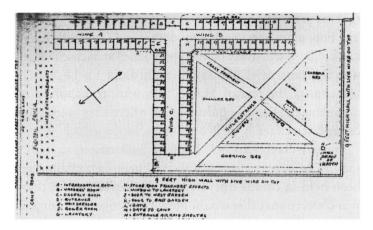

Plan of the Zellenbau.

day before he left, and 'handed Suttill a pencil as I (and also my three friends) believed that we were going to be executed when we learned about departure from the Zellenbau and therefore I thought that my only (illegal) pencil was no more good for me'. One of his colleagues, Petersen, saw my father the next morning just before the Danes left for Flossenburg.[7]

Dowse, Day and their fellow Stalag Luft III escaper, Jimmy James, were held in the first of the three wings of the Zellenbau whilst the Danes were held in the central wing where my father, Grover-Williams and at least two of the Locksmith party were held, although Eccarius gave my father a cell number in the first wing. As well as the main entrance where the three wings met, there were also doors at the end of each wing so it would have been easy to move prisoners from the middle wing to one of the others in such a way as to make other prisoners think that they had been removed altogether when in fact they had only been moved within the Zellenbau. None of those who went to Flossenburg mention seeing my father there. Eccarius told his British interrogators that my father had been taken to Berlin but gives no date. The only person to say that my father and Grover-Williams had not been sent away but had been killed at Sachsenhausen was Schroeter who last saw them around 15–18 March. 'At approx the end of March they were transported by ambulance car to the Industriehof where they were most certainly executed.'

As early as April 1945, Maurice Buckmaster wanted to send to Moscow a list of SOE prisoners who might have been held in camps liberated by the Russians, but there was concern that this would blow their cover. Buckmaster considered that saving their lives was more important and a list of some of those 'reasonably believed to be in Russian hands', including my father, was sent to the Soviets in May, but there is no record of any response.[8]

My mother was still being informed in late July 1945:

I have had news from a reliable informant that your husband was alive and well in late January or early February of this year. I am pursuing this clue and will certainly keep you informed if it should give results. In any case it is good news that at the time he was well.

It was only in November that she was informed otherwise:

I am sorry to say that it is now felt that there is now only the slightest hope that your husband may still be found to be alive and, should no further information come to light in the meantime, an approach will be made on 8th May 1946 to the War Office Casualties Branch to presume his death. We shall of course continue to make every endeavour to trace him but I feel that in the circumstances you are entitled to know the position as we see it today.[9]

This approach presumed his death on or after 1 February 1945. Finally in September 1946, in the light of Schroeter's evidence, she was told that this date had been amended to on or shortly after 18 March 1945.

Sachsenhausen was liberated by the Russians on 22 April 1945 and they immediately started to prepare a list of camp staff to be prosecuted, most of whom had ended up as British prisoners. The British had prepared their own list of people whom they wished to prosecute for 'Ill-treatment of Allied POWs and Internees' but in May 1946 it was agreed that the Soviets should take over the Sachsenhausen prosecutions and all of the files and prisoners were handed over. At the end of the year, 'after months of interrogations by the NKWD officers and military public prosecutors, all of the defendants gave in to the burden of incriminating evidence and to the massive psychological pressure. They offered general confessions.' The trial started in Berlin in October 1947, the accused being:

> charged with participation in the murder of Soviet prisoners and co-responsibility for the entire camp regime. These were regarded as war crimes and crimes against humanity. After the charges had been read aloud, each of the defendants confessed audibly and distinctly to their guilt in all of the crimes charged against them.[10]

After only eight days of proceedings, Kaindl and others were sentenced to various years of forced labour. The death sentence in the Soviet Union had been suspended in May 1946 and was not reinstated until 1950. The men were sent to the northern coalmines and Kaindl died there in the first winter. Eccarius and others who survived this regime were released in 1955 but were tried again in Germany and given long prison sentences.

I thought that this might be as far as I could go when a researcher at Sachsenhausen went to Moscow and found some evidence from the Russian War Crimes Trial in the old KGB archives. These were two witness statements by a Russian officer who had met another of the orderlies from the Zellenbau; Hans Apel looked after the prison boiler and one of his tasks was to burn the possessions of those who had been killed. One of the things he had been given to burn was a notebook listing in German the names of 112 prisoners from the Zellenbau. One page confirmed what I already knew – that 'Dowa, Dei, Dames and Churchill' were released on 15 February – suggested that the record was accurate.[11]

The notebook gave seven examples of persons who had been 'released to the crematorium' and much to my surprise, one of these was, '*Sutil, Francis, seit dem 3.9.43, geb. 1910 Max-Boronell (England) geschikt IV – A 2, am 23.3.43 ... ins Krematorium entlassen*'. This gives his date of arrival at Sachsenhausen as 3 September 1943 on the orders of the Section of the RSHA dealing with sabotage and then indicated his release to the crematorium. All the death dates in the other entries are for 1945. Clearly my father was not killed in March 1943 so this must be a typing error for 1945. One of the statements ended by saying that a complete copy of the notebook was attached. Unfortunately it no longer is, nor was, the notebook found in the archives.[12]

On a later visit to the archives in Moscow, an interrogation of Eccarius by the Russians was found dated after the death penalty was repealed in Russia and it appears that, with the death penalty no longer a threat, Eccarius had been persuaded to give a fuller version of events and one closer to the truth as to his involvement. He describes all of his activities and admits that between the end of 1944 and his leaving the camp in April 1945, forty prisoners from the Zellenbau were killed.

Fourteen of these he escorted personally to the Industriehof, including one group of four comprising: two members of the English army, Grover-Williams and Suttill; an Italian, Bacigalupi, and a Norwegian, Peer Nilson. He stated that all four were shot at the end of February.[13]

Schroeter said that those who left the Zellenbau in their prison clothes were going to their deaths as those being released invariably left in their uniforms or own clothes. What Schroeter did not know was the existence of a special facility for shooting prisoners that did not impair their clothing. Prisoners were taken out of the prison in a field ambulance ostensibly for a medical examination at the Industriehof where there was a neck shot installation:

> In turn they were told to undress and were led into a 'medical inspection' room where stood a 'doctor' in a white coat who instructed the prisoner to stand against a wall to have his height measured; when the measuring bar touched the top of his head an SS man fired through a slit in the wall. Loud music piped through a loudspeaker deadened the noise of the shot. The body was dragged out to the crematorium, the blood was wiped away and the next victim was brought in.[14]

Next to the Industriehof was the 'execution trench' where prisoners were shot or hanged in groups. It is possible that my father was shot there but he would have had to be undressed if Schroeter is correct.

In the light of this new evidence, my father's Death Certificate was officially amended to read, 'Executed, Sachsenhausen Concentration Camp, on or shortly after 23/3/1945.'

The British recognised his achievements by making him a Companion of the Distinguished Service Order (DSO), at the

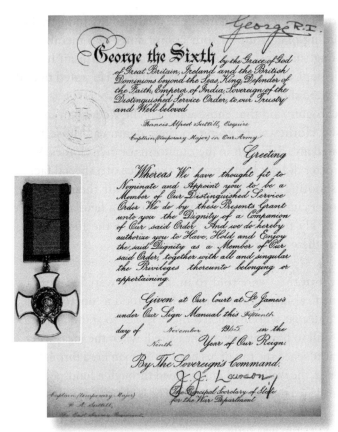

DSO medal citation. (Author)

time the second highest military award. The French have not given him any recognition. In the 1950s he was considered for the award of the Croix de Chevalier de la Légion d'Honneur but the decree used was not considered appropriate as it only covered French nationals.[15]

At his trial in 1948, Déricourt made the extraordinary claim that Prosper's real name was Lord Cole, an English traitor, and that he had heard that Churchill had talked of Cole's treachery being responsible for a delay in the invasion.[16] This is nonsense, but it was referred to in the official reports of the trials of both Déricourt and Culioli. This, together with the fact that much of the material my father received was given to the communists, may be the real reason he has been given no recognition by the French.

Notes

1. Interrogation of Eccarius, 21.02.1946, WO 309/853, TNA.
2. Interviews 05.07.1946 & 21.08.1946, HS 8/882, TNA.
3. www.air-photo.com/english/tgeb.html.
4. Statement by Hoess, WO 309/439, TNA.
5. Following a British raid on Sark at the beginning of October 1942 when some German prisoners were killed, Hitler ordered that in future all Commandos caught should be executed immediately, despite being in uniform, unless a delay in their execution might lead to useful information being revealed under interrogation. The first group to suffer the consequences of this order were seven Commandos from Operation Musketoon caught in Norway a month before the order was made but on 22 October they were taken to Sachsenhausen, held in the Zellenbau overnight and killed the next morning. The Checkmate team had been captured in May 1943 but were not killed immediately and, even when sent to Sachsenhausen in September, they were held in the main camp initially on easy duties in the kitchens but later made to make long marches testing boots.
6. Briefing report for the British Commanders'-in-Chief Mission to the Soviet Forces in Germany (BRIXMIS) 1988, IWM.
7. Vera Atkins' papers, IWM.
8. HS 4/331, TNA.
9. HS 9/1430/6, TNA.
10. Sachsenhausen Information Leaflet 24, 1999. Information Leaflet 24, Gedenkstatte und Museum Sachsenhausen, 1999.
11. The statements are in German and I was informed by a German that they seem to have been written originally in Russian from information in German and then translated back into German by a Russian, which probably explains the phonetic spelling of the names of Dowse, Day and James and other errors.
12. Statements 12.10.1946, in Sachsenhausen archives.
13. Interrogation 20.12.1946, in Sachsenhausen archives.
14. B.A. James, *Moonless Night*, William Kimber, 1983.
15. 16P 300559, SHD.
16. Henri Déricourt: TMP Paris, jgt n° 576/597, 07/06/1948.

AFTERWORD

Having, I hope, removed the layers of confusion laid over my father's story by the conspiracy theorists, it is now possible to look at what he actually achieved. Despite the loss of his orders, it is possible to discern what they probably were by looking at how his organisation developed. His only identifiable contacts when he first arrived were Carte contacts provided by Germaine Tambour and contacts established by Raymond Flower along the Loire between Tours and Orléans. Although no direct contacts appear to have been taken over from the earlier Autogiro circuit of Pierre de Vomecourt, use was made of the experience of two refugees from the collapse of that circuit, Octave Simon and Henri Garry, but in a completely different area from that in which they had operated previously, where they were able to use completely new contacts. When my father met Heyermans, the Carte representative in the north of France, he was surprised to find that this part of Carte still considered itself to be operational, so he disengaged from the contacts he had made and took no further steps to be active in their areas at that time.

My father's first parachute operation was in Étrépagny, to the west of Gisors in the eastern Eure, where his contact came from one of Flower's recruits, Pierre Culioli, who had worked there as a tax inspector before the war. Having made contacts in that area, my father decided that Culioli would be of more use in the area where he had worked with Flower, so he sent him back there to expand these contacts. In the Gisors area he was somehow put into contact with Georges Darling to whom he gave the task of recruiting further groups in this area. Darling also started a group near St Quentin and this was handed over to Beiler at the end of March 1943, when he recovered from the injury he had sustained on landing and found that his original mission was no longer relevant. Beiler developed this into the Musician circuit but it only became independent when he was sent a wireless operator of his own in September 1943.

By February 1943, Darling around Gisors, Culioli south of Blois and Simon and Garry near Le Mans had all found DZs to which Physician operations were flown. The DZ near Le Mans was used again in March and April whilst Culioli activated three new DZs and Darling found another four. Edward Wilkinson was sent by my father to Angers to set up groups there under his operational name Privet, whilst Jean Worms organised the first Juggler drop south of Châlons-en-Champagne. Just to the south of Juggler's area, two groups were established around Troyes to which Physician operations were flown but without success, and these were then handed over to Ben Cowburn to become the start of the Tinker circuit. The old Carte contacts in the north were also picked up again and Physician operations were flown to DZs near Hirson and further west along the Franco-Belgian border.

The organisation's activities continued to be expanded in May. The DZ north-west of Le Mans was replaced by one to the north-east whilst a new DZ much further north near Falaise in Normandy was also tried. Wilkinson moved to Nantes to take over a Physician group and Richard Heslop took over in Angers but both used the operational name of Privet. Darling and Culioli continued their expansion in June; the group started by Culioli in Meung-sur-Loire in the Loiret

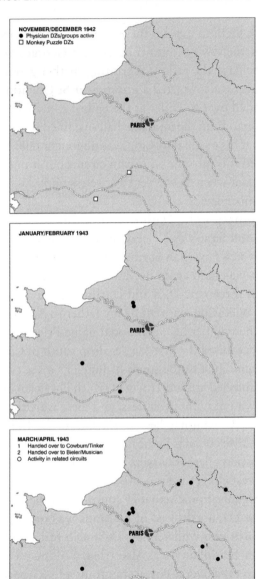

Development of the Physician circuit.

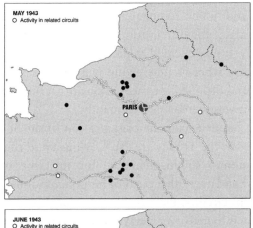

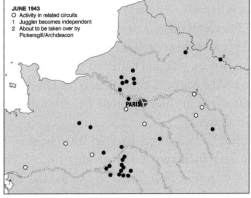

Development of the Physician circuit.

received its first operation; and a completely new southern group was started based in Montargis at the eastern end of the Loiret. Another new group was formed based on the National Agricultural College to the west of Paris. Although the drop at Falaise had been successful, it was decided that it would be too dangerous to have further drops this near the closely guarded coast. As material was needed in Normandy, it was decided to drop material further south to the DZ to the north-east of

Le Mans and to another near Ancinnes, and then take it by lorry to Falaise for distribution into other parts of western Normandy. It was decided to do the same at the eastern end of the region where a new group was formed in Évreux to take material dropped for them at one of Darling's DZs and transport it westwards into Normandy.

Having handed over the organisation of the St Quentin area to Beiler, the Troyes area to Cowburn and the Nantes/Angers region to Wilkinson and Heslop, my father was ready in June to hand over other parts of his organisation to become independent circuits. Pickersgill with Macalister as wireless operator was to take over the Physician groups in the north of France and develop them into the Archdeacon circuit whilst the arrival of two other wireless operators, Noor Inayat Khan and Gaston Cohen, enabled Garry to take over the Physician groups around Le Mans to develop into the Phono circuit, and Jean Worms to run his Juggler circuit free from dependence on Prosper wirelesses.

If my father had not been arrested when he was, he would have been left with two large groups for which he saw completely different functions. In the south, some of the material dropped was being used for sabotage locally and in Paris but most stored for use when the Allied invasion took place. In the north, only the minimum amount of material was kept in the area; the majority was distributed to groups who were not under his control but were organising sabotage in Paris, or, was taken west into Normandy. When the Allies landed, which he thought would be in the second half of 1943, he intended to split his command in two, taking charge of the northern area himself and handing over the southern groups to Norman. He considered that it would be impossible to continue to operate from Paris due to much stricter curfews that would be imposed and more frequent round-ups and checkpoints.

This break-up of the organisation into two parts had been mentioned in one of his reports in March so even at that earlier date he foresaw that large parts of his organisation would soon be dispersed to other organisers. This strategy is mentioned again in a report by Agazarian at the end of June, so it was clearly a long-term strategy that must have been discussed with London and agreed by them, probably during my father's visit in May.

SOE's policy was that circuits should be completely independent and have no contact with each other. This separation proved to be impossible to maintain, mainly due to the chronic shortage of wireless operators and London's frequent instructions to agents to inter-connect. When my father first arrived in France, the only operator available in the Occupied Zone was Marcel Clech, trying to work in Tours with Flower's Monkeypuzzle circuit but finding it almost impossible due to the intensity of German detection activities. Charles Grover-Williams had been sent in even before Flower but not with a wireless operator. Claude de Baissac had been sent in July with a wireless operator but the latter had been so badly injured on landing that he could not work. His replacement, Roger Landes, arrived with Gilbert Norman in November 1942 but was based in Bordeaux. Although Norman was quickly transferred to Prosper, he was not able to transmit for three months. Trotobas arrived six weeks after my father with an operator but Arthur Staggs was not able to make his set work so he looked to my father for communication with London. Opportunities for communicating with London were improved at the very end of 1942 with the arrival of Jack Agazarian as a second operator for Prosper but this still meant that five organisers were having to use two operators. Although Norman at last received a set and made contact with London in March just as Clech was leaving France, two more organisers, Jean Worms

340 PROSPER: MAJOR SUTTILL'S FRENCH RESISTANCE NETWORK

and Henri Déricourt, had arrived by then, so that by the end of March the situation was even worse with seven organisers using two operators. SOE's policy of keeping circuits separate was seriously compromised by its failure to provide enough wireless operators.

April saw the arrival of four more organisers and the return to action of two others. Ben Cowburn brought his own operator and, after contacting my father for introductions to his groups there, he and Barrett operated independently. Jean Bouguennec also arrived to set up the Butler circuit and Michel Fox, the Publican circuit. They came with a wireless operator but Rousset lost his set on landing and they went to my father for help until a new set was dropped for them in May. The returnees were Edward Wilkinson and Richard Heslop in the Nantes/Anger region, who should have had their own operator but Denis Rake was arrested before he could join them. Liewer also arrived in April to set up the Salesman circuit in the Rouen/Le Havre area together with Dubois, now trained as an SOE operator. Dubois returned to Tours to work and, although Liewer used him for communications with London, he had to make contact with the Prosper organisation in order to find safe accommodation in Rouen.

May saw the return of Clech. He was meant to act as the wireless operator for a new circuit, Inventor, and to be the link with London for Frager's Donkeyman circuit, but Déricourt stole his schedules and he was not able to operate for a couple of months. The June arrivals were swept up in the June arrests as has already been noted and so made no difference to the situation.

The problem of having too many people relying on too few wireless operators is well illustrated by Agazarian, who reported that he had sent messages for more than twenty people. As expected he sent messages for members of the

Prosper organisation and its sub-circuits – my father, Norman, Amps, Garry, Worms and Déricourt – and those dependent on Prosper for other reasons – Beiler, Wilkinson, Antelme, Grover-Williams, Trotobas, Bouguennec, Fox, Rousset, Jones of Inventor and Clech – but he also sent them for both Claude and Lise de Baissac and Flower. Even more surprisingly he sent messages for agents from RF and DF sections – Lejeune, Natzler, Gerson and Racheline.

This near monopoly on wireless communication between London and northern France in the first half of 1943 undoubtedly helped my father to start organising parachute operations so quickly. His first operation was just six weeks after his arrival. Of those who had arrived before him, Flower was almost as quick as he also had a wireless operator initially, but he only managed to organise four drops in total. Grover-Williams, who had arrived even earlier, had to wait over four months for his first delivery and he only managed one more in total than Flower. Claude de Baissac, who went in straight from training at the end of July, organised his first operations after three months but his first success was not until November and he then received nothing more until April 1943. However, by the end of June that year sixty-six Scientist operations had been flown in all, of which half were successful.

Trotobas, who was the next organiser to arrive after my father, did not have a successful operation until April. By the end of June 1943, twelve Farmer operations had been attempted but only two were successful, although he had more success in the second half of the year until his death in November. When at the end of March Beiler was given the group started by Darling for my father near St Quentin, a drop had already been arranged for 14 April. After that he concentrated on expanding the circuit and only arranged two more drops before his arrest in January 1944. Similarly

Cowburn was able to receive his first operation within a month of his arrival to the established group that he had taken over, but he only organised two more before returning to London in September. The injuries that Bouguennec sustained on landing in April, and the loss of their wireless, delayed the start of the Butler and Publican circuits until a new set arrived for Rousset in May. Fox only managed one successful drop before his arrest in September whilst Bouguennec was more successful, organising six.

The last successful Physician operations were flown on the night of 21/21 June. These brought the total number of Physician operations flown to over 100 with just under half being successful. They delivered seven agents and 400 containers.

Some writers take it for granted that because of all the interactions, the collapse of the Prosper organisation caused many arrests in other circuits later in the year. There is no evidence for this. Indeed all of the arrests outside the Prosper organisation, and even some within it, were due to other factors.

Edward Wilkinson's arrest on 6 June was brought about by his pre-Prosper contacts. The arrest of Pickersgill and Macalister on 21 June was one of the causes of the Prosper crisis; it was not a consequence. The capture of Jean Worms and the Guernes on 1 July was due to their own carelessness in returning to a meeting place they knew to be blown. The Chestnut circuit's collapse in August was the result of the Germans tracking down Dowlen whilst he was transmitting and Beiler's Musician succumbed in January 1944 for the same reason. In September 1943 the chiefs of the Butler and Publican circuits, now operating independently as they had received a replacement wireless, were all three caught together due to a local betrayal. The arrest of the Garrys, now running an independent Phono circuit, followed the arrest of their wireless operator, who had been in contact with Gestapo agents posing as Pickersgill and Macalister.

The arrests of the wireless operators from the Butler, Phono and Musician circuits enabled the Germans to take over their wirelesses, as they had already done with that of Macalister/ Archdeacon, and play them back so convincingly that London thought that these four circuits were still operating normally. They had previously played back the set of Norman but only for six weeks, although this did enable them to catch Agazarian.

Almost 300 operations were flown to German-controlled circuits between October 1943 and May 1944, of which almost 200 were successful. These delivered not just large amounts of arms (just over 1,900 containers), sabotage material and money straight into the hands of the Germans but also seventeen agents, some of whose wirelesses were also played back successfully for a short while. The seventeen agents dropped directly to the Germans, together with two others who were caught whilst trying to make contact with these circuits, were all killed in concentration camps.

Before the release of the French Circuit Liquidation files, it was difficult to calculate accurately how many people were arrested following the capture of the leaders of Prosper. Some reports have claimed as many as 1,000, of whom over 400 died.[1] In fact the number arrested in 1943 and deported as a direct consequence of the collapse of the organisation was 167 of whom just under half survived. In addition, three others were shot when the Germans tried to arrest them; two died in France as a result of ill-treatment in prison; two died in prison in France; and two escaped from the train taking them to Germany. I have listed all of these in Appendix 3 and, if I have missed out some names, I hope readers will let me know so that the list can be as complete as possible. I have not included the many who were arrested and released after a period of detention.[2] (I have also listed in Appendix 3 the names of the RAF crews who died whilst flying Physician operations.)

Most of the men who were deported were among the 1,944 on a transport that left France on 17 January 1944, arriving in Buchenwald two days later. The transport consisted of closed cattle wagons with 100 men in each. It was the sixth such transport but was twice the size of any of the earlier ones and was the first of an accelerated programme of deportations, which resulted in a total of 5,500 male deportations from France in January. From Buchenwald, many were moved to Dora, Flossenburg and Mauthausen. In total, 37 per cent died or disappeared in the camps and about 50 per cent returned, the fate of the rest being unknown.

One hero of this transport was Alfred Balachowsky, the biologist from my father's group at the National Agricultural College. He was initially sent on to Dora but soon returned to Buchenwald to help with an outbreak of typhus. When it was realised that French agents were to be killed, he was able to help three of them, Forest Yeo-Thomas, Harry Peuleve and Stephan Hessel, to avoid execution by a ruse that they had died of typhus and substituting their identities for prisoners who had really died. He also gave evidence at the Nuremburg trials. He was not able to save Pickersgill and Macalister, who were killed there on 14 September 1944.

Most of the women deported were among the almost 1,000 who left France on the last day of January and arrived in Ravensbrück three days later, from where they were sent to work in various satellite camps, although some were gassed, including the Tambour sisters. In total 20 per cent died or disappeared and some 75 per cent returned. The Swedish Red Cross negotiated the release of almost 100 in April 1945 just before the camp was liberated and several Prosper women were included, although some were already too ill and died before they could be returned to France. Yvonne Rudellat had been moved to Belsen, but when it was liberated she was not found immediately as she was not registered under a name known to those looking for her and, by the time she was found, she had died.

As has already been noted, my father was shot in Sachsenhausen on 23 March 1945. Gilbert Norman was killed in Mauthausen on 6 September 1944. Jack Agazarian, James Amps and Jean Worms were killed in Flossenberg on 29 March 1945. Andrée Borrel was killed in Natzweiler on 6 June 1944. She and three other women agents were given lethal injections and then put straight into the crematorium ovens, possibly even before they had died. One of the women managed to scratch the face of the doctor giving the injections. It could have been any one of them but it reminded me of the spirit Borrel showed in training when she shocked her fellow trainees by suggesting that a good way to kill a Nazi would be to plunge a sharpened pencil in his ear.

Unlike the names of most SOE agents who died in Europe, my father's is not on the memorial at Brookwood Cemetery in Surrey, just 20 miles from his home. It has instead been placed on the Groesbeek memorial, part of the Canadian Cemetery, in a small village in the Netherlands. Although this is clearly totally inappropriate, the Commonwealth War Graves Commission refuses to correct it.

Notes

1. R. Marshall, *All the King's Men*, HarperCollins,1988.
2. Livre Memorial, http://www.bddm.org/liv/recherche.php.

ACKNOWLEDGEMENTS AND SOURCES

My primary written sources were the:

- SOE and Air Ministry files in The National Archives in London;
- circuit files in the 17 P series in the Archives nationales in Paris;
- personal files in the 16 P series in the archives of the Service Historique de la Défense in Paris;
- archives of Libre Résistance Amicale Buck in Paris and the Université de Nanterre;
- books and articles that I have referred to in the text and listed at the end of this section.

Many of the latter were of dubious value either for reasons already given in the chapter titled Theories and Lies or because they lack references supporting what is written.

Mainly due to the loss of vital Air Ministry files, I made several research visits to France and found people who were able to fill in the many gaps in my knowledge, and these meetings are recorded in the book.

I would not have even thought of publishing the results of my research without the prompting and encouragement of the late Professor Michael Foot backed by two colleagues from the Special Forces Club Historical Sub-Committee, Duncan Stuart and Mark Seaman.

I must say a special thank you to David Harrison and Steven Kippax for a constant supply of information and to Annette Biazot, Josette Bossard and Fabrice Dury for their help with French sources and with research.

I was helped in many ways by many others: Dodo Anderson, Platon Alexiades, Alain Antelme, Roger Beam, Jacqueline Bieler, Fabrice Bourée, Tim Buckmaster, Richard de Courson, Howard Davies of The National Archives, Joseph Esteves, Gerard Fournier, Caroline Griffith of the Special Forces Club, Gerard Larue, Guy Laurent, David List, Ken Merrick, Gerard Metais, Teddy Meunier, Nigel Perrin, Laurent Quillichini of the Blois Museum, Stephen Tyas, Martine Vallon of the Romorantin Museum, staff of the Archives départementales of the Oise, Loir-et-Cher and Sarthe, and researchers and archivists at the Gedenkstatte und Museum Sachsenhausen.

Books and Articles

Allbeury, T., *A Time without Shadows*, Hodder, 1990

Basu, Shrabani, *Spy Princess*, Sutton Publishing, 2006

Biazot, Annette, and Lecler, Philippe, *Face à la Gestapo*, Euromedia, 2011

Buckmaster, Maurice, *Prosper*, Chambers's Journal, January 1947

Buckmaster, Maurice, *Specially Employed*, Batchworth, 1952

Buckmaster, Maurice, *They Fought Alone*, Odhams, 1958

Bureau, J., *Un Soldat menteur*, Laffont, 1992

Carre, M-L., *The Cat*, Four Square, 1961

Cave Brown, Anthony, *Bodyguard of Lies*, Harper and Row, 1975

Clark, Freddie, *Agents by Moonlight*, Tempus, 1999

Collins, L., *Fall from Grace*, Granada, 1985

Colvin, Ian (ed.), *Colonel Henri's Story*, William Kimber, 1954

Cookridge, E.H., *Inside SOE*, Arthur Baker, 1966

Cowburn, Benjamin, *No Cloak, No Dagger*, Adventurers Club, 1960

Dalton, Hugh, *The Fateful Years*, Frederick Muller, 1952

Foot, M.R.D., *SOE in France*, HMSO, 1966 and 1968; New edition Frank Cass, 2004. (A French edition was published in 2008 by Tallinder under the title, *Des Anglais dans la Resistance*)

Foot, M.R.D., *SOE: An Outline History*, BBC, 1984

Foot M.R.D., *SOE in the Low Countries*, St Ermin's Press, 2001

Fuller, J.O., *Double Webs*, Putnam, 1958

Fuller, J.O., *Double Agent?*, Pan Books, 1961

Fuller, J.O., *The German Penetration of SOE*, William Kimber, 1975

Guillaume, Paul, *L'abbé Emile Pasty: pretre et Soldat*, Loiret, Orléans, 1946

Guillaume, Paul, *La Résistance en Sologne*, Orléans, 1946

Guillaume, Paul, *La Sologne au temps de l'héroïsme et de la trahaison.*Imprimerie Nouvelle, 1950

Hany-Lefebvre, Noemi, *Six mois à Fresnes,* Edition Flammarion, 1946

Helm, Sarah, *A Life in Secrets*, Little Brown, 2005

Heslop, Richard, *Xavier*, Rupert Hart-Davis, 1970

Howard, Michael (Sir), *Strategic Deception*, HMSO, 1990

James, B.A., *Moonless Night*, William, 1983

King, Stella, *Jacqueline,* Arms and Armour Press, 1989

Kramer, Rita, *Flames in the Field*, Michael Joseph, 1995

Larteguy, J. and Maloubier, B., *Triple Jeu*, Laffont, 1992

Lheureux, Danièle, *La Résistance 'Action-Buckmaster' Sylvestre-Farmer avec le capitaine 'Michel' Trotobas*, Geai Bleu, 2001

Mackenzie, W., *The Secret History of SOE*, St Ermins Press, 2000

Marks, Leo, *Between Silk and Cyanide*, HarperCollins, 1998

Marshall, Robert, *All the King's Men*, William Collins, 1988

Ménard, Christian, *39–45 La Résistance dans le Vexin*, Les cahiers de la Société Historique et Geographique du Bassin de l'Epte, No. 25, 1990

Merrick, K.A., *Flights of the Forgotten*, Arms and Armour, 1989

Morgan, General Sir Frederick, *Overture to Overlord*, Hodder & Stoughton, 1950

Nicholas, Elizabeth, *Death be not Proud*, Cresset Press, 1958

Perrault, G., *Le Secret du Jour J*, Fayard, 1964

Pioger, André, *Les Circuits Satirist, Physician and Bricklayer dans la Sarthe*, Gens de la Lune 180/183, 1978

Ryan, Robert, *The Spy who came back from the Dead*, Sunday Times Magazine, 16 December 2001

Seiler, Richard, *La Tragédie du Réseau Prosper*, Pygmalion, 2003

Vader, John, *The Prosper Double-Cross,* Sunrise Press, 1977. (French translation by C. Leburn, *Nous n'avons pas joue*, Le Capucin, 2002.)

Verity, Hugh, *We Landed by Moonlight*, Ian Allen, 1978; Revised edition Air Data Publications, 1995

Vivier, Jack, *Montrichard, ville occupé, cite libérée (1939–1945),* Editions CLD, Chambray-les-Tours, 1984

Wighton, Charles, *Pin-Stripe Saboteur*, Odhams, 1959

Wynne, B., *Count Five and Die*, Souvenir Press, 1958

AGENT TRAINING – HS 7/286

DEPOT SCHOOLS – [My father and group 27N comprising eleven men went to Wanborough Manor, Special Training School (STS) 5 near Guildford in Surrey]

Naturally most agents proceed to take particular courses designed to fit them for the actual missions which they are to perform in the field but there are certain matters which must form part of the training of every agent and these are taught at the Depot Schools. The Depot School syllabus is designed to cover a period of three weeks but can be extended to four weeks. The course consists of the following subjects:

(1) Weapon Training

Instruction is given in the rifle, Bren Light Machine Gun, grenades, Sten and automatic. The students are taught elementary stripping of these arms and how to clean and prime a grenade. There is firing practice and students should be able to throw a grenade 25 yards. The object is to give students a sound knowledge of the elements of each subject before they reach the para-military schools. This takes twenty-four hours in all, most divided into one hour periods.

(2) Signalling

Students are taught the morse code and should reach a genuine minimum standard of 8 words a minute (sending and receiving). The course takes nineteen hours, mostly one hour periods divided equally into sending and receiving.

(3) Physical Training

This is carried out with a view to the strenuous para-military course which follows and close attention is paid to the breaking in of the students' boots and the hardening of their feet. Not including games, the physical training course takes eighteen hours of one hour a day.

(4) Map reading

This is the longest course and covers not only reading but the practical use of maps, the taking of bearings and the sketching of maps including panorama sketching. There are a considerable number of field tests which include following a route by the map and compass and the description and plotting of routes taken by day and night. The course takes in all thirty hours, composed of one hour and two hour periods and one three hour period devoted to memorising, following and describing a route.

(5) Fieldcraft

This is the second longest course and is devoted to all types of crawling and silent movement and the use of cover and camouflage. There is a good deal of practical work in stalking, moving about and reconnaissance by day and night and there are practical schemes involving the reconnaissance of ground, targets and houses and an attack on a guarded place. The course takes twenty-seven hours.

(6) Demolitions

This syllabus includes only the elementary principles of demolitions and aims at providing the student with a thorough elementary knowledge (both practical and theoretical) of all British explosives in common use. Instruction is given in the use of safety fuses and cordtex (or primacord) and in the firing of simple cutting and mining charges but students are not taught the use of plastic explosives, booby-traps, incendiaries or devices. The students are taught to prepare dummy made-up charges which are later used in night schemes. The course takes twenty-five hours in all.

(7) Miscellaneous

Under this heading come security addresses by the school commandant, an explanation of the course, the issue of kit and preparation for and discussion of day and night schemes. There is no set time for training in P.A.D. but all students should be thoroughly conversant with the fitting and use of respirators and accessories and should wear their respirators for at least two 15 minute periods each week. They should also be taught how to decontaminate weapons. Miscellaneous subjects take fifteen hours in all.

If the course is extended to four weeks the additional time is taken up with revision of the syllabus.

PARA-MILITARY SCHOOLS in Scotland. [My father and seven others were based in Meoble Lodge, STS 23]

This course lasts four weeks and physically is much the hardest of the three. Its main objects are twofold:

(a)   to teach the use of the offensive weapons and 'special' stores with which it is hoped that the students will be equipped;

(b)   to train students in raid tactics, both as individuals and in small groups.

The main subject taught is Demolition, i.e. the destruction of communications and supplies. The other subjects taught are those which enable an approach to the target and the withdrawal from it to be carried out.

(1) Demolition

At first the training is mainly technical. The work done at the Depot Schools is made more difficult by such practical additions as working against time and doing dangerous work needing delicacy of touch, like the fitting of fuses into detonators, in the dark and after violent physical exertion. The use of Plastic is taught and the students' knowledge of other forms of High Explosive is thoroughly revised. This is followed by full instruction in Delayed Action Devices, both Mechanical, Chemical and Electrical, and including the ordinary Household Candle for use both as means of firing charges and starting fires. Students then go through a full course in Incendiaries and Incendiarism and revise this with Delayed Action Devices used in conjunction with Incendiaries. Next comes instruction in the setting and use of traps, laying special emphasis on the doubling of the firing mechanism, so that even if the trap is found and its wire cut or switch removed it will still operate. This section also includes the use of traps to fire a charge laid with a Delayed Action Device if the enemy tries to remove either the device or the charge itself.

The training then becomes more operational. Students are taught to calculate the amount of explosive to use in various cases and the best means of carrying the charge to the objective and of fixing and firing it when there. They receive special instruction in railway and marine sabotage, the firing of charges under water and the method of handling limpets. They are given considerable practice in the making up of charges and taught the use of a Cavity Charge for obtaining increased cutting effect on steel plate. The most effective methods are indicated of sabotaging everything except telegraphic communications and machinery (which are considered too technical). This includes action against aeroplanes, A.F.V.s and personnel.

The rest of the course consists of further practice in the preparation and use of all incendiary, direct action, electrical and home-made devices and of further hints on the concealment and camouflage of charges both in transport and when in position.

The course concludes with two examinations, one written and one practical. The written examination consists of a number of questions to which a quick and brief answer must be given. The time allowed for giving answers is 1.5 minutes and the students are expected to get over 80%. The practical examination is in two parts. The first is done in the dark, or blindfolded, and consists of fitting fuses to detonators, setting a device with detonator in operation and setting a booby-trap with a trip wire connected to a detonator and dummy charge. The second is to prepare a fairly large charge in two sections with a system of firing and some method of fixing it quickly in position.

(2) Appreciation, Planning and Reports
Stress is laid on the importance of getting extremely full information before even beginning to plan any operation and on considering the action to be taken carefully in the light of this so that when formulated the plan will be as concise and simple as possible. The method taught of issuing orders is that laid down by the Army, but the orders are given more individually and with necessary additions to allow for factors like a danger signal or last minute cancellation. The lectures on this subject are followed by a Sand Table exercise and one or more exercises on the open ground.

(3) Map Reading and Compass
The very full instructions already given at the Depot School are merely revised practically by this figuring in all schemes on the ground.

(4) Silent Killing and Weapon Training
The Silent Killing syllabus is an extension and elaboration of the Unarmed Combat taught in the Army, with more emphasis on the killing and with special additions such as fighting when in a crowd, and the use of the knife. The training is designed to inspire the necessary self-confidence and ruthlessness and to put it fully into practice. All the weapon training given is in the use of the revolver and Tommy or Sten gun, stress being laid chiefly on quickness in getting off an accurate shot. Practice is given in shooting in the dark and in firing up and down.

(5) Fieldcraft
Like the map reading, this subject, which has also been very fully taught at the Depot School, is merely revised practically by being brought into all the schemes.

(6) Physical Training, Rope Work and Tumbling
The Physical Training consists of the Trained Soldiers Tables 1 & 2 for the first fortnight and of Logging Exercises and Special Tables for the second. Similarly the Rope Work, which is Standard Climbing, is done first in PT kit, then in

denim and boots plus pack. The tumbling is mainly instruction in landing from a height. After the first week the Assault Course is introduced progressively and finally there is a competition run over the whole of it.

(7) Signalling

This begins with a test on what has been learned already, and thereafter consists mainly of practice in sending and reading, in instruction on the procedure used in sending messages, and on the Q code which has to be memorised. Lamp work is introduced except for those who read 12 w.p.m. who specialise in sending and reading instead.

(8) Raid Tactics

In these the students practice the drill and formation of a party attacking different objectives.

(9) Schemes and Exercises

These bring out in practice all the lessons already taught.

(10) Para-Naval Training

This is given to more or less selected personnel to enable them to sabotage small ships and to overcome any water obstacle in the approach to and withdrawal from an objective. It includes silent rowing and other boatwork.

[**Ringway airfield,** Manchester – STS 51 – is not mentioned in this document but agents did a short parachute training course after leaving Scotland.]

FINISHING SCHOOLS at Beaulieu in Hampshire [My father and three other potential organisers stayed in The Rings, STS 31.]

The training here is mental as compared with the largely physical work of the preparatory and para-military schools.

(1) Preliminary Talk

On the arrival of a party the duty officer attached to it explains who he is and that he is the link between the student and headquarters. The students are told of the local security precautions and arrangementsfor correspondence. They are given the hours of work (9.30 to 12.15 and 5.00 to 6.00 every day except Sundays, not including practical exercises and unarmed combat in the afternoons and certain night exercises) and they are given an outline of the course which covers the agent's life in the field, his protection and security, the German army, propaganda, codes, ciphers, secret inks, railways and fieldcraft.

(2) Guerrilla Warfare

The object, effects and types of guerrilla warfare are taught as well as the ingredients necessary for success as a leader or guerrilla soldier.

(3) Security

Students are taught the necessity for a good cover story, of being inconspicuous and discreet and of taking precautions with their documents and communications as well as familiarising themselves with the enemy counter-espionage methods and of being prepared for an emergency.

(4) Informant Service

This part of the course deals with obtaining information by personal observation and by using such persons as priests, inn-keepers, doctors, servants and discontented enemy soldiers with the object of learning about local conditions, counter-espionage and targets.

(5) Cover

This instruction deals with the necessity for a cast-iron background which will at the same time leave sufficient leisure for the agent's work. The obvious pitfalls in the use of false names and false occupations are pointed out as well as the necessity for being able to answer a close interrogation into the assumed background.

(6) Control of Civil Population

This part of the course deals with the methods used by the enemy to eliminate hostile elements by identity cards and the control of movement, action, communication and publications.

(7) Arrival

This subject covers the first forty-eight hours of an agent's arrival at the scene of an operation. He is warned to conform with all the necessary formalities and not to attempt subversive activities too soon. Instruction is given in the disposal of parachutes and containers, assembling the party and contacting friends. The advantages and disadvantages are pointed out of staying at hotels, boarding houses or as paying guests. Stress is laid on the necessity for building the cover and establishing suitable headquarters.

(8) Descriptions

Under this heading instruction is given in recognising unknown persons and in giving recognisable descriptions.

(9) Observation and Surveillance

It is explained that observation is the power to observe and surveillance the method of carrying out observation for a set purpose. Students are instructed to analyse the attributes of things that please them, then of things they dislike and finally of things to which they are indifferent. In this way they become sensitive to the presence of strangers or unusual happenings. From this they proceed to study the surveillance of people without themselves being noticed.

(10) House Searches and Raids

Instruction is given in police methods, routine searches, special searches and snap controls. Students are taught possible hiding places in houses or on the person and the importance of being orderly so as to be able to detect a search which has taken place during their absence.

(11) Body Search

Under this heading further instruction is given in places of concealment on the body and clothes, the importance of remaining calm and methods of distracting the searcher's suspicions.

(12) Approaching and Recruiting Agents

The importance is pointed out of not rushing into this activity which should be preceded by a survey of local opinion and a consideration of the types required. These include members of industrial groups, specialists, cut-outs, letter-boxes, accommodation addresses and couriers. The first recruits are likely to be drawn from the informant service (see above). The first steps are to learn all about a potential agent before approaching him, to know his weaknesses and interests, to be careful about the method of instruction and not to recruit an agent at the first interview. It is pointed out that it is advisable to let concrete suggestions come from the agent in the early stages, to give him time to think the matter over, to pretend to be an intermediary and to give the effect of belonging to a powerful and well-organised body.

(13) Handling of Agents

It is pointed out that finance must be arranged promptly and scrupulously and may take the form of goods instead of money or of some service to the recruit or his family. The recruit must be instructed to continue in his job and should be tested on something small before being entrusted with real work. An agent who becomes inefficient should be laid off gently: if he is inefficient through overwork or nerves he may recover; if he is inefficient through being won over by the enemy he may have to be killed. The impression should always be given that sooner or later treachery will be punished.

(14) Organisation of Agents

Under this heading is taught the importance of the cell system, the use of cut-outs and the departmentalising of the work.

(15) Communications

The advantages and disadvantages are pointed out of personal meeting, the post, telegraph and telephone. Agents are advised to meet at unusual rendezvous and never to go straight there from their residence. Instruction is also given in indirect methods of communication such as poste restante, letter boxes, accommodation addresses, advertisements and couriers. Students are taught methods of concealing messages (for example in tramcar seats) but it is pointed out that practically every method has been tried and is known.

(16) Establishment and Organisation Headquarters

Students are taught the importance of accessibility and good cover; for example a barber's shop is open to all but provides no security control whereas a a lawyer's office is open only to a particular type of client and provides good security control as well as cover for the possession of safes, etc. Visitors should have a good reason for visiting headquarters and special signals should be prearranged to avoid contact when the place is being watched.

(17) Passive Resistance

Students are taught that the objects of passive resistance are to reduce the enemy war effort, to make his life uncomfortable and to raise the civilian morale. Methods are indicated and the importance is stressed of avoiding reprisals.

(18) Selection of Targets

It is pointed out that targets should be selected with a view to damaging the enemy war effort or morale over a wide area and that the value of the result should be weighed against the inevitable reprisals with their probable effect for good or evil on the local population. Indications are given of how reprisals can be avoided by making the damage appear accidental or caused by a landing party or Allied aircraft.

(19) Planning and methods of attack

The importance is pointed out of good preliminary intelligence and reconnaissance followed by an attack on the weak point or bottleneck, either by explosives or by natural elements such as fire and water. Instruction is also given on the formation and organisation of the attacking group and the security principles to be observed afterwards.

(20) Interrogation

Under this heading are taught the various methods of interrogation, such as the use of sympathy, trickery, firmness or cruelty. The importance is stressed of a cast-iron story firmly and calmly delivered.

(21) Defensive Measures

This section covers the final arrangements before departure (checking up on personal appearance, clothes and effects), the question of carrying weapons, the drugs that will be taken and the procedure to be followed in the case of action by enemy police. Agents are given instruction in their personal behaviour if they are being pursued by the police and in the necessity of warning others when an agent has been arrested and of looking after his family. Further instruction is given on the subject of interrogation and the necessity for suicide in the last resort.

(22) Intelligence Reports

This covers the gathering of intelligence as far as it concerns SOE agents and the necessity for providing accurate and detailed information.

(23) German Organisation

Under this heading a fairly detailed resume is given of the Nazi party, armed forces, police and counter-espionage organisations.

(24) Propaganda

It is explained that propaganda is the art of persuasion with a view to producing action. It may be political, regional or religious and may take into account economics, age and sex.

There are fundamental themes such as the certainty of Allied victory, hatred of Germany, the future of the country and national pride. There is also subversive propaganda to the German army based on general dissatisfaction, fear and anxiety and deprivation of the comforts of home. It is pointed out that propaganda must be simple, accurate and repetitive. It must come from the right source and be directed to the right people at the right moment. Successful propaganda work involves an intelligent investigation of local opinion and interests. Some instruction is given in the reproduction of propaganda by printing, typewriting, duplicating and its distribution by chain letter, rumour, hand or post.

(25) Railways

Instruction is given in the sabotage of the permanent way, telephones, signalling installations, wagons, locomotives, etc.

(26) Codes and Ciphers

It is explained that a code is a method of concealing a message so that it appears innocent but a cipher is a method of converting a message into symbols which do not appear innocent but which have no meaning to an outside person. Instructions are given in various methods.

(27) Secret Inks

It is explained that secret inks are used for the purpose of using the ordinary postal service but that except in a few cases the reagents are known. Instruction is given in the methods of using secret inks and the precautions to be observed.

(28) Fieldcraft

Instruction is given in finding a way, where to hide and live in the open, how to detect the presence of others, how to find food and water and how to make a fire and cook.

Source HS 7/286, TNA.

APPENDIX 2

PHYSICIAN AND RELATED PARACHUTE DROPS

INCLUDING Déricourt Pick-ups and Landings

KEY: PHYSICIAN = SUCCESSFUL OPERATION
1M/10C/1P = number of men, containers and packages dropped
PHYSICIAN
nc = OPERATION not completed
nr = no reception
138/161 = Squadron number
BBC messages and number in approved list where known
'Pilot's comments'

NB The coordinates given are those of the pinpoints used by the RAF; they are *not* the location of the DZs for which see the main text for those that are known.

1942

23/24 Sept	as per 24/25 – 138 nc/wrong lights	
24/25 Sept	WHITEBEAM (Andrée Borrel)	
	ARTIST (Lise de Baissac)	
	MONKEYPUZZLE 1 – completed 138	2M/1C/3P
	47.40.10N 01.35.39E	
	Bois Renard, Nouan-sur-Loire, Loir-et-Cher	
	Les singes ne posent pas des questions	
01/02 Oct	PHYSICIAN (Francis Suttill)	

	CHEMIST (Jean Amps) – completed 138	2M/1P
	48.56.40N 03.10.25E	
	Blind near La Ferté-sous-Jouarre	
01/02 Oct	CHESTNUT 1 – completed 161	4C
20/21 Oct	MONKEYPUZZLE 2 – completed 161	4C/3P
	47.40.10N 01.	35.39E
	Bois Renard, Nouan-sur-Loire, Loir-et-Cher	
20/21 Oct	SCIENTIST 1/ACTOR – nc	
27/28 Oct	SCIENTIST 1 – nc	
31/10–01/11	ACTOR (Roger Landes)	
	BUTCHER (Gilbert Norman)	
	MONKEYPUZZLE 3 – completed 138	3M/4C/3P
	47.40.10N 01.35.39E	
	Bois Renard, Nouan-sur-Loire, Loir-et-Cher	
	Les écrevisses marchent de travers	
16/17 Nov	PHYSICIAN 1 – 138 nc/nr (Étrépagny)	
17/18 Nov	PHYSICIAN 1 – completed 138	4C
	49.20.40N 01.36.05E – Étrépagny	
17/18 Nov	SCIENTIST 2 - nc	
18/19 Nov	PRINTER (Hayes)	
	BRICKLAYER (France Antelme)	
	MONKEYPUZZLE 4 – completed 138	2M/4C/2P
	47.12.55N 00.33.00E	
	La Crepellerie, Saché, Indre-et-Loire	
	Michel monta très tard/haut dans la pommier	
18/19 Nov	FARMER (Trotobas)/BAKER(Staggs)	
	MUSICIAN (Beiler) – completed 161	3M/2P
20/21 Nov	SCIENTIST 2 – completed 161	4C
28/29 Nov	SCIENTIST 1 – nc	
23/24 Dec	GLAZIER (Agazarian)	
	SCULPTOR (Natzler DF)	
	PHYSICIAN 2 – 138 nc/weather (Sérifontaine)	
23/24 Dec	BUTLER/BARBER/FARRIER – 138 nc/weather	
	46.33.20N 00.13.44E	
29/30 Dec	GLAZIER (Jack Agazarian) – completed 138	
	TOBACCONIST (Hamilton)	2M/2P
	49.20.40N 01.36.05E	
	Le Génétray, Étrépagny, Eure	
	'Dropped together to reception'	
29/30 Dec	SCIENTIST 1 – nc	
29/30 Dec	BUTLER/BARBER/FARRIER – 138 nc/weather	

1943

22/23 Jan	**JUGGLER (Jean Worms)**	
	FARRIER (Henri Déricourt) – completed 138	2M/2P
	48.02.20N 02.39.34E – NW of Montargis	
09/10 Feb	PHYSICIAN 2 – 138 nc/nr	
	49.22.02N 01.18.38E – (Sérifontaine)	
	PHYSICIAN 7 – 138 nc/nr (Eporce)	
09/10 Feb	PHYSICIAN 4 – 138 nc/not sure as to reception	
	47.24.28N 01.19.59E – (St Lomer)	
	PHYSICIAN 6 – 138 nc/nr	
	47.41.40N 01.20.37E – (Hameau-Mézières)	
	Les sauterelles arrivent par milliards	
13/14 Feb	PHYSICIAN 4 – 138 nc/nr (St Lomer)	
	PHYSICIAN 6 – 138 nc/nr (Hameau-Mézières)	
14/15 Feb	ARTIST 2/BUTLER/BARBER – nc	
	46.25.22N 00.20.42E	
15/16 Feb	**PHYSICIAN 7 – completed 138**	4C
	48.03.50N 00.01.09E	
	Champ Failly, Neuvy-en-Champagne, Sarthe	
	La baleine aime les eaux froids	
15/16 Feb	PHYSICIAN 2 – 138 nc/nr (Sérifontaine)	
	PHYSICIAN 8 – 138 nc/nr (Flavacourt)	
15/16 Feb	FARMER 1 – nc	
18/19 Feb	FARMER 1 – nc	
24/25 Feb	PHYSICIAN 4 – 138 nc/weather (St Lomer)	
	PHYSICIAN 6 – 138 nc/weather (Hameau-Mézières)	
25/26 Feb	PHYSICIAN 2 – 138 nc/nr (Sérifontaine)	
	Marcel et Jeanne se rencontrent ce soir	
	PHYSICIAN 8 – 138 nc/nr (Flavacourt)	
25/26 Feb	FARMER 1 – nc	
26/27 Feb	**PHYSICIAN 8 – completed 161**	3C/1P
	49.19.44N 01.51.02E	
	Le Pre, Flavacourt, Oise	
	Le laitier passera demain à onze heures	
26/27 Feb	PHYSICIAN 6 – 161 nc – weather (coords as above)	
26/27 Feb	BUTLER/BARBER – 161 nc	
26/27 Feb	FARMER 1 – nc	
26/27 Feb	FARMER 2 – nc	
12/13 Mar	PHYSICIAN 11 – 161 nc/not attempted, weather (Eporce)	
12/13 Mar	PHYSICIAN 18 – 161 nc/nr (Origny)	
12/13 Mar	FARMER 1 – nc	

14/15 Mar	PHYSICIAN 11 – completed 161	4C/1P
	48.03.50N 00.01.09E	
	Champ Failly, Neuvy-en-Champagne, Sarthe	
17/18 Mar	TRAINER. (Dericourt Operation)	
	B19 46.24.30N 00.20.44E, S of Poitiers	
	Landed – F. Agazarian, J. Goldsmith, P. Lejeune and R. Dowlen	
	Picked up – C. de Baissac, Antelme, R. Flower and Dubois	
23/24 Mar	BUTLER (Bouguennec)/BARBER (Rousset)/	
	PUBLICAN (Fox) – completed 138	3M/1P
	47.36.30N 00.29.14E	
11/12 Apr	PHYSICIAN 12 – completed 138	2M/5C/2P
	TINKER (Cowburn)/INNKEEPER (Barrett)	
	47.24.28N 01.19.59E	
	Bois de St Lomer, Thenay, Loir-et-Cher	
	Les petits cochons seront farcis (BBC April/82)	
	PHYSICIAN 19 – 138 nc/nr (Champ Failly)	
11/12 Apr	PHYSICIAN 17 – completed 161	5C/1P
	47.34.31N 01.54.44E	
	Miraillon, Chaumont-sur-Tharonne, Loir-et-Cher	
	Marcel souhait le bonjour à Marcel	
11/12 Apr	PHYSICIAN 20 – completed 161	5C
	49.06.39N 01.33.21E	
	Le Petit Bois, Bois Jérôme St Ouen, Eure	
11/12 Apr	PRIVET 1 – completed 138	4C/1P
	47.25.48N 00.32.36W – Angers	
	Il faut rattraper le temps perdu (BBC April/44)	
12/13 Apr	PHYSICIAN 19 – completed 138	5C/1P
	48.03.50N 00.01.09E	
	Champ Failly, Neuvy-en-Champagne, Sarthe	
	SCIENTIST 14	
13/14 Apr	PHYSICIAN 18 – completed 138	5C
	49.54.23N 04.02.56E	
	Origny-en-Thiérache, Aisne	
	FARMER 1 – completed 138	5C/1P
	MUSICIAN 1 – nc	
13/14 Apr	PHYSICIAN 9 – 138/nc	
	'Insufficient time owing to time wasted on other 2 receptions'	
	PHYSICIAN 23 – 138 nc/nr (Troyes)	
14/15 Apr	PHYSICIAN 10 (1st) – completed 138	5C*
	49.16.36N 01.51.09E	
	Les Groux(?), Trie-Château, Oise	
	PHYSICIAN 15 – completed 138	5C

	49.16.18N 01.43.43E	
	Les Marais, Neaufles-Saint-Martin, Eure	
	Tabac 6 francs, Place Blanche (BBC April/78)	
	(*5C for Trie-Château also delivered to Neaufles by mistake)	
14/15 Apr	PHYSICIAN 14 – 138 nc/nr (Lalandelle)	
14/15 Apr	**JUGGLER 1 – completed 138**	5C/1P
	48.54.46N 04.12.27E – Thibié, west of Troyes	
	CHESTNUT 2	4C
14/15 Apr	**SALESMAN (Dericourt Operation)**	
	B28 BRONCHITE 47.26.20N 00.59.41E Pocé-sur-Cisse	
	Landed – Dubois, Frager, Liewer and Chartrand	
	Picked up – Clech	
	The second Lysander ran into a tree on landing.	
15/16 Apr	**PHYSICIAN 21 – completed 138**	5C
	47.26.58N 01.10.44E	
	Les Motteaux, Chaumont-sur-Loire, Loir-et-Cher	
	Il y a des lunettes à la suite (BBC April/73)	
15/16 Apr	**PHYSICIAN 13 – completed 161**	5C
	47.24.28N 01.19.59E	
	Bois de St Lomer, Thenay, Loir-et-Cher	
15/16 Apr	PHYSICIAN 9 – 138 nc – (Troyes)	
	PHYSICIAN 23 – 138 nc – (Troyes)	
15/16 Apr	**SCULPTOR (Dericourt Operation)**	
	B17 (L+L not found) 1km ENE of La Chartre-sur-Loir	
	Landed – Natzler +1	
	Picked up – J. Aisner	
20/21 Apr	**PHYSICIAN 14 – completed 161**	5C/1P
	49.22.46N 01.50.26E	
	Forêt de Thelle, Lalandelle, Oise	
20/21 Apr	PHYSICIAN 22 – 138 nc/insufficient time	
	49.42.40N 05.09.49E (Ardennes but see 15/16.05)	
	Quelle omelette mes aieux (BBC April/146)	
22/23 Apr	**TOMY. (Dericourt Operation)**	
	B30A TORTICOLIS 47.45.50N 00.42.04E 2km E of Couture-sur-Loir	
	Picked up Déricourt (to discuss accident on 14/15.)	
05/06 May	Déricourt returns by parachute near Mer	
12/3 May	PHYSICIAN 33 – 138 nc	
	48.59.14N 03.19.23E (Aisne but see 13/14.05)	
	'Could not positively identify ground'	
12/13 May	**CHESTNUT 3**	5C

13/14 May	**PHYSICIAN 35 – completed 161**	10C/1P
	47.29.25N 01.37.22E	
	Courmemin 1, Courmemin, Loir-et-Cher	
	La surprise est au fond de la boîte (BBC June/22)	
	PHYSICIAN 36 – completed 161	4C/1P
	47.33.15N 01.37.16E	
	Neuvy, Loir-et-Cher	
	Quatre gangsters assis sur l'herbe (BBC May/56)	

'Only 4 containers came away on first run. A second run was
made but the container still hung up and it was not possible
to jettison because P35 load was still on board. After the
completion of P35, we returned to P36 and attempted without
success to jettison the container.'

13/14 May	**PHYSICIAN 9 – completed 138**	5C/1P
	48.53.40N 00.16.53W	
	Falaise, Calvados	
	Le serpent chauve devient zazou.(BBC May/5)	
	PHYSICIAN 27 – completed 138	5C/1P
	48.18.16N 00.38.18E	
	l'Hermitière, Orne	
	L'amateur de roses et de porcelaine (or) Dolly est une belle friponne	
13/14 May	**PHYSICIAN 23 – completed 138**	10C/1P
	49.22.46N 01.50.26E	
	Forêt de Thelle, Lalandelle, Oise	
13/14 May	PHYSICIAN 10 (2nd) – 161 nc/crashed	
	49.16.36N 01.51.09E (Trie-Château)	

'F/O Noble flying Halifax BB328 crashed at Pont-Audemer, 30km
SE of Le Havre – no survivors.'

13/14 May	PHYSICIAN 32 – 138 nc/reception lost on circuit	
	47.25.37N 01.33.59E – (Courmemin 2) (see also 11/12.06)	
13/14 May	PHYSICIAN 33 – 138 nc/nr (Theillay) (see also 12/13.05)	
13/14 May	FARMER 2 – 5C/1P	
14/15 May	**INVENTOR (Dericourt Operation)**	
	B28A GRIPPE 47.21.29N 00.52.12E 1.5km ENE of Azay-sur-Cher	
	Landed – J. Aisner, V. Leigh, S. Jones and M. Clech + 14 packages	
	Picked up – F. Suttill	
14/15 May	**PHYSICIAN 28 – completed 138**	10C/1P
	47.26.58N 01.10.44E	
	les Motteux, Chaumont-sur-Tharonne, Loir-et-Cher	
	Les cornichons sont marines. (BBC May/57)	

15/16 May	**PHYSICIAN 25 – completed 138**	10C/1P
	49.06.39N 01.33.21E	
	Le petit Bois, Bois Jérôme St Ouen, Eure	
15/16 May	**PHYSICIAN 22 – completed 138**	10C/1P
	49.24.56N 01.41.45E	
	La Rouge-Mare, Neuf-Marché, Seine Maritime	
	Ôte-toi de là que je m'y mette (BBC 5/63)	
15/16 May	**PHYSICIAN 34 – completed 161**	10C/1P
	47.15.45N 01.16.38E	
	Bois de Juchepie, Mareuil, Loir-et-Cher	
	La main microscopique amorce l'operation (BBC May/62)	
16/17 May	PHYSICIAN 26 –138 nc/not definitely found	
	49.16.18N 01.43.43E	
	Les Marais, Neufles-Saint-Martin, Eure	
	Pierrette regarde la feuille a l'envers (BBC May/59)	
16/17 May	JUGGLER 2 – 138 nc/nr	
	48.54.46N 04.12.27E (Thibié)	
16/17 May	**TINKER 1 – Voulains, west of Troyes**	5C
17/18 May	**PHYSICIAN 24 – completed 138**	9 out of 10C/1P
	49.22.46N 01.50.26E	
	Forêt de Thelle, Lalandelle, Oise	
	'One container hung up and could not be released. It was not	
	possible to jettison as the load for Roach 26 was still on board.'	
18/19 May	**PHYSICIAN 37 – completed 138**	5C
	47.49.21N 01.40.04E	
	Meung-sur-Loire, Loiret	
	Les genets ardennais sont fleuris (BBC May/49)	
	JUGGLER 3 – 138 nc/nr	
18/19 May	PRIVET 4 – 138 nc/nr (coords as below 22/23.05)	
19/20 May	**PRIVET 3 – completed 161**	5C/1P
	47.19.49N 00.33.15W – Angers	
20/21 May	**CHESTNUT 4 – completed 138**	10C
	PHYSICIAN – completed 138	
	BRICKLAYER – completed 138	2M/2C/3P
	47.34.31N 01.54.44E	
	Miraillon, Chaumont-sur-Tharonne, Loir-et-Cher	
	'Jumped when told.'	
	Les bicyclettes du châtelain ne valent rien (BBC May/55)	
21/22 May	**PHYSICIAN 29 – completed 138**	10C/1P
	49.43.10N 05.09.32E	
	Le Monty, Muno, Ardennes Belgium	
	Nous irons chercher les oeufs de Paques (BBC May/42)	

21/22 May	**PHYSICIAN 30 – completed 138**	10C/1P
	49.54.23N 04.02.56E	
	Origny-en-Thierache, Aisne	
	FARMER 3 – nc	
21/22 May	**PHYSICIAN 31 – completed 161**	12C/1P
	47.34.31N 01.54.44E	
	Miraillon, Chaumont-sur-Tharonne, Loir-et-Cher	
21/21 May	FARMER 5 – nc	
22/23 May	PHYSICIAN 33 – 161 nc/weather (Theillay)	
22/23 May	**PRIVET 4 – completed 138**	5C
	47.34.42N 00.37.25W – Angers	
23/24 May	**PHYSICIAN 33 – completed 161**	10C/1P
	47.20.40N 01.59.09E	
	Les Bretonnieres, Theillay, Loir-et-Cher	
	N'oubliez pas l'Alsace (BBC May/61)	
23/24 May	PHYSICIAN 26 – 138 nc/nr	
	49.16.18N 01.43.43E – (Neaufles-Saint-Martin)	

'When pinpointing on Gisors, saw reception to E of town flashing L. This must have been PHYSICIAN 16.'

23/24 May	PHYSICIAN 38 – 138 nc/nr	
	49.34.25N 02.05.08E (Rotangy, Oise)	
23/24 May	PHYSICIAN 16 – 138 nc/weather	
	49.16.40N 01.50.12E – (Trie-Château)	
23/24 May	PRIVET 2 – 138 nc/weather – Nantes	
10/11 Jun	**PHYSICIAN 54 – completed 138**	5C

Pinpoint unknown

'Halifax aircraft N317 took off at 2255 on operation ROACH 47 and 48/PHYSICIAN 54 captained by F/Lt HOOPER and crew. Target FRANCE. Operation PHYSICIAN 54 only completed.'

Neuvy – *Le chien eternu dans les drapes (BBC June/15)*

Dr Segelle, a nephew of one of the reception team, is reported *in La République du Centre* of 13/14 September 1947 as saying that there was a drop near Neuvy on 10 June when some of the containers exploded. This would be Physician 54 as it is recorded in HS 8/143 (TNA) that some of the containers from this operation blew up.

| 10/11 Jun | **PHYSICIAN 53 – completed 138** | 10C |

Pinpoint unknown

'Halifax aircraft F252 took off at 2303 on operation ROACH 43/PHYSICIAN 53 captained by Sgt Brown and crew. Target FRANCE. Operation PHYSICIAN 53 only successful.'

Doulcay – *Leblanc va au marché noir (Trochet statement)*

Aerial photo of my father's pick-up point annotated by Déricourt to show where he was standing. (AIR 20/8493)

A letter from the *maire* of Mennetou of 28.11.1963 noted in the Blois archives states that there was a drop to a DZ at the farm of Doulcay, Maray, Loir-et-Cher, on this night so this must have been Physician 53.

10/11 Jun   PHYSICIAN 38 – 138 nc/nr
49.34.25N 02.05.08E if same as 23/24.5 above = Rotangy
PHYSICIAN 52 – 138 nc/nr
47.20.40N 01.59.09E if same as 22/23.6 below = Theillay
'Halifax aircraft P155 took off at 2257 on operation
PHYSICIAN 38/PHYSICIAN 52 captained by F/O Malinowski
and crew. Target FRANCE. Operation not successful.'

10/11 Jun   PRIVET 2 – 138 nc

11/12 Jun   PHYSICIAN 32 – 161 nc/missing (10C) (with CHARLOTTE – 4P)
49.20.09N 01.59.38E – near Beauvais
'Later news received from a secret source to the effect that
aircraft fitting the description of DG406 was seen to be shot
down in flames by ground flak at a position in the vicinity of
Beauvais, which was near his second pinpoint. Reported that
first operation had been carried out successfully.' (AIR 27/1068)
Charlotte was an operation to drop four packages to an
intelligence circuit near Lyons-le-Forêt, 45km west of Beauvais,

and must have been the first pinpoint as Norman reported on
16 June that nothing was received at the Physician DZ.

11/12 Jun   PHYSICIAN 16 – 138 nc/weather
49.16.40N 01.50.12E – if same as 23/24.5 above = Trie-Château
PHYSICIAN 26 – 138 nc/weather
49.16.18N 01.43.43E – if same as 16/17.5 above = Neufles-St-Martin
'Halifax aircraft C330 took off at 2303 on operation
PHYSICIAN 16/26 captained by F/O DOWNES and crew.
Target FRANCE. Operation not successful.'

11/12 Jun   PHYSICIAN 48 – 138 nc/weather
'Halifax aircraft R364 took off at 2300 on operation ROACH
24/PHYSICIAN 48 captained by Sgt BROWN and crew. Target
FRANCE. Operation not successful.'

11/12 Jun   PHYSICIAN 46 – 138 nc/weather
'Halifax aircraft E666 took off at 2257 on operation ROACH
35/PHYSICIAN 46 captained by F/O WILKINSON and crew.
Target FRANCE. Operation not successful.'

11/12 Jun   **JUGGLER 2 – completed 138**   **10C**
48.54.46N 04.12.27E – Thibié, west of Troyes
FARMER 3 nc

12/13 Jun   PHYSICIAN 60(1st) 138 nc – (see 21/22.6 below)
WATCHMAKER – completed 138
48.56.18N 01.53.10E - Grignon
Le Roncey, Bazemont, Yvelines
PHYSICIAN 42 – completed 138   **5C/2P**
Pinpoint unknown
'Halifax aircraft V154 took off at 2310 on operation PHYSICIAN
60/WATCHMAKER & PHYSICIAN 42 captained by F/Lt
HOOPER and crew. Target France. Operation successful.'
Watchmaker was Gaston Cohen and he reported his successful
drop on this date to the Grignon group. Although the
Operations Record Book for 138 Squadron records that all three
operations were successful, Cohen reported that the bomb door
jammed after he jumped, preventing the release of the Physician
60 containers. This explains why there is another Physician 60
(2nd sortie) on
16/17 June – see below. Physician 42 would have been delivered
to the Bois-Jerome-Saint-Ouen group to be collected by Marcel
Gouju as it is the only possible date for his material to have
arrived before his depot was inspected by my father on 17 June.

12/13 Jun   **CHESTNUT 5**   **10C/1P**

13/14 Jun	**PHYSICIAN 44 – completed 138**	10C/1P

Pinpoint unknown

'Halifax aircraft W156 took off at 2355 on operation PHYSICIAN 44/ROACH 24 captained by F/Lt DODKIN and crew. Target FRANCE. Operation successful.'

This operation was the Sunday drop at Langlochère – see Chapter 8.

13/14 Jun   PHYSICIAN 58 – 138 nc/not enough time

49.43.10N 05.09.32E if same as on 21/22.06 below = Muno

'Halifax aircraft V154 took off at 2305 on operation LABRADOR 2/PHYSICIAN 58 captained by F/Lt HOOPER and crew. Target BELGIUM. Operation LABRADOR 2 only completed'

13/14 Jun	**BUTLER 1 – completed 138**	8C/1P

13/14 Jun   FARMER 3 nc

13/14 Jun   **SACRISTAN (Floege) AND CARDINAL (Reeve) - completed**

14/15 Jun	**PHYSICIAN 45 – completed 138**	5C/1P
	PHYSICIAN 61 – completed 138	10C/1P

'Halifax aircraft D378 took off at 0009 on operation PHYSICIAN 45/61 captained by F/Sgt ARMSTRONG and crew. Target FRANCE.'

Ancinnes – *Elle est bleue aux fleurs rouge. (BBC June/67)*

l'Hermitière – *Mieux vaut voler que de nager (BBC June/27)*

14/15 Jun	**PHYSICIAN 56 – completed 138**	10C/2P

'Halifax aircraft F253 took off at 2320 on operation ROACH 30/PHYSICIAN 56 captained by Sgt BROWN and crew, Target FRANCE. Operation PHYSICIAN 56 only successful.'

14/15 Jun   PHYSICIAN 41 & 43 – 138 cancelled, 'rear turret useless' (Physician 43 was successful on 17/18 June but Physician 41 was not repeated.)

14/15 Jun	**PHYSICIAN 46 – completed 138**	5C
	PHYSICIAN 48 – completed 138	10C

'Halifax aircraft P171 took off at 2319 on operation PHYSICIAN 48/46 captained by F/O WILKINSON and crew. Target FRANCE.'

Local reports show that there was a first drop to Ancinnes in the Sarthe and a second to l'Hermitière in the Orne, which would have been one of the combined operations. A report from the ground records that Physician 46 was dropped to the group waiting for Physician 41 and this would suggest that this was the second June drop at Langlochère – see Chapter 8. As the DZs for Physician 41 and 46 were in the south, Geelen's report of

a successful operation to the group at Origny-en-Thiérache on
this date would suggest that this was Physician 56. The drops
to Ancinnes and l'Hermitière were as expected so they must
have been Physician 45 and 61, and one of the reception team
remembered that he had received ten containers and a wireless set
at Ancinnes, which would be Physician 61.

14/15 Jun	PHYSICIAN 58 – 138 nc/not found (as 13/14.6 above)	
	'Halifax aircraft W156 took off at 2315 on operation PHYSICIAN 58/ROACH 44 captained by F/Lt DODKIN and crew. Target France. Operation not successful.'	
14/15 Jun	JUGGLER 4 – 138 nc/nr	
15/16 Jun	PHYSICIAN 55 – completed 138	5C/1P
	ARCHDEACON (Pickersgill) – completed 138	2M
	PLUMBER (Macalister) – completed 138	
	Les dieux s'installent au balcon – (Blois archives)	
	PHYSICIAN 64 – completed 138	10C

Pickersgill and Macalister were dropped at Meusne/Châtillon probably with
Physician 55 as the package would have been their luggage. Physician 64 is likely
to have been destined for a group in the same area.

16/17 Jun	PHYSICIAN 60 (2nd) – completed 138	10C
	48.56.18N 01.53.10E – Grignon	
16/17 Jun	PHYSICIAN 71 – completed 138	10C
	PHYSICIAN 75 – completed 138	5C
16/17 Jun	PHYSICIAN 72 – completed 138	10C
	MISTRAL 1 – 5C	
16/17 Jun	PHYSICIAN 46 (2nd) – completed 138	10C
	PHYSICIAN 43 – 138 nc/nr	

The daughter of the leader of the Montrichard group told me
that her father received two drops in June and in each case the
operation was combined with a Mistral operation, which means
that Physician 72 was dropped at Montrichard. Physician 46
was meant to have been dropped on 14/15 June – see above – so
the DZ for that and for Physician 43 must have been near that
for Physician 41, which was in the Courmemin area – see 17/18
June below. Guillaume claims that 3 tonnes were dropped either
this night or the night before to a group at Chuelles to the east
of Montargis with the message – *L'ersatz est superflu. (BBC
June/72)*

16/17 Jun	PHYSICIAN 51 – 138 nc	
	PUBLICAN 1 – 138 nc	
16/17 Jun	BUTLER 2 – completed 138	5C/1P
16/17 Jun	TEACHER (Dericourt operation)	

B20A INDIGESTION   47.34.05N.00.27.54W Indigestion, NNE of Angers

Landed – Lefort, Inayat Khan, Rowden and Skepper

Picked up – Mme Pierre-Bloch, J. and F. Agazarian, Lejeune and ?

17/18 Jun   PHYSICIAN 43 – completed 138   10C/1P

Guillaume reports a drop on this night to the Chambord group's new DZ at Chassenais near Courmemin, from which the material was taken to Culioli's HQ at Veillens.

17/18 Jun   PHYSICIAN 49 – completed 161

LINKMAN (Raynaud)   1M/10C/1P

47.26.58N 01.10.44E

les Motteaux, Chaumont-sur-Tharonne, Loir-et-Cher

Raynaud claimed that they were chased by a German night fighter but the pilot had 'No incidents to report.' (AIR 27/1068)

Mon vieux Julien, quelle aventure. (BBC June/16)

17/18 Jun	PHYSICIAN 66 – 138 nc/nr	
17/18 Jun	JUGGLER 3 – completed 138	10C/1P

48.39.28N 04.24.31E – SW of Vitry-le-François

17/18 Jun   JUGGLER 4 – completed 161   10C/1P

48.53.43N 04.11.02E – Thibié, west of Troyes

TINKER 2 – Nogent-sur-Aube, NE of Troyes   5C

17/18 Jun   PUBLICAN 1 – 138 nc/not found

(18/19 June – full moon.)

20/21 Jun	PHYSICIAN 76 – completed 138	10C
20/21 Jun	PHYSICIAN 73 – completed 138	5C
	PHYSICIAN 79 – completed 138	10C
	MISTRAL 2 – 4P	
20/21 Jun	PHYSICIAN 50 – completed 138	5C
	PHYSICIAN 70 – completed 138	10C

Either Physician 73 or 79 was to the Montrichard group – see 16/17 June. Guillaume states that there were three other drops to terrains in the Sologne – at a new DZ near Villeny; at a DZ near Courmemin where containers had fallen into a lake on a previous operation = Courmemin 1; and to a new DZ near Menettou-sur-Cher or Préjeux in the neighbouring commune of Langon.

Montrichard – *Venez quand méme, en s'arrangera*

Courmemin 1 – *La moto grate l'auto*

20/21 Jun PUBLICAN 1 – 138 nc/weather

20/21 Jun CURATOR/ACOLYTE Failed – no reception – see 23/24 Jun below

21/22 Jun **PHYSICIAN 67 – completed 161**   10C/2P
            DENTIST (Connerade)
            48.56.18N 01.53.10E
            Le Roncey, Bazemont, Yvelines.
            Le commisaire devient agent de change

21/22 Jun **PHYSICIAN 58 – completed 138**   5C
            49.43.10N 05.09.32E
            Le Monty, Muno, Ardennes, Belgium.
            A drop to the Muno DZ on this date is recorded in the testimony
            of three of those involved.
            La location est ouverte. (BBC June/43)
            PHYSICIAN 68 – 138 nc

21/22 Jun **PRIVET 2 – completed 138**   10C/1P
            47.28.40N 01.34.35W

21/22 Jun **PUBLICAN 1 – completed 138**   10C

22/23 Jun PHYSICIAN 68 – 138 nc

22/23 Jun PHYSICIAN 51 – 138 nc
            PHYSICIAN 77 – 138 nc

22/23 Jun PHYSICIAN 59 – 138 nc

22/23 Jun PHYSICIAN 52 – 161 nc/nr
            47.20.40N 01.59.09E – (Theillay)

22/23 Jun PHYSICIAN 74 –161 nc/nr
            47.43.20N 01.01.29E – (Huiseau-en-Beauce)

When Culioli was taken to Blois after his arrest, he told the
Germans about two planned receptions that were due: one in the
region of Maves and the other in the region of Courmemin. The
first would be Physician 74, where Guillaume records that the
DZ was in the grounds of the château Plessis-Saint-Armand and
that Georges Buhler and the *maire* of Huisseau-en-Beauce were
in the reception team. The team did not go out because they had
been told of the arrest of Culioli. The second would have been in
the commune of Gy-en-Sologne, where records from the archives
in Blois reveal that there was no reception because Germans
had occupied the ground. There was no reception at Theillay as
this would have been a team from Romorantin and their leader
Couffrant had been arrested. (Dossier judiciaire – Pierre Culioli,
TMP Metz, jgt n° 183/4526, 17/031949)

22/23 Jun   Abandoned – generator failed – see 23/24 Jun below
23/24 Jun   **CURATOR/ACOLYTE (Dericourt Operation)**
              B28 BRONCHITE 47.26.20N 00.59.41E Pocé-sur-Cisse
              Landed – R. Lyon and Col. Bonoteaux
              Picked – up – R. Heslop and P. Taylor

Sources in The National Archives

AIR 20/8252	Daily Summary of Tempsford Operations		
AIR 20/8459	138 Squadron's Rough Diary of Operations		
AIR 20/8461	161 Squadron's Rough Diary of Operations		
AIR 20/8452	Pilot's Reports	138 Squadron	24.08.42 – 30.12.42
AIR 20/8476	Pilot's Reports	138 Squadron	15.01.43 – 24.05.43

(138 Squadron Pilot's Reports for June and July are missing)

AIR 20/8456	Pilot's Reports	161 Squadron	??.04.42 – 27.01.43
AIR 20/8498	Pilot's Reports	161 Squadron	26.02.43 – 24.07.43
AIR 20/8256	Operational Instructions		10.11.42 – 03.03.43
AIR 20/8257	Operational Instructions		08.03.43 – 01.05.43

(Operational Instructions for May and June are missing)

AIR 20/8474	Pilot's Reports	161 Squadron Pick-up Operations 1943
AIR 27/956	Operations Record Books	138 Squadron

HS 8/8841 BBC messages for April to June 1943

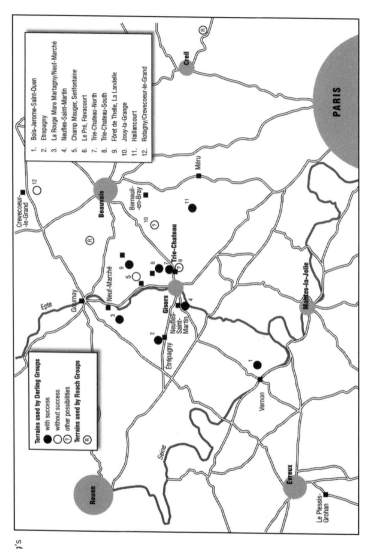

Georges Darling's DZs.

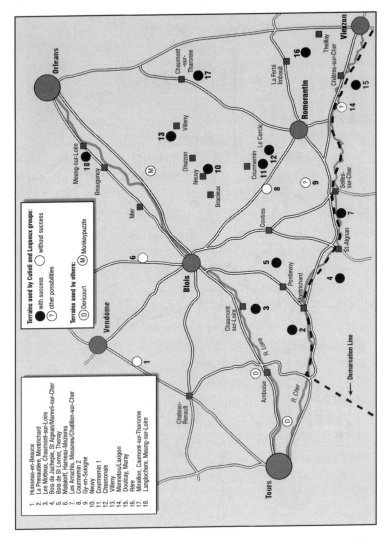

Piere Culioli and
Maurice Lequeux
DZs.

APPENDIX 3

CASUALTIES

1. People Killed or Arrested and Deported or Interned in 1943

The information below lists people killed or arrested and deported or interned in 1943 as a direct result of their involvement with the Prosper organisation, including dates of arrest and deportation.

It does not include those who were released shortly after their arrest or those who were killed or arrested in 1944 as these were unlikely to have been the consequence of their activities in the organisation. Conversely some of those arrested at the end of 1943 who have been included may have been arrested for other reasons. I have included the Dutems brothers who were part of the Monkeypuzzle circuit as their arrests were a direct result of the arrest of Gilbert Norman. Other difficult decisions are noted in the text.

The Leaders

SUTTILL Francis	24.06.1943	Not known	Killed
NORMAN Gilbert	24.06.1943	Not known	Killed
AMPS James	Not known	Not known	Killed
BORREL Andrée	24.06.1943	13.05.1944	Killed

Trie-Château Groups and Western Oise

ALLAIS Sylvain	29.06.1943	17.01.1944	Died
ARGENCE Jean	09.08.1943	17.01.1944	Survived
AUBRY Maxime	29.06.1943	17.01.1944	Died
AUBRY Francine	29.06.1943	–	Died in Fresnes 22.07.1943

Neaufles-Saint-Martin monument. (Author)

AUBRY Paul	29.06.1943	–	Interned to 28.06.1944
BARBIER Alexandre	09.08.1943	17.01.1944	Died
BIGOT Camille	29.06.1943	17.01.1944	Died
BOULANGER Ginette	29.06.1943	31.01.1944	Died
BOYELDIEU Roland	29.06.1943	17.01.1944	Died
DARLING Georges	Shot 26.06.1943		Died 27.06.1943
DAVESNE René	24.06.1943	17.01.1944	Survived
DAVESNE Jeanne	24.06.1943	31.01.1944	Survived
DELFOSSE André	29.06.1943	17.01.1944	Died
FOURNIER Joseph	26.06.1943	17.01.1944	Died
HEBERT Gaston	29.06.1943	17.01.1944	Died
HENAFF Leon	09.08.1943	17.01.1944	Died
HÉRISSET Raymond	09.08.1943	17.01.1944	Died
HEUILLARD Georges	09.08.1943	17.01.1944	Survived
IGLEZIAS Jose*	09.08.1943	17.01.1944	Died
LAURENT Alexandre	29.06.1943	17.01.1944	Died
LAURENT Antonine	29.06.1943	31.01.1944	Died
LHOMME Gabriel	??.06.1943	17.01.1944	Died
LUCAS Victor	29.06.1943	17.01.1944	Died
PERRET Alfred	29.06.1943	17.01.1944	Survived
PERRET Lucien	29.06.1943	17.01.1944	Survived
PERRET Marcel	29.06.1943	17.01.1944	Survived
PERRET Yvonne	??.??.1943	31.01.1944	Survived

PONLÉVE Marcel	29.06.1943	17.01.1944	Survived
REDELSPERGER Adolphe	26.06.1943	17.01.1944	Died
SAILLY Marcel	04.11.1943	27.01.1944	Survived
SCHWARZ Marcel	29.06.1943	17.01.1944	Died
SÉNÉCAUX Sylvain	29.06.1943	17.01.1944	Died
TIERCELIN Gilbert	02.08.1943	28.10.1943	Survived
VILLEGAS Jules	29.06.1943	17.01.1944	Survived

* Originally I could not find any record of Iglezias being part of this group but a subsequently opened file confirms that he was. (GR 16 P 301000, SHD archives)

Évreux Group

BERNARD Georges	??.??.1943	17.01.1944	Survived
GOUJU Marcel	29.06.1943	17.01.1944	Survived

Grignon Group

ABGRALL Guillaume	01.07.1943	17.01.1944	Died
BALACHOWSKY Serge	02.07.1943	17.01.1944	Survived
BARBIER Paul	14.07.1943	17.01.1944	Survived
DOUILHET Robert	04.07.1943	17.01.1944	Died
MAILLARD Marius	04.07.1943	17.01.1944	Died
VANDERVYNCK Eugene	10.07.1943	17.01.1944	Died

A LA MÉMOIRE DE :

Alfred BALACHOWSKY, déporté à DORA et à BUCHENWALD,
Robert DOUILHET, déporté, mort le 5 mars 1944 à BUCHENWALD,
Désiré MAILLARD, dit Marius, déporté, mort en avril 1944 à DORA,
Eugène VANDERVYNCKT, déporté, mort le 1er mai 1945 à DACHAU
Résistants du réseau "PROSPER" sur le site de GRIGNON

" Ils se sont sacrifiés pour la cause de la France
sans que nulle loi humaine ne les y contraignit ! "

Grignon memorial. (C. Dury)

Sologne Groups

BEIGNET Sylvain	28.08.1943	08.11.1943	Gassed
BIGOT Maxime	01.08.1943	11.10.1943	Died
BOUCHER René	08.07.1943	02.09.1943	Survived
BOUTON René	?.?.1943	18.10.1943	Survived
BRAULT Georges	21.06.1943	18.10.1943	Survived
BUHLER Georges Marcel	16.08.1943	17.01.1944	Survived
CAILLARD Marius	15.07.1943	Not known	Died
CANARD Henri	28.08.1943	08.11.1943	Died
CHARMAISON Jean	03.07.1943	11.10.1943	Survived
CORBEAU Maurice	23.09.1943	17.01.1944	Died
CORDELET Auguste	03.07.1943	18.10.1943	Died
COUFFRANT Roger	21.06.1943	08.11.1943	Survived
CULIOLI Pierre	21.06.1943	08.08.1944	Survived
DAGUET Henri	21.06.1943	21.06.1943	Died
DE BERNARD Pierre	09.09.1943	27.04.1944	Survived
DE BERNARD Anne-Marie	09.09.1943	31.01.1944	Survived
DRUNAT Michel	23.09.1943	17.01.1944	Survived
FERME Henriette	11.09.1943	31.01.1944	Survived
FOUQUET Pierre	16.09.1943	14.12.1943	Survived
FROMENTIN Germaine	25.08.1943	31.01.1944	Survived
GALLIOT Joseph	08.10.1943	27.01.1944	Died
GATIGNON André	03.07.1943	08.11.1943	Survived
GIRARD Bernard	23.09.1943	14.12.1943	Survived
GOLEAU Armand	28.08.1943	18.10.1943	Died
GRIGNOUX Lucien	12.03.1943	22.04.1943	Survived
HABERT André	21.06.1943	08.11.1943	Died
LECLERC Jacques	23.09.1943	28.10.1943	Survived
LEGOURD Prosper	02.07.1943	18.10.1943	Died
LEMEUR Albert	02.07.1943	08.11.1943	Survived
LEVEQUE Renée	24.09.1943	31.01.1944	Survived
MANDARD Robert	02.10.1943	17.01.1944	Died
MERCIER Albert	21.06.1943	08.11.1943	Died
MERCIER Guy	06.06.1943	15.07.1944	Died
MIREAU Jean	13.08.1943	17.01.1944	Survived
MORAND Juliette	17.08.1943	Not known	Survived
OURY Gerard	28.08.1943	11.10.1943	Survived
PETIT Marcel	15.09.1943	15.08.1944	Survived
RABIER André	16.12.1943	06.04.1944	Survived
RUDELLAT Yvonne	21.06.1943	??.08.1944	Died
SAUSSET Paul	02.07.1943	18.10.1943	Died
SYDNEY Jean	21.06.1943	08.11.1943	Died

| THÉNOT Marcel | 24.08.1943 | 08.11.1943 | Died |
| VAUZELLE Jacques | 30.08.1943 | 04.06.1944 | Survived |

Monkeypuzzle Circuit

| DUTEMS Jean | 29.07.1943 | 22.11.1943 | Died |
| DUTEMS Guy | 29.07.1943 | 08.11.1943 | Died |

Meung-Sur-Loire Group

BILLARD, Marie-Thérèse	05.07.1943	31.01.1944	Survived
BOQUEHO Robert	05.07.1943	27.04.1944	Survived
BORDIER Jean	05.07.1943	27.04.1944	Died
DE ROBIEN Alain	05.07.1943	17.01.1944	Died
DE ROBIEN Marie	06.07.1943	31.01.1944	Survived
DURAND Jacqueline	01.07.1943	Not known	Survived
FLAMENCOURT Edouard	01.07.1943	17.01.1944	Died
FLAMENCOURT Jean	01.07.1943	27.04.1944	Died
FLAMENCOURT Marguerite	01.07.1943	31.01.1944	Survived
LEQUEUX Maurice	01.07.1943	Not known	Survived
PASTY Emile	05.07.1943	–	Died in Fresnes 1944
PHILBÉE Jean	04.08.1943	17.01.1944	Survived
PHILBÉE Paul	05.07.1943	Not known	Survived
RAIMBAULT André	05.07.1943	27.04.1944	Survived
RIVIÈRE Louis	05.07.1943	27.04.1944	Died
VAPPEREAU Georges	30.07.1943	27.04.1944	Died

Baule monument. (Author)

Montargis Group

Name			
CARMIGNAC Lucien	–	–	Killed 08.07.1943
CARMIGNAC Marguerite	08.07.1943	31.01.1944	Survived
CARMIGNAC Norbert	–	–	Killed 08.07.1943
CARMIGNAC Roger	08.07.1943	12.05.1944	Survived
CASSIER Pierre	28.06.1943	04.10.1943	Died
CASSIER Jean	28.06.1943	11.10.1943	Died
COAVEC Jeanne	08.07.1943	01.07.1943	Survived
COMPIN Henri	30.06.1943	25.10.1943	Survived
CONTER Micheline	28.06.1943	16.12.1943	Survived
FELIN Marcel	30.06.1943	Not known	Died
GAUTHIER Kleber	09.07.1943	27.04.1944	Died
GIRON Jacques	25.07.1943	11.10.1943	Died
GIRON Pierre	25.07.1943	04.10.1943	Died
GUILLEMIN Albert	09.07.1943	27.01.1944	Survived
HARRY Gabrielle	07.07.1943	04.08.1944	Survived
JAILLON Gaston	08.07.1943	04.10.1943	Died
LEHMANN Charles	09.07.1943	27.01.1944	Survived
LEHMANN Georgette	09.07.1943	31.01.1944	Died
NARCY Roger	30.06.1943	04.10.1943	Survived
NIERADZIK Joseph	08.07.1943	22.11.1943	Survived
PERNET Gerard	01.08.1943	17.09.1943	Died
PERNET Jean-Louis	01.08.1943	17.09.1943	Died
POGET Olivier	08.07.1943	11.10.1943	Survived
THONONT Maurice	30.06.1943	04.10.1943	Survived
VESSIÈRES Jacques	08.07.1943	17.01.1944	Died

Sarthe and Orne Groups

Name			
CELIER Jean	13.07.1943		Died 1944 from maltreatment in internment
DE COURSON Germaine	16.07.1943	31.01.1944	Died
DE MONTALEMBERT Arthur	02.10.1943	17.04.1944	Died
LAUMAILLET Constant	Not known	17.01.1944	Survived
LOTTIN Paul	09.07.1943	28.10.1943	Gassed

Falaise Group

Name			
BAR Pierre	01.07.1943	17.01.1944	Survived
BERTIN Georges	03.07.1943	17.01.1944	Died
BESNIER Robert	03.07.1943	17.01.1943	Died
CAUCHY Jean-Michel	01.07.1943	14.12.1943	Died
CAUCHY Marie	01.07.1943	31.01.1944	Survived

Falaise plaque. (Author)

CHENE Paul	05.07.1943	Not known	Died
DE LA ROCHEFOUCAULD B	08.07.1943	17.01.1944	Died
DE LA ROCHEFOUCAULD Y	10.09.1943	31.01.1944	Survived
LANGLOIS André	03.07.1943	17.01.1943	Died
LEROY Louis	03.07.1943	17.01.1944	Died

Origny-en-Thiérache Group

MANESSE Elisse	20.08.1943	17.01.1944	Died
PLANCOULAINE Claude	08.09.1943	27.01.1944	Died
PLANCOULAINE Emile	08.09.1943	27.01.1944	Survived

Ardennes Group

BIAZOT Gaston	02.09.1943	17.01.1944	Survived
GODFRIN Marcel	02.09.1943	17.01.1944	Survived
LEFÈVRE Georges	01.09.1943	17.01.1944	Survived

Paris Area

ANDRÈS Raymond	11.10.1943	03.09.1943	Died
BUREAU Jacques	??.??.1943	Not known	Survived
FREMEAUX Charles	03.07.1943	16.09.1943	Died
GUERNE Armel	01.07.1943	17.01.1944	Escaped in transit
GUERNE Jeanne	01.07.1943	31.01.1944	Survived
LAURENT Maud	24.06.1943	31.01.1944	Survived
LAURENT Nicolas	24.06.1943	17.01.1944	Survived
MONNET Leonie	28.07.1943	31.01.1944	Survived

MONNET Marie-Louise	28.07.1943	14.06.1944	Died
TAMBOUR Germaine	22.04.1943	31.01.1944	Gassed
TAMBOUR Madeleine	22.04.1943	31.01.1944	Gassed
VASSEL Jacques	08.07.1943	04.10.1943	Died

Others

CHOUPAULT Joseph	18.08.1943	17.01.1944	Died (from Versailles?)
BOURGOGNAT Maurice	29.06.1943	17.01.1944	Survived (from Humblingny, Cher?)

Juggler Circuit

DE LA FOURNIERE Jacques	18.07.1943	–	Died under torture
DELHOMMEL Georges	08.07.1943	17.01.1944	Died
GERMEMONT Renée	23.10.1943	13.01.1944	Survived
GUERRE André	20.07.1943	17.01.1944	Escaped in transit
LAMBERT Edouard	10.07.1943	17.01.1944	Survived
MARTIN ????	01.07.1943	Not known	Died
MOREAU Henri	18.07.1943	17.01.1944	Survived
NICOLAS Angeline	03.07.1943	13.05.1944	Died
NICOLAS Marcel	03.07.1943	15.08.1944	Died
NICOLAS Paulin	03.07.1943	17.01.1944	Died
PIERRET Louis	16.07.1943	17.01.1944	Survived
THIBAULT Emile	07.07.1943	17.01.1944	Died
TRIOULET Denise	19.07.1943	Not known	Survived
TRIOULET Françoise	19.07.1943	Not known	Survived
TRIOULET Juliette	18.07.1943	Not known	Survived
WORMS Jean	01.07.1943	Not known	Killed

SOURCES

Circuit Liquidation files from the 16 P Series in the SHD archives, Château Vincennes Livre Memorial: http://www.bddm.org/liv/recherche.php

2. Royal Air Force Crew Lost on Physician Operations

13/14.05.43 Halifax BB328 NF – U of 138 Squadron on Operation PHYSICIAN 10/ROACH 6. Crashed at Pont-Audemer (Eure), France.

F/O Thomas NOBLE RAFVR – Pilot – killed
Sgt Douglas Albert BALL RAFVR – Gunner – killed
Sgt Kenneth HUBBARD RAFVR – Wireless Op – killed
F/Sgt John Patrick KEATING RCAF – Gunner – killed
Sgt Dudley Frank WEST RAFVR – Navigator – killed
Sgt James WOODS RAFVR – Flight Engineer – killed

11/12.6.43 Halifax DG406 MA – V of 161 Squadron on Operation
PHYSICIAN 32/CHARLOTTE. Shot down by Flak near Beauvais,
France.

F/Lt Alfred Francis FOSTER DFC RAFVR – Pilot – killed
Sgt Arthur MOON RAFVR – Dispatcher – killed
P/O James Thomas O'BRIEN DFM, RAFVR – Navigator – killed
Sgt John Smith RIDDELL RAFVR – Engineer – killed
P/O Llewellyn ROBERTS DFM, RAF – Wireless Op – killed
S/L Anthony de Quincey WALKER DFC RAFVR – 2 Pilot – killed
P/O Frederick Lionel WILLIAMS RAFVR – Rear Gunner – killed

www.roll-of-honour.com /Bedfordshire/TempsfordAircrewLost1943.html
Abbeville 42

INDEX

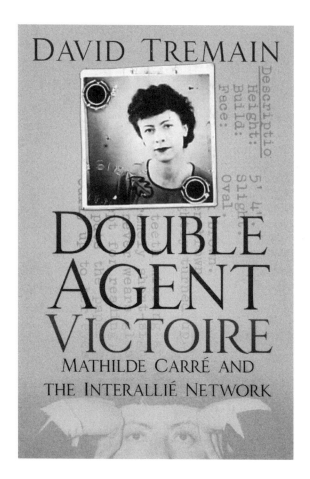

DAVID TREMAIN

DOUBLE
AGENT
VICTOIRE

MATHILDE CARRÉ AND
THE INTERALLIÉ NETWORK

978 0 7509 8804 9

JERRY ROBERTS MBE
FOREWORD BY PADDY O'CONNELL

LORENZ

BREAKING HITLER'S TOP SECRET CODE AT BLETCHLEY PARK

978 0 7509 8770 7

The History Press

The destination for history
www.thehistorypress.co.uk